Janaab' Pakal of Palenque

Janaab' Pakal of Palenque

Reconstructing the Life and Death of a Maya Ruler

Edited by Vera Tiesler and Andrea Cucina

The University of Arizona Press
Tucson

Frontispiece: Sarcophagus lid (redrawn by
Mirna Sánchez from Greene 1983 : Fig. 99).

The University of Arizona Press
© 2006 The Arizona Board of Regents

This book is printed on acid-free, archival-quality paper.
Manufactured in the United States of America

11 10 09 08 07 06   6 5 4 3 2 1

Library of Congress Cataloging-in-Publication Data
Janaab' Pakal of Palenque : reconstructing the life and death
of a Maya ruler / edited by Vera Tiesler and Andrea Cucina.
p. cm.
Includes bibliographical references and index.
ISBN-13: 978-0-8165-2510-2 (hardcover : alk. paper)
ISBN-10: 0-8165-2510-2 (hardcover : alk. paper)
1. Pakal, Maya king, 603–683—Death and burial. 2. Mayas
—Kings and rulers—Mexico—Palenque (Chiapas)—Biography.
3. Mayas—Anthropometry—Mexico—Palenque (Chiapas)
4. Maya architecture—Mexico—Palenque (Chiapas)
5. Palenque Site (Mexico) 6. Tombs—Mexico—Palenque
(Chiapas) 7. Human remains (Archaeology)—Mexico—
Palenque (Chiapas) 8. Palenque (Chiapas, Mexico)—
Antiquities. I. Tiesler, Vera. II. Cucina, Andrea, 1966–
F1434.P35J36 2006
972'.75092—dc22
2005035582

Half a century after the initial exploration of Pakal's tomb,
we dedicate this book to:

the pioneers of Palenque's osteological studies,
whose stimulating pursuits provided
the starting point of this reassessment

the new generations of Maya bioarchaeologists

the ancient Maya and their living descendents,
whose cultural and biocultural heritage will never cease to
trigger our amazement and admiration

Contents

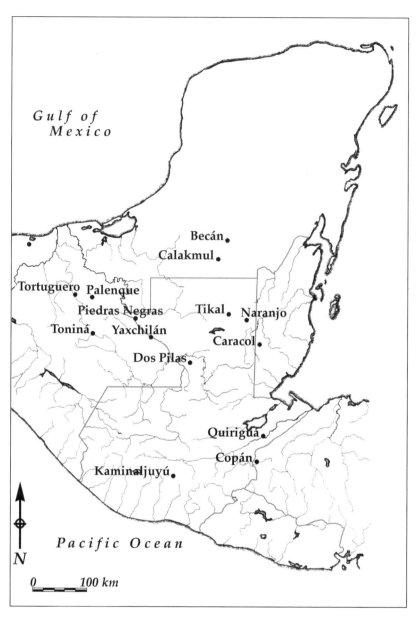

Maya area with locations of major pre-Columbian sites mentioned in this volume (by Vera Tiesler)

Prologue

Sergio Raul Arroyo

Former General Director,
Instituto Nacional de Antropología e Historia

When John Lloyd Stephens explored Palenque in 1840, searching for imaginary secrets hidden within the ruins of the Temple of the Inscriptions (the name refers to the abundant hieroglyphs carved on its walls), he expressed his admiration in his travel notebook: "Here were the remains of a cultivated, polished and peculiar people, who had passed through all the stages incident to the rise and fall of nations; reached their golden age, and perished entirely unknown" ([1841] 1969:356).

His amazement derived from the recognition of a civilization that had been able to develop a hermetically gorgeous writing as well as unheard of architectural fortunes. Stephens's admiration was to have two unsuspected consequences. First, he gave rise to the romantic American fantasies of an Egypt-like culture that once had flourished and then was devoured by the forest. Second, his narrative represented the first step toward the encounter between science and an enigmatic Maya civilization.

The ancient city of Palenque, which had been completely unknown to Stephens, soon incited incessant public attention and scientific curiosity. A second milestone in explorations was set little more than a century after Stephens's exploration. The year 1952 witnessed the discovery of the luxurious tomb of a Maya ruler, hidden in the very core of the Temple of the Inscriptions. Today almost everyone knows how archaeologist Alberto Ruz Lhuillier made the discovery of the monolith harboring the remains of K'inich Janaab' Pakal. His astonishment mirrored Howard Carter's feelings when he discovered the tomb of Tutankhamen 30 years earlier in the Valley of the Kings in Egypt. Ruz wrote: "Out of the dark shadows emerged a fairy-tale sight, a fantastic and transcendental view of another world. It looked like a magic cave sculptured out of ice, the walls shimmering and bright like crystals of snow. . . . It gave the impression of an abandoned chapel. Bas-relief stucco figures were walking along the walls. Then my eyes looked at the floor, which was taken up almost completely by a huge, perfectly preserved carved stone" (1953:95–96).

Since Ruz's discovery, the history of Palenque and its inhabitants has been rewritten with ever more subtle detail. At the same time, this reconstructed history has laid an enormous responsibility on the shoulders of its explorers to translate and spread the voices of the ancient Maya. The new explorers must re-create the lives of a divergent people, of their governors' dynasties and reigns, of their military strategies, of their artists' accomplishments, of their priests' rituals and scientific achievement, and of the language spoken by their protector gods. In this quest, the ancient Maya Weltanschaung poses a crucial challenge because it entangles mythical archaeotypes with historical facts, all woven into the calendric inscriptions, as all-embracing witnesses of the Mesoamerican civilization. The ancient worldviews were expressed both in everyday life and in the celebrations of the sacred, funerary, or festive. The carved and chiseled expressions of these fundamental events bear the clues to identity and belonging, the knowledge of the past, the perception of the moment, and at the same time a clear desire to transcend. Thanks to advances in anthropology, it is possible now to evaluate and reinterpret this material evidence of the past and to clarify secular academic controversies on the developments and achievements of individuals and ancient societies, of which Pakal and Palenque are no exception.

In this volume, ample new insights provide a more complex and precise image of the biography of Palenque and its king. Addressed to the academic community and interested amateurs, this book brings together the contributions of a group of experts of different institutions and disciplinary backgrounds—including distinguished epigraphers, anthropologists, archaeologists, and historians. Their investigations offer an integrated view of Pakal's life and death in ancient Maya society. His physical appearance is brought to life jointly from the iconographic and bony information, and the reconstruction of his lifestyle is founded on scientific proposals gleaned mainly from biocultural frames of reference.

Pakal, Palenque, and the pre-Hispanic Maya still guard secrets that puzzle us with the same mystery as other enigmas of the past. We should ask ourselves, as did Italo Calvino (1998) so eloquently when he was faced with the supremacy of pre-Hispanic civilization: Can we be sure that the gods still speak the same language of the forest from their decaying temples? Maybe they are no longer those who conversed in ancient times and who repeated the terrible, though not desperate accounts of the endless circle of destruction and resurrection. Maybe gods speak to us today, aware that what has gone never comes back.

It is in this sense that one central question arises within this thorough interdisciplinary examination of Pakal's personal attributes and biography: Will the novel insights on the individual level be the window to a much more complex and astounding collective vital history? This book provides the new framework and reference for a major adventure in Maya scholarship: the joint re-creation of the life and death histories of those people who inhabited the ancient Maya world.

Janaab' Pakal of Palenque

1

Studying Janaab' Pakal and Reconstructing Maya Dynastic History

Vera Tiesler and Andrea Cucina

The quest for reconstructing Classic Maya noble history is becoming ever more popular in the academic community. Still, Maya biographic research is warranted mainly by the intricate written records on Maya courtly life, deciphered through epigraphy, although its efforts also are receiving increasing input from investigation of skeletal remains. As part of physical anthropology and—in the past few decades—bioarchaeology,[1] osteological and dental studies have contributed to the interpretation of ancient societies with a broad range of biographic and demographic data, health records, and biocultural practices. Recent advances in microscopic and molecular analysis have added to the interpretation. In Maya research, this holds especially true for the groundbreaking studies of stable isotopes and mtDNA (Wright 1996, 1999a; Merriwether et al. 1997; Whittington and Reed 1997; White 1999; González-Oliver et al. 2001; Burton et al. 2003; Matheson et al. 2003; Buikstra et al. 2004). Their results have made osteology increasingly attractive, more so for the study of dynastic burials with their great demand for detailed biocultural information.

Along with more conventional methods, many of the new powerful analytical tools have been put to work to generate detailed information of rulers' lives, such as their natality and residential histories, physical regimes and impairments, childhood diseases, dental health, and nutrition and diet, providing valuable new insights on the aristocracy of Copán, Piedras Negras, Dos Pilas, Calakmul, and Palenque (Demarest et al. 1991; Carrasco et al. 1998; Tiesler, Cucina, and Romano 2002; Burton et al. 2003; Houston et al. 2003; Buikstra et al. 2004). A second line of skeletal research draws from human taphonomy, providing data on posthumous body treatments both as part of a personalized death cult, directed by and toward the elite, and as part of the rituals involving their sacrificial escorts (Tiesler, Cucina, and Romano 2002, 2003; Tiesler and Cucina 2003; Weiss-

Krejci 2003; Buikstra et al. 2004). A third application, which has just started drawing scholars' attention, centers on facial reconstructions and recognition of famous Maya nobles. This approach can add an important facet to the biographic research by providing an image and potential identity match for historic personages (Tiesler, Cucina, and Romano 2003, 2004). It is relevant because the actual burial place may not necessarily be related to the inscription references on the dignitaries' death and commemoration, a limitation illustrated by the ongoing discussions on the identity of the so-called Red Queen, recently discovered in Palenque's Structure XIII (López-Jiménez and González-Cruz 1995; González-Cruz 1998, 2001).

Interpreted jointly with iconographic portraiture and the written record, the study of noble life and death now permits the reconstruction of aristocratic history on a regional level, similar in many ways to the approaches used in the study of the entangled European history of nobility. However, the different data sets do not always reconcile harmonically to cast a unified documentation of life and death. Many ambiguous or even plainly contradictory results have generated academic controversies centered on the credibility of both the osteological information and the written record (see Marcus 1992a; Martin and Grube 2000).

In this volume, we center our attention on one notorious example of conflicting sources of information: the investigation of Janaab' Pakal of Palenque. The discovery of this famous ruler inside Palenque's Temple of the Inscriptions a little more than half a century ago triggered a renovated enthusiasm regarding this ancient city on the western fringes of the Maya world (figure 1.1). Since the initial documentation of Palenque during the eighteenth century, it has figured prominently in Maya research. The town is located scenically at the feet of the Chiapanec Highlands, from where it overlooks the plains of the Usumacinta basin, gradually descending toward the Gulf of Mexico to its north. The city gained prominence in the regional political network during the Classic period (ca. AD 250–900), as it emerged as capital over the B'aakal kingdom in the western Lowlands. Concurrently, its urban area grew to an extraordinary 3.5 square kilometers, leading to a vast depopulation of the surrounding hinterland (Liendo 2002). During Pakal's reign in the seventh century AD, Palenque expanded and consolidated its political authority in the region until suffering the same fate as all fellow central Lowland kingdoms. Its dynastic sequence came to an end during the early ninth century, after which the city was

FIGURE 1.1 Temple of the Inscriptions and Temple XIII, Palenque (photograph by Andrea Cucina)

gradually depopulated and abandoned in the aftermath of what has been coined the "Maya Collapse" (Martin and Grube 2000).

Since the discovery of the Palenque ruins in modern times, generations of scholars have been mesmerized by the beauty of its imposing natural surroundings, its architecture, and the harmony and anatomical detail of its skillfully executed sculptures. They have been joined more recently by epigraphers who have deciphered much of the kingdom's tangled noble history (see also chapters 2, 7, and 10 in this volume).

The Discovery

On the afternoon of 27 November 1952, during the fourth field season at Palenque, Dr. Alberto Ruz Lhuillier made a public announcement that was to be remembered for a long time. He declared that the megalithic block inside the "secret chamber" below the Temple of the Inscriptions was a sarcophagus that held the remains of an unknown dignitary, constituting at that time the most extraordinary tomb finding of the pre-Columbian world (Romano 1980, 1989) (figure 1.2).

FIGURE 1.2 Dr. Alberto Ruz entering the funerary chamber in the Temple of the Inscriptions, Palenque (photograph by Arturo Romano)

Upon discovery, the huge block of stone was thought to serve merely as a support for the delicately stone-carved slab it was carrying. Its real use was suspected only after the monolith was perforated diagonally from the side. As the drill hit the stone's inner space, it came out stained with red pigment. The research team's suspicion was soon confirmed after they lifted the heavy sarcophagus slab and sustained it with six robust wooden logs. Below it, a womb-shaped inner lid appeared, embedded to perfection into the hollow funerary monolith. White stucco filled the slits between both blocks and the four lithic plugs, thus sealing off hermetically the tomb's interior (Arturo Romano, personal communication, 2001). Once cleared, the plugs permitted a first sight into the spectacular inner space that revealed a richly furnished primary interment of a single skeleton completely coated with vermilion pigment (figure 1.3). The skull was partially covered by a mosaic green jadeite mask, the thorax resting beneath a pectoral plaque made of large jadeite beads.

During the following three days, a support team was entrusted with the exploration: medical doctor and physical anthropologist Eusebio Dávalos Hurtado, art expert José Servín Palencia, and Arturo Romano Pacheco, who had been commissioned to take photographs and assist in the general tasks of onsite recording and analysis. For the occasion, heavy photographic and lighting equipment and specialized osteometric tools (spreading and sliding caliphers, an osteometric board, and index tables) were brought in from Mexico City in preparation for a detailed, up-to-date exploration (Romano 1980:285–86).

The delegation and the material had to be flown from Villahermosa into Palenque because no paved road led to the community. Poet Carlos Pellicer, at that time in charge of Tabasco's regional museum, joined the incoming party (Romano 1980, 1989). Several intensive working days of detailed onsite recording ensued until interrupted by the holiday season. It was decided that only the objects of personal attire were to be lifted from the tomb, along with the dignitary's skull, which was to undergo a thorough lab analysis by physical anthropologists Eusebio Dávalos Hurtado and Arturo Romano Pacheco.

The investigators' report, extended and verified 20 years later, describes an articulated skeleton of a robust male adult in his forties, with an estimated stature of 1.65 meters, who lacked visible signs of skeletal pathology (Dávalos and Romano 1955; Ruz 1978; Romano 1980, 1989). The

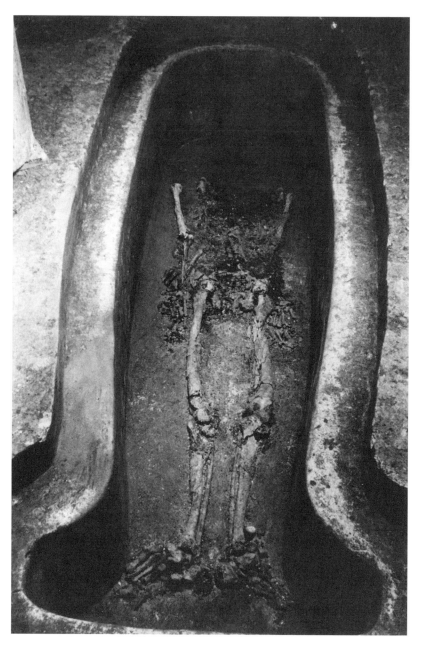

FIGURE 1.3 The opened tomb, 1952 (photograph by Arturo Romano)

age estimate was based in part on the degree of dental attrition, which the anthropologists found to be slight. They considered the dignitary's teeth to be "well developed and only slightly worn on their occlusal surface," and "the sockets of both inferior second molars were reabsorbed" (Dávalos and Romano 1955:108).

The Aftermath

Twenty years after the finding in 1952, some of the original appraisals of the personage from the sarcophagus tomb began to be challenged because epigraphic deciphering of the inscriptions in the 1970s soon provided the dignitary with a name and basic biographic information. The readings document that K'inich Janaab' Pakal I, divine ruler of the B'aakal reign, was born in AD 603 and enthroned at the age of 12. He died on AD 28 August 683 at the age of 80 (9.12.11.5.18), to unite with his ancestors at an altar place in the House of the Nine Figures, prepared by his son and follower to the throne, Kan B'alam (Schele and Mathews 1998; Martin and Grube 2000; Martin 2003a) (figure 1.4). Besides age, the determination of Pakal's physical health was put into question because portraits of him were claimed to display a clubfoot and possibly supernumerary toes as distinguishing features (Greene, Rosenblum Scandizzo, and Scandizzo 1976:70; Greene 1980:277).

Two additional discussions have been raised on Pakal that are of more recent origin and are dealt with in chapters 7 and 8 in this volume. In 1994, Mexican archaeologists discovered the remains of a female dignitary inside a sarcophagus tomb in Structure XIIIsub, right next to the Temple of the Inscriptions. She was soon named "Red Queen" for the intense red cinnabar color of her remains and for lack of any confirmed identity. The chronology of associated funerary vessels indicates that her interment falls roughly in the same time as Pakal's own deposition (López-Jiménez 1996). This concurrence—together with her elaborate mortuary arrangements, including two sacrificial victims, and her privileged location right next to Pakal's mortuary edifice—soon came to raise questions on her potential family ties to this ruler. So far different historical identities have been attributed to her remains, ranging from Lady Ix S'ak' K'uk', mother of the ruler; Lady Ix Kinuw; and Janaab' Pakal's wife Ix Tz'akb'u Ajaw (Ahpo Hel), mother of Kan B'alam (López-Jiménez and González-Cruz

FIGURE 1.4 Pakal's funerary chamber (photograph by Patricia Tamés)

1995; González-Cruz 1998, 2001; Tiesler, Cucina, and Romano 2002, 2004; López-Jiménez 2003).

The other recent debate takes up Ruz's original appraisal of the mortuary box that sealed the entrance of the monolithic chamber. Ruz (1973) had interpreted the human deposit as five or maybe six sacrificial victims laid down at the same time. Estella Weiss-Krejci (2003), in her critical review on Maya tombs containing more than one individual, challenges this assessment on the grounds of reduced space and lack of affirmative evidence. She offers the alternative explanation of mortuary reuse by successive interments of members of Pakal's "house" in a now energy-laden place (2003:374–75).

In light of the ongoing debates, it is surprising that the original investigation was not followed up by a second thorough in situ study of the skeleton during the 1970s, designed to resolve the increasingly irreconcilable arguments. In the time between the discovery of the sarcophagus in 1952 and our recent study in 1999, it was reopened at least two more times. In 1978, Arturo Romano was commissioned to return Pakal's fragmented skull to Palenque, where it was repatriated during a solemn act (Valencia 1978). Despite consolidation efforts in 1952 with "duco" cement, the pieces had much deteriorated, presumably because of the microclimatic changes in humidity and temperature that occurred once the burial was unsealed (Romano 1977; see also Alvarado 1999 and Orea-Magaña 1999). The mandible and neurocranium displayed a marked taphonomic (i.e., postmortem) deformation that hampered all efforts at reconstruction. Some of the long skull's outer bone layers were exfoliating; fissures had formed in most fragments; and various teeth had separated from their roots.

Similar findings were reported in an official letter by Arturo Solano for the remainder of the skeleton. The restorer had visited the tomb for two weeks during the month of November 1978 before the repatriation of the skull. On this occasion, the remains' state of preservation had to be examined and action taken if necessary (Solano 1978). The bones were in a "state of powder and fragmentation that did not even permit touching for the fear of destruction" (Solano 1978). Facing the advanced progress of deterioration, Solano proceeded with photographic recording and resolved to inject the bones in situ with Paraloid b-72, diluted with thinner. Once these goals were concluded, the sarcophagus lid was heaved back on top of the monolith.

In the meantime, Ruz had the original osteological age estimate revised and confirmed by Arturo Romano (Ruz 1978). Romano himself entrusted physicians Mario Antonio Balcorta and Francisco R. Villalobos with a histomorphological appraisal of a cranial fragment from the personage for additional evidence (Ruz 1978:293). Their results, which appeared in Ruz's article titled "Gerontocracy at Palenque?" (1978), described a uniform mineralization of the bone matrix that they considered to be consistent with an age between 30 and 40 years. Ruz added to this evidence historical documentation and skeletal life-span data from several large collections from Mesoamerica and North America that had been gathered by Carlos Serrano, Johanna Faulhaber, and Douglas Ubelaker. His review of their results underscored that ancient populations were generally short-lived, with few individuals exceeding 50 years of age (see chapter 5). Ruz went on to suggest a reading for Pakal's birth and death dates, referring to a long count date on the south side of the sarcophagus as Pakal's birth reference and another one on the west side as that of his demise. Both dates provided an age just short of 40 years, very different from the 80 years suggested by Mathews and Schele (1974), which Ruz emphatically refused, along with the reading of the personage's name as "Pacal" or *shield*. Ruz explained that it is

> difficult to accept as a scientific means of determining the age of an individual, who did in fact exist and whose remains have been discovered in his tomb, the exclusive study of such inscriptions, whether definitely related to the person buried (tombstone) or found in other monuments and therefore not indisputably referring to the said person, without any concern whatsoever for the person's bodily remains. ... On the other hand there is the complete skeleton of the individual whose age is to be established. And at no point do the authors who "decipher" his age from the hieroglyphic texts allude to the results of the anthropological analysis, even to compare them with the epigraphic study, criticize them and refute them. They roundly affirm the personage's age, completely ignoring the osteological evidence. (1978:292)

During the 1980s, new details on Pakal's life and death were provided by Arturo Romano (1980; see chapter 6 in this volume). He referred to the artificial head form as "tabular oblique" and reiterated that Pakal was a physically normal individual with no signs of congenital afflictions in the form of hypertrophies or supernumerary bony segments. Referring to the work of Greene, Rosenblum Scandizzo, and Scandizzo (1976), Romano strongly disapproved any possibility of clubfoot or polydactily in the remains of the dignitary and at the same time denied the scientific value of these authors' iconographic study. By that time, the discussion had grown field specific and had developed nationalistic facets. At the time that the two noncommunicating factions were forming, the arguments surrounding the ruler's potential deforming disease and, more so, his age at death were growing irreconcilable. One faction supported the physical anthropologists' interpretation, whereas the other shared the opinion of the rapidly evolving international circles of Maya epigraphers and art historians.

By now, the advancing field of Maya epigraphy has come to confirm the birth and death data originally deciphered by Mathews and Schele (1974). It has also been able to determine a full phonetic reading of the ruler's name and full title, now read as K'inich Janaab' Pakal I (Martin and

Grube 2000; see also Grube, chapter 10, in this volume). The current debate on Pakal's age has shifted accordingly. No longer the translations, but the misuse of monumental Maya inscriptions as official documents has been held potentially responsible to account for the discrepancy in the age assignments (Marcus 1992a). On the side of skeletal studies, the reliability of morphological age estimates has been put into question, especially in the advanced age classes (Hammond and Molleson 1994; Urcid 1993; see also chapters 2, 3, 4, and 11 in this volume).

The Study

In view of the ongoing debate on Pakal's skeletal record and the evanescent physical evidence, the recent in situ study of Pakal's remains was driven by two major goals. First, the processes and agents that were disintegrating the already much deteriorated skeleton had to be diagnosed and halted if possible. The second objective addressed the need for an updated reappraisal of the skeleton because further data and new assessments were essential to provide satisfactory answers to the ongoing debates surrounding Pakal. These assessments benefit both from the new frames of regional bioarchaeological research and from the potent analytical tools only recently made available to bioarchaeology.

The reappraisal of the personage's skeleton was first contrived in the course of a short stay at Palenque in preparation for the Third Palenque Round Table of the Instituto Nacional de Antropología e Historia (INAH). During a visit to the Temple of the Inscriptions in late 1998, the senior author scrutinized parts of the ruler's skeleton from the outside through the four plug holes. On this occasion, vestiges of insect infestation and bat excrement were observed in the tomb's inner space, motivating the project Conservación, Restauración y Estudio in Situ de los Restos Humanos de K'inich Janaab' Pakal I, Personaje Hallado en el Recinto Funerario del Templo de las Inscripciones, Palenque, Chiapas. The study, with Vera Tiesler in charge, was financed by the INAH technical secretary upon approval by its archaeological council.

The onsite recording of the remains was conducted during three days in 1999. It was guided by the useful practical advice of Arturo Romano (figure 1.5). Almost half a century after his original participation in Ruz's team, he now assisted in the interventions from the site camp and was in-

FIGURE 1.5 Arturo Romano revisits Palenque in 1999 (photograph by Vera Tiesler).

formed periodically on the state of progress. Polaroid pictures taken from inside the funerary chamber aided his evaluation of the skeleton's condition.

In the course of the in situ study, a detailed drawing was made, and the bones were treated by the expert hands of restorer Haydée Orea-Magaña (figure 1.6). Photographer Patricia Tamés conducted the recording of the assemblage and of specific diagnostic skeletal traits. Metric and morphological skeletal data were obtained using caliphers and entered in a set of recording sheets designed by Buikstra and Ubelaker (1994) and Tiesler (1999). Twenty-four red-pigment, skeletal, and unidentified organic samples were taken for posterior histological, chemical, and molecular evaluation.

Back home, the team proceeded with a thorough data assessment, aiming to gain new insights into the ruler's basic biographic data. Maya epigraphers Nikolai Grube and Simon Martin were consulted repeatedly on epigraphic issues. Additional special analyses were conducted on Pakal's remains:

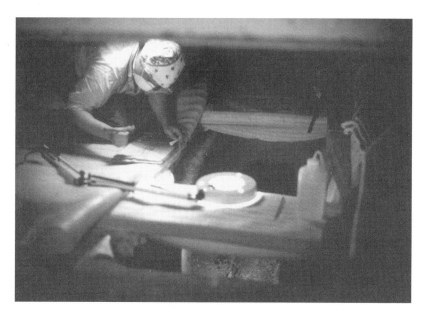

FIGURE 1.6 Restorer Haydée Orea-Magaña at work (photograph by Vera Tiesler)

Paleodiet by trace elements (Samuel Tejeda, Laboratorio de Fluorescencia de Rx, Instituto Nacional de Investigaciones Nucleares [ININ]).

Microscopic identification of organic samples (José Luis Alvarado, Laboratorio de Paleobotánia, INAH).

Study of pigments in thin sections (Javier Vázquez, Escuela Nacional de Restauración, INAH).

Taphonomic and paleopathological evaluation, age determination in thin sections (Samuel Stout and Margaret Streeter, University of Missouri at Columbia; Vera Tiesler and Andrea Cucina, Universidad Autónoma de Yucatán).

Application of new parameters in chronological age determination, using the pubic simphyses, auricular surfaces, and cranial suture closure (Jane Buikstra, University of New Mexico; George Milner, Pennsylvania State University; Jesper Boldsen, Odense University, Denmark)

Study of mtDNA and nuclear DNA (Carney Matheson, Lakehead University, Canada).

Pigment identification (Samuel Tejeda, Laboratorio de Fluorescencia de Rx, ININ; Iván Oliva and Patricia Quintana, Centro de Investigaciones Avanzadas/Politécnico Nacional, Unidad Mérida).

Evaluation of diagenetic changes in bone (Patricia Quintana, Centro de Investigaciones Avanzadas/Politécnico Nacional, Unidad Mérida; Samuel Tejeda, Laboratorio de Fluorescencia de Rx, ININ).

Scanning electron microscopy of histological thin sections (Iván Oliva, Centro de Investigaciones Avanzadas/Politécnico Nacional, Unidad Mérida).

Reconstruction of dietary components and provenience through strontium stable isotope ratios (Douglas Price and James Burton, University of Wisconsin at Madison, coordinated by Jane Buikstra).

Chronological age estimation through dental evaluation (Della Cook, Indiana University, coordinated by Jane Buikstra).

As regards Pakal's death ritual, new insights were to be gained on the body treatment and the circumstances of death of his sacrificial companions. For this purpose, additional data were compiled between 2002 and 2003 through the study of fragments of Pakal's skull, vertebrae, and ribs, housed in the headquarters of the INAH Dirección de Antropología Física in Mexico City. On these occasions, we also investigated some of the skeletal remains of Pakal's companions. A deeper understanding of the ruler's life and death within Palenque society was gleaned from a previous study of at least twenty-eight other skeletal individuals from the city's core area, excavated between 1951 and 1972 and now housed in the INAH headquarters (Tiesler 1999). Rib samples from this collection proved to be of valuable help also in interpreting the histology of Pakal's rib.

Still another bioarchaeological investigation turned out to be crucial for this project. For the past seven years, Tiesler, Cucina, and Romano have studied the remains of the Red Queen and her two sacrificial companions from Temple XIII. The results of this study and the other skeletal data were designed to put into a collective perspective the individual information retrieved from Pakal and his sacrificial companions.

This Volume

This volume grew out of the papers presented on a chilly Saturday morning at the symposium "Bioarchaeological Investigations of a Royal Tomb at the Temple of Inscriptions, Palenque, Mexico: Shedding New Light on Hanab Pakal and Dynastic Maya History." It was held in April 2003 at the Sixty-eighth Annual Meeting of the Society of American Archaeology in Milwaukee, Wisconsin. The eleven presentations given there were meant to communicate the broad scope of applied interdisciplinary research conducted on the Pakal remains in order to provide additional information, fresh insights, answers to old disputes, and, most important, new relevant questions in the field of Maya dynastic research.

The chapters are organized accordingly. Chapter 2 discusses the dignitary's life, appearance, and mortuary treatment from a regional bioarchaeological perspective. Because Pakal's age at death is likely the most important debate, the contributions dealing specifically with this issue follow immediately. In chapter 3, Jane E. Buikstra, George R. Milner, and Jesper L. Boldsen revisit the age-at-death controversy. Apart from new results regarding conventional age markers in the pelvis, the authors put to work a new macroscopic ageing method called Transition Analysis, which is especially designed for advanced age ranges. The authors conclude that Pakal did live well into his second half-century. Sam D. Stout and Margaret Streeter, in chapter 4, reach a similar conclusion by use of a histomorphological approach validated by comparative data from Palenque's Classic population. Pakal's life and age at death in Palenque's demographic context is also the topic of chapter 5 by Lourdes Márquez, Patricia Hernández, and Carlos Serrano, underscoring the scarceness of such an advanced age in the reconstructed demographic mortality curve.

Subsequent chapters explore additional facets of Pakal's life and death. In chapter 6, Arturo Romano employs taphonomic and new osteological images to refute claims that the dignitary had deforming diseases. In chapter 7, T. Douglas Price, James H. Burton, Vera Tiesler, Simon Martin, and Jane E. Buikstra compare stable isotope ratios in enamel and bone samples obtained from Pakal and the Red Queen of Temple XIIIsub to the written information on Palenque's nobility with the aim of providing new evidence of the king's residential history and clues on his family ties to the female dignitary buried next to his temple shrine. In chapter

8, Andrea Cucina and Vera Tiesler provide new insights on sacrifice and ritual posthumous body treatments in elite tombs. The chapter centers on the attendants from Palenque's Temple XIII and the Temple of the Inscriptions whose death was part of the elaborate ancestral cult reserved to Maya paramounts.

Chapters 9 and 10 shift from a Pakal or Palenque framework in the age-at-death issue to wider or different contexts. Chapter 9, the controversial contribution by Patricia Hernández and Lourdes Márquez, reconsiders the supposed longevity of rulers from Yaxchilán, Shield Jaguar and Bird Jaguar, documented in the written record and investigated through the skeletal evidence. Nikolai Grube analyzes royal Maya life and death histories based on the written record from a regional perspective in chapter 10, providing a broad panorama of the twisted power politics of rulers' families and the entangled genealogies of the Maya Classic, also more than applicable to Pakal's lineage.

The discussion by John Verano in chapter 11 furnishes a unified perspective on the volume contributors' joint conclusions, centering on the age question as the main issue of the debate. His remarks should hold true for most investigations of past societies because no absolute truth should be expected in the re-creations of past life histories from the material record. Even the most thorough and detailed investigation will eventually be rendered obsolete and become a piece of history in itself as scientific methods advance and the frames of reference gradually grow ever more complex. Progress may lead to enrichment through additional information and confirmation of the original panorama or may in some cases oblige researchers to reconsider and reshape their previously held interpretations, as Norman Hammond pointed out during his Pakal symposium discussion. Interestingly enough, the present reappraisal of Janaab' Pakal's remains cover all these possibilities. In this sense, we hope not only to share an updated study of a well-known historical personage, but also to introduce and furnish further elements of reflection, to trace new lines and caveats in regional investigation, and to offer some innovative approaches to biocultural and interdisciplinary reconstruction of Maya dynastic history.

ACKNOWLEDGMENTS

The editors thank the participants in the Pakal Project for their important contributions, their shared effort, and their enthusiasm. We appreciate very much Arturo Romano's collaboration, solidarity, perspectives, and timeless answers to our many questions. Professor Romano is the only living witness among Ruz's original inner circle of investigators during the initial recovery of Pakal's tomb in the 1950s. Special thanks go to Jane Buikstra (now at Arizona State University), for sharing this "adventure number 1,001" in bioarchaeology with us through all its stages. We also gratefully acknowledge the spirited teamwork of and contribution by the other participants of the investigation: Carlos Serrano (Universidad Nacional Autónoma de México), Haydeé Orea-Magaña (INAH), Sam Stout (now at Ohio State University), Margaret Streeter (now at Boise State University), George Milner (Pennsylvania State University), Jesper Boldsen (Odense University, Denmark), Javier Vázquez (INAH), José Luis Alvarado (Laboratorio de Paleobotánia, INAH), Samuel Tejeda (ININ), Valeria García Vierna (INAH), Daniela Rodriguez (INAH), Carney Matheson (Lakehead University, Canada), Douglas Price and James Burton (University of Wisconsin at Madison), Della Cook (Indiana University), and Iván Oliva and Patricia Quintana (Centro de Investigaciones Avanzadas/Politécnico Nacional, Unidad Mérida). We also thank Patricia Tamés for her professional photographs.

We are likewise indebted to those who joined forces for the Sixty-eighth Annual Meeting of the Society for American Archaeology in Milwaukee, Wisconsin, to share their valuable insights and viewpoints during the symposium "Bioarchaeological Investigations of a Royal Tomb at the Temple of Inscriptions": Lourdes Márquez and Patricia Hernández (INAH), Nikolai Grube (University of Bonn), John Verano (Tulane University), and Norman Hammond (University of Boston).

Marco Ramírez Salomón provided detailed radiographies; Mirna Sánchez supplied skillful drawings; and Simon Martin generously shared his stimulating recent work on Palenque, which proved of much help in envisioning the "big picture" of Pakal's biography. We also thank the editorial staffs of the University of Arizona Press for their support and assistance in making this English version a reality, as well as Nydia Lara and Hernán Lara for sharing their enthusiasm and interest in our endeavors during many inspiring discussions, enlightened from philosophical angles that only Nydia can imagine. Elizabeth Dunkel gave editorial assistance, and two anonymous reviewers supplied many helpful comments.

Last but not least, we express our enormous gratitude for the institutional support lent by INAH staff Alejandro Martínez, Joaquín García Bárcena, and Francisco Ortíz in allowing us the opportunity to study the skeletal materials housed in INAH's Dirección de Antropología Física. Ethnologist Sergio Raúl Arroyo's generous funding, support, and academic vision made this dream investigation come true.

Life and Death of the Ruler
Recent Bioarchaeological Findings
Vera Tiesler

This chapter is intended as a preamble to the subsequent contributions, which specifically address most of the questions on Pakal's life and death. I provide a general osteobiographic profile of this ruler, his lifestyle and appearance, as well as new insights on some of the posthumous treatments of his body.

Before turning to Pakal's biography from the bioarchaeological point of view, I briefly address some key issues of his record and insights into his historic role and place in ancient Maya society. This information is crucial for subsequent discussions because it provides the historical frame within which the skeletal data set can be viewed. In this attempt, I broadly follow the recent accounts by Schele and Mathews (1998:95–132), Martin and Grube (2000:159–68), and Martin (2003a), who have provided a detailed chronicle of the king's life and epoch.

Chronicles of Janaab' Pakal's Life and Death

K'inich Janaab' Pakal, divine ruler of the reign of B'aakal, stands out as a pivotal figure of Classic Maya dynastic history. His name identifies his attributions: *k'inich* alludes to the sun god, and *pakal* means "shield." No translation of the clause *janaab'* exists yet despite its transparent phonetical reading (Martin 2003a). Epigraphy provides detailed accounts of Pakal's long life and successful reign, equaled by few other Classic Maya paramounts (Schele and Freidel 1990; Schele and Mathews 1998; Martin and Grube 2000; see also Grube, chapter 10, in this volume). Inscriptions record Pakal's date of birth as 9.8.9.13.0 or 8 Ajaw 13 Pop in the long-count and short-count cycles, corresponding to 23 March 603 in the Gregorian calendar. Apparently, the prince was born during times of turbulence and crises; the city of Lakanhá (Palenque) had just been attacked by Calakmul, marking the unsuccessful end of Lady Yohl Ik'nal's K'atun-long reign. Equally calamitous was the eight-year term of her successor, Aj Ne'Ohl Mat, who experienced a second defeat by the same enemy. The king died in 612, and no clear information exists on the three crisis-plagued years to follow. Pakal's own accession in 615 is commemorated on the Oval Tablet from the Palace. The scene depicts the youngster being invested with the insignias of power by his mother, Lady S'ak' K'uk', who probably also oversaw the first years of the boy's reign (figure 2.1). Surprisingly little is known about the first 30 years of Pakal's rulership. In 626, he wedded Lady Ix Tz'akb'u Ajaw, who apparently came from outside Lakanhá (see chapter 7) and who gave him at least three sons, two of whom were to succeed him to the throne: K'inich Kan B'alam II was born in 635, followed by K'inich K'an Joy Chitam II in 644. A third child, Tiwohl Chan Mat, saw the light of day in 648, but died at the young age of 32 (Ringle 1996; Martin 2003a). Pakal himself is mentioned in the record as the presiding authority over his son's burial in 680, possibly inside Temple XVIII (Martin 2003a). Lady Ix Tz'akb'u Ajaw did not live on to witness the loss of her son; her demise is recorded on 16 November 672 (Schele and Mathews 1998:108).

Nikolai Grube argues in this volume (chapter 10) that rulers tend to wait to erect monuments until their reigns are stable and their tenure appears secured, which is usually quite late in time. This holds true also for Pakal's rulership; it was only in the second half of his long reign that he started to commission an impressive bulk of commemorative writings and constructions, including the Olvidado and the Palace. In several of the Palace rooms, the inscriptions and imagery highlight the king's military achievements and commemorate his diplomatic feats.

Around 675, well before his death on 28 August 683 (9.12.11.5.18), Pakal started to work on his own massive mausoleum: the Temple of the Inscriptions, with its vaulted inner chamber and spectacular monolithic tomb (Schele and Mathews 1998:97) (figure 2.2). It is likely that he also commissioned the remodeling of the companion temples to its west, including the Temple of the Skull, housing a richly furnished tomb, Structures XIIsub and Structure XIIIsub, the famous resting place of the "Red Queen" (López-Jiménez 1996) (see figure 1.1).

The final preparations of Pakal's own tomb inside the Temple of the Inscriptions were supervised by Kan B'alam II, his son and follower to the throne. The inscription panels read that "he [Kan B'alam] gave caring to

FIGURE 2.1 Oval Tablet (redrawn by Mirna Sánchez from Greene 1985:fig. 91)

the House of the Nine Figures, its holy name, the tomb of the Sun-faced Hanab Pakal, Holy Palenque Lord" (Schele and Mathews 1998:108). There, at the altar place, Pakal was laid down to unite with his ancestors (Eberl 2005:43–66). This "altar" most likely refers to the decorated monolithic coffin with its heavy outer slab and inner lid, held in place by six supports (Marquina 1964; Ruz 1973). Red pigment covered the inside of the hollow monolith, which housed the mortal remains of the king along with most

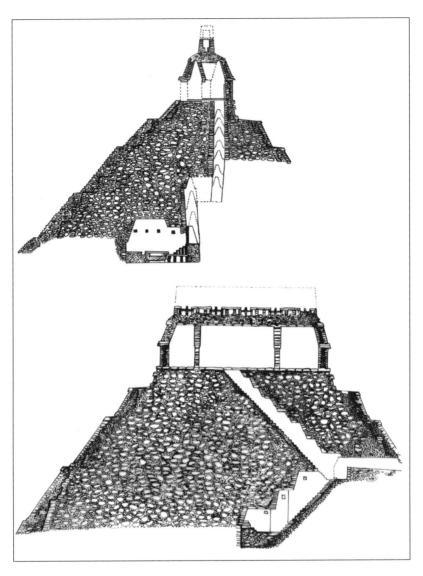

FIGURE 2.2 Temple of the Inscriptions; cut north-south and east-west
(redrawn by Mirna Sánchez from Ruz 1973:319, figs. 261e and 261f)

of his personal adornments and offerings. The attire includes a mosaic facial mask, a mouth ornament, earflares, a pectoral plaque, wrist bracelets, and finger rings. Sculptured images of Sak Hunal and the Maize God were also placed in the sarcophagus, alluding to Pakal's divine attribute and to the Maya mythological concepts of rebirth and resurrection (Ruz 1973; Quenon and Le Fort 1997; Schele and Mathews 1998).

Kan B'alam II was already a 48-year-old mature man when he assumed the rulership of the B'aakal realm in January of the year 684, 132 days after his father's demise. The ostentatious funerary paraphernalia that he organized during that time in honor of his father surely provided an apt opportunity for the king-to-be to legitimate publicly his own claims to the throne and to assure his place in the dynastic line (Schele and Mathews 1998; Martin and Grube 2000). As Grube points out in chapter 10, the interregnum period before Kan B'alam's accession might have been less smooth than he wanted to communicate in the monumental imagery he commissioned.

Although selective, this historical account still allows for unique insights into Late Classic dynastic life and death and into Janaab' Pakal's own role within its sociopolitical arena. It has to be stressed, however, that the epigraphic record is far from complete, as Grube underscores in chapter 10. Documented life events, which the ruler in power commissioned retrospectively, usually center on key episodes of ritual and public importance, but other episodes and facets of aristocratic biography do not appear in the chronicles. Pakal's written history and monumental portraiture is not an exception. We do not learn much from the inscriptions about daily concerns. What was family life like at the upper end of Palenque society? How did nobles pass their childhood? How did the aristocracies from within and between sites relate to each other? How segregated from the remainder of society were the upper sectors and rulers such as Pakal? What did they eat? What were the prevailing living conditions? How did diseases affect nobles typically? Which pastimes did they indulge in? How did they look? And how were their bodies prepared for the last journey, after their life had come to an end?

The following paragraphs explore some aspects of Pakal's course of life and death from a bioarchaeological perspective, and I interpret the specified data sets from a social and cultural viewpoint. With this description, I hope to confirm and enrich the previous inventory and to add new facets to Pakal's biography, especially concerning his lifestyle and appearance and the mortuary treatment he underwent. As noted earlier, this information introduces some key issues in the Pakal investigation, which subsequent chapters deal with more specifically.

Material and Methods

The information given here is based primarily on the osteological, dental, and taphonomic data recorded during the onsite study of the opened sarcophagus in 1999 (figure 2.3). Some vertebral and isolated rib fragments from the personage have been stored since the 1950s at the Dirección de Antropología Física of the Instituto Nacional de Antropología e Historia (INAH) in Mexico City and were studied separately. Red-pigment, bone, and unidentified organic samples were taken to perform histological analyses and for chemical evaluations (figure 2.4). I discuss some results of these special analyses in this chapter.

During the visit to Palenque, the investigative team drew Pakal's skeletal segments to scale with the help of a grid and a plumb line. We then transferred this draft to a detailed layered 1:2 tracing. Anatomical identification, orientation, degree of articulation, and taphonomic conditions were reported for each recorded bone segment. The latter include surface color and erosion, degree of fragmentation, pigment covering, and specific faunal and cultural postmortem changes. The drawing was used for the interpretation of general skeletal distribution. To infer the original conditions of placement and further potential cultural disturbances, I employed a set of practical concepts derived and adapted from different sources of general taphonomic investigation, mainly the French *anthropologie de terrain* (Duday 1997) and an array of burial observations from the region (Tiesler 2004).

General procedures were based on osteometry and macroscopic observation, aided by magnification and complemented by X-ray, optical, and scanning electron microscopy (SEM). The data were recorded onsite on eleven data sheets and entered in a database of skeletal attributes from the Maya area. Particles of pigment adhering to rib fragments were embedded in polymeric resins, thin-sectioned, and analyzed to determine material properties, diagenetic changes, and bone contamination. Iván Oliva and Patricia Quintana of the Departamento de Física Aplicada, Centro

FIGURE 2.3 The opened tomb, 1999 (photograph by Patricia Tamés)

de Investigaciones Avanzadas/Politécnico Nacional, Unidad Mérida, conducted these studies using low-impact SEM, energy dispersive X ray, and
X-ray diffraction methods. Samuel Stout, Margaret Streeter, and Andrea
Cucina of the University of Missouri at Columbia obtained thin sections
from the midportion of an uncalcified rib. With them, I studied the histological properties and taphonomic contamination of these sections.

In determining sex, common parameters were used, complemented
by metric discrimination of single and multiple variables (Steele and
Bramblett 1988; Buikstra and Ubelaker 1994; Tiesler 1999). Age estimation
rested on the examination of the morphology of the auricular and pubic
surfaces, dental wear, degenerative changes, and degree of ectocranial suture obliteration (Suchey et al. 1984; Meindl and Lovejoy 1985; Meindl and
Mensforth 1985).

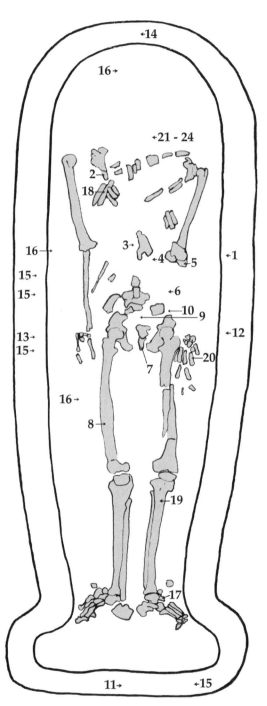

FIGURE 2.4
Distribution of samples
taken in situ (drawing
by Vera Tiesler)

The maximum living stature was calculated from preserved long bones, using the corrected regression formula by Genovés (1967; see also del Ángel and Cisneros 2004). The assessment of patterns of physical constitution relied on the external geometry and expression of muscle-attachment areas, considered in the context of Classic Maya skeletal populations (Tiesler 1999). Regarding pathology, general inflammatory processes (osteomyelitis-periostitis, arthritis, porotic hyperostosis, cribra orbitalia) were recorded on the cranial and postcranial skeleton after Schultz (1988) and Merbs (1983). Presence and extent of carious lesions and enamel hypoplasia were evaluated for each tooth following the parameters established by Schultz (1988); each lesion was expressed in grades from 0 (absent) to 4 (extreme or deforming). Overall rates of dental wear were scored in first molars according to Hillson (1986) and Brothwell (1987).

To determine the presence, degree, and type of head shaping, we employed only nonmetric parameters due to poor preservation. The classification of form and technique was based on the scheme established by Imbelloni (1938; Dembo and Imbelloni 1938) and adjusted by Romano (1965) and Tiesler (1998, 1999). The dentitions were evaluated according to the presence or absence of artificial decoration. The modified dental patterns were classified according to techniques and formal types, using Romero's (1986) classification; from there, the overall visual dental pattern was inferred following the classification by Tiesler (1999, 2001a).

Body Treatment and Entombment

Although the ruler's remains were not altered by secondary funerary rites, looting, or rodent activity, time and environmental conditions had left their marks on them. When discovered, Pakal's skeleton was found in a highly deteriorated state due to high temperatures and humidity. Preservation today is even poorer than it was 50 years ago because the previous interventions have left their toll. Before 1952, the inner cavity of the monolith had been covered by a heavy outer slab and an adapted inner lid. The slits left by the latter were found sealed completely with white stucco (Arturo Romano, personal communication, 2001). Since then, the sarcophagus has been exposed to bat excrement, insects, microorganisms, and fluctuating high temperature and humidity. Mass tourism has proved detrimental to conservation over the years (Orea-Magaña 1999). These factors together have contributed to the very poor state of preservation in which the remains were found in 1999. Apart from solid shreds of cinnabar coating, crumbs of calcite, and disintegrated bone splinters, the bottom of the cavity was littered with remains of recent origin, which the team identified as vestiges of vegetal stalks, wood splinters, cotton wool, threads, and insect keratin shells (Alvarado 1999; Orea-Magaña 1999).

Some alterations must have occurred directly during the course of the earlier explorations. Longitudinal cracks and exfoliating outer layers of bones appear associated to inappropriate use and concentrations of consolidants (figure 2.5a). There is evidence of postdiscovery misplacement of various skeletal segments. Most noticeably, the bones of the right forearm are inverted, a position already depicted in the 1950s. As for the lower extremities, the right talus was found rotated backward 180 degrees, just like it appears in the original 1950s record, but the right patella pointed upward as we recorded it, probably a more recent modification (figure 2.6). The primary anatomical relationship was lost completely in the skull, which was first removed and then reunited with the postcranium in 1978 (see chapter 1). It is very likely that other minor positional changes occurred during the removal of Pakal's personal attire, such as his mask, his heavy pectoral plaque, and the finger rings, in the 1950s. The disturbances should have affected most severely the hand segments and the thoracic cage, but it was difficult to trace any modifications because of lack of preservation.

Apart from the recent perturbations, no taphonomic indication points to a reopening of the tomb after its initial sealing in the seventh century. The skeleton had preserved its primary position, indicating that corpse decomposition had occurred completely inside the hollow monolith. A straight horizontal line had formed on the inner walls of the monolith slightly above the floor, marking the maximum level of liquid produced during the decomposition process, an estimated total volume of 20 to 25 liters, a quantity that could well correspond to the amount of fluids produced during the first phases of decay (see figure 2.3).[1] Interestingly, this volume falls within the range of the displacement volume calculated in the Red Queen's sarcophagus, where a similar line had formed (Romano and Tiesler 2002). In her case, it marked an estimated 24 liters.

Through the centuries, the bones had turned brownish, almost blackish, in most of Pakal's skeleton, except for the yellowish pelvic bones. A pa-

FIGURE 2.5 *(a)* Exfoliation of outer layers of cortical bone; *(b)* layers of pigment coating, 1999 (photograph by Patricia Tamés)

FIGURE 2.6 The skeleton, in situ, 1999 (photograph by Patricia Tamés)

tina was visible on the bone segments that were not destroyed or covered by cinnabar. The effects of decomposition have left their traces also in the thin sections in the form of tiny cracks, diagenetic substitution, and congestion of the medullar cavities. The external cortical surfaces are eroded, with some areas destroyed completely.

The body's original position is reflected by the distribution of the preserved skeletal parts (figure 2.7). At the time of the initial opening in the 1950s, most of the vertebral bodies were found still in anatomical articulation, suggesting that the corpse had been placed directly on the center of the floor of the tomb's inner space, the head positioned northward, and the feet facing the triangular door.

Pakal's skull was still face up at the time of discovery, which is unusual for decomposition in free space. Instead of rolling toward its side, the neurocranium had disintegrated and fallen to pieces in its original place, quite similar to the state of the Red Queen's skull (Romano and Tiesler 2002). The bony face had preserved its unity despite fragmentation as the remains of the zygomatic arches retained their anatomic relationship with the mandible. Its chin rested on top rows of beads in the area between the clavicles. Fragments of the mask's base still covered parts of the forehead.

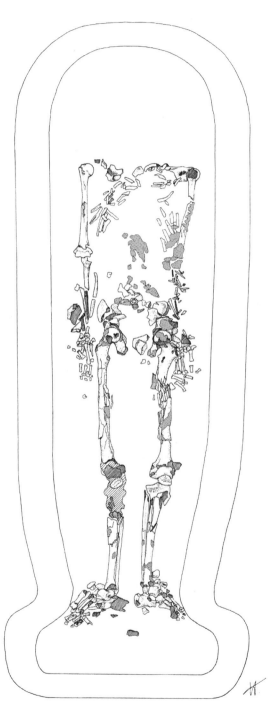

FIGURE 2.7
Taphonomic skeletal
drawing (by Vera
Tiesler)

I assume that the pectoral and collar ornaments held the skull in position. The heavy mosaic mask and abundant head adornments, made up mostly of shell and jadeite, very likely further stabilized the skull and prevented it from collapsing toward the side.

The legs and arms were extended, with the hands resting at the height of the upper thighs. Some disarticulation had occurred in these segments due to decomposition in free space. The cavity's inner walls merged close to the skeleton at ankle level. Along with gravity, these lateral contentions most likely caused the metatarsals and phalanges to fall distally, creating a plantar flexion of both feet. The anatomical cohesion of most phalanx segments of the feet, which appear to have collapsed en bloc, indicates the presence of some sort of footwear, although we cannot rule out other factors (see Romano, chapter 6, in this volume).

No constriction effects were visible on the shoulder girdle, as could be indicated by the clavicles shifting into a vertical position or the reduction of shoulder width by medial rotation of the humeral heads. On the contrary, both humeral heads had slightly shifted laterally, extending the width of the bony shoulder girdle to approximately 40 centimeters. Both legs had collapsed laterally during decomposition, causing the feet to fall laterodistally. Whereas both knees and ankles came to rest quite apart from each other, the femoral heads had not separated from the hip bones, but had rotated inside the acetabular cavity, indicating some sort of constricting effect only in this part of the body. This interpretation is strengthened by the detection of textile remains and imprints found in the left acetabular area of the pelvis, which had already been noted in the 1950s (Ruz 1973; Romano 1989), leading to the representation of a loincloth in the well-known reproduction drawing of Pakal (Garza 1992:89).

The skeletal distribution pattern is thus consistent with Ruz's original interpretation. According to Ruz (1973), Pakal's loincloth was the only clothing on Pakal's dead body when it was laid to rest in the sarcophagus. At the same time, this interpretation rules out any tight wrapping in the fashion known from Calakmul and other Classic sites (García-Vierna and Schneider 1996; García-Moreno and Granados 2000; Tiesler 2004). Bundling was probably not a generalized mortuary treatment for the local elite, considering that it was not displayed by the Red Queen in Temple XIII (Tiesler, Cucina, and Romano 2002).

A last observation concerns the red pigmentation of Pakal's remains (figure 2.8; see also figures 2.5b and 2.7). Compact layers of red pigment covered the whole body. The pigment was identified as cinnabar with a small hematite component, very similar to the composition of the pigment in the Red Queen tomb (Tiesler, Cucina, and Romano 2002; Iván Oliva, personal communication, 2002). On Pakal's skeleton, the vermilion coating varied in thickness between half a millimeter and six millimeters. The trunk was covered by the thickest layers of pigment, whereas other parts—such as the ventral surface of the right scapula, the iliac bones, the lingual surface of the mandible, and the endocranium—had largely preserved their original brownish surface color. The distribution of pigmentation thus seems to have been concentrated in the axial skeleton and in those bone surfaces that are anatomically close to the body surface, with all the spared areas corresponding to internal portions. The pattern suggests that Pakal's body was painted with the vermilion pigment before disintegration. This interpretation is confirmed by a consideration of the king's funerary mask. Its surfaces were found mostly clean of the red pigment, indicating that it was placed over the dead king's face after his body was painted red.

Additional information is provided by the sectioned rib samples that had preserved their original pigmentation. Microscopic inspection of them revealed an elaborate stratigraphy of cinnabar and a blackish organic material with a high carbon component. Each coating appears to have been applied with an organic agglutinant, alternating with some natural resin (Patricia Quintana, personal communication, 2002). Our findings are similar to the ones by Javier Vázquez (2000), who thin-sectioned other pigment samples from this context. The results indicate that Pakal's body did undergo an elaborate embalming procedure, accomplished with alternating applications of red cinnabar and blackish coating, before being sealed inside the tomb and most probably even before being placed inside it. It is worth mentioning that Pakal's pigment cover appears much more elaborate than the single-layered coating conceded to the Red Queen's body, as revealed by thin sections of samples from different parts of her skeleton (Tiesler, Cucina, and Romano 2002, 2003).

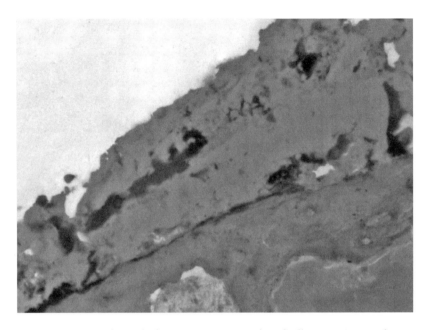

FIGURE 2.8 Histological rib section, stratigraphy of adhering pigment layers (40x microscrope magnification)

Fragments of a Lifetime

The results of the general macroscopic analysis identify the deceased as a mature adult older than 55 years of age. Chapters 4 and 5 provide specific morphological indicators on the age estimation. The sex is undoubtedly male, considering the prominent mastoid processes, well-expressed supraorbital area, and general robust constitution. Measurements of humeral epiphyseal width, maximum vertical diameter of femoral head, and combined values of both taluses equally identify the individual as a male. The latter formulated value of 105 millimeters is considerably above the breaking point of 95.195 for sex discrimination based on pre-Hispanic Maya skeletal samples (Tiesler 1999). Less evident is Pakal's low mandible and the vertical diameters of his right humeral head, features classified as "feminine" (see also Buikstra, Milner, and Boldsen, chapter 3, in this volume). However, these attributes are less-secure indicators and do not alter the overall determination as male.

Pakal's maximum living stature, taken in situ, was calculated at 163 centimeters. A combined estimate from his left tibia and right humerus is 161 centimeters. This stature falls within the established range of 160–65 centimeters for males among the pre-Hispanic Maya (Márquez and del Ángel 1997; Tiesler 2001b) and slightly above the average for Palenque's male population, 159.3 centimeters (standard deviation 2.9), measured from the humerus (Gómez 1999).

The preserved skeletal segments do not show signs of healed trauma or deforming disease (see Romano, chapter 6, in this volume). Not a single sign of carential disease was determined that may point toward chronic deprivation or episodes of growth interruption and stress, such as cribra orbitalia, porotic hyperostosis, enamel hypoplasia, or periosteal reactions. Similar to the case of the Red Queen (Tiesler, Cucina, and Romano 2002, 2003), the lack of evidence points toward a healthy growth period and general favorable living conditions prior to death when compared to the remainder of Palenque's skeletal population available for study. The gap becomes compellingly clear when compared jointly with the proportions of selected stress indicators, reported by Gómez (1999) on 201 skeletons, retrieved by the recent explorations at Palenque. According to her findings, 39.7 percent of Palenque's male adults suffered from periosteal reaction, another 36.2 percent from porotic hyperostosis, and 46.4 percent from cribra orbitalia, a lesion that has been associated with anemia or parasitosis (Larsen 1997). Stress episodes in the form of enamel hypoplasia were recorded in 38.4 percent of male adults' permanent incisors and in 42 percent of their permanent canines, respectively.

As regards biomechanical markers, no reliable measurements of long bone indices could be obtained, and the preserved muscle insertion areas are expressed discretely in the skull and the postcranium when compared to those for the male population from the region (Tiesler 1999). The observable portions of the skeleton do not display any enthesopathic lesions or hypertrophied muscle-attachment sites that could be indicative of harsh habitual physical labor involving specific groups of muscles and ligamentous tissue.

During the 1999 project, the ruler's dentition and associated bone structure were thoroughly registered. The ruler's two second molars and one lower central incisor were lost antemortem, and advanced active periodontal disease is witnessed by a general alveolar retraction and sharp resorptive edges. His reduced occlusal wear, barely reaching the dentine, is remarkable, as well as the heavy tartar accumulation concentrated on the lingual side of his lower anterior mandibular teeth and surrounding the molars.

In general, dental attrition is produced by tooth-on-tooth contact, whereas dental abrasion is the result of the interaction of the occlusal surface with external elements (i.e., usually food) (Hillson 1996). The overall result of both is the general loss of dental material. Despite the fact that wear can only increase with age, its pattern and extent vary from person to person and depend on a large array of intrinsic and external factors, including diet, daily habits in food intake, bruxism, and extramasticatory activities (Larsen, Shavit, and Griffin 1991; Hillson 1996; Larsen 1997). Diet-related occlusal wear is directly associated with the relative degree of softness or coarseness of the food as well as with the way it is prepared, which makes it difficult to generalize a pattern (Molnar 1971; Larsen 1997). The use of stone mortars and metates (in Mesoamerica) increase the extent of wear by introducing grinding particles in the food (Larsen 1997).

Dental calculus is the product of the mineralization of the dental plaque. Its etiology is not clearly understood; nonetheless, alkaline pH and salivary production play a role in its formation (Hillson 1986). Besides physiological and pathological factors, dental calculus can also result from the combined consequences of behavioral habits, such as lack of oral hygiene, a diet rich in animal proteins, and a less-abrasive diet. On the contrary, food rich in carbohydrates and refined sugars creates an ideal environment for the growth of the oral bacteria, whose acid by-products trigger the development of carious lesions (Hillson 2000). Although caries and calculus can be present at the same time in an individual's mouth, they tend to be mutually exclusive (Larsen 1997).

Regarding Pakal's own dentition, the reduced overall rate of occlusal wear is consistent with a very soft, refined diet, in which animal proteins could have represented an important constituent, along with soft tamale maize cakes, chocolate beverages, and *atole* soups (Houston, Stuart, and Taube 1989), foods that might also be responsible for the amount of calculus in his incisors and molars. Indeed, the calculus accumulation and the reduced attritional rate displayed by the ruler's teeth appear to be a common feature among Maya male nobles, significantly different from the commoners (Tiesler 1999, 2000; Cucina and Tiesler 2003). The twenty-four teeth recovered from the sarcophagus do not show a single case of caries, which again supports the hypothesis of a diet based more on proteins than on carbohydrates, evidence that Cucina and Tiesler (2003) encountered in the male elite of the northern Petén area (1.4 percent of teeth affected in elite males versus 6.3 percent in male commoners). This interpretation is coherent also with the results obtained by trace element analysis (Tejeda 2000), which suggests a higher intake of animal-derived proteins among elite individuals than was the case for most of the other inhabitants of Palenque of Pakal's time.

Pakal should have suffered from back ailments during the last years of his life due to bone loss. General osteopenia was noted in the axial skeleton and to a lesser degree in the appendicular segments. Osteoporotic changes affect both compact and spongy bone. The latter displays trabecular thinning, sparsening of its general architecture, and the formation of reinforcement lines, as highlighted in the mediolateral radiography of the fragmented left talus (Murray and Jacobson 1982) (figure 2.9).

Other portions of the skeleton show irregular remodeling readily visible with macroscopic screening—for example, the mandible or skull cap with its almost completely obliterated sutures (see chapter 3 for age implications). In the skull cap, the irregular sparse bone architecture resulted in alternating thick and thin bone portions, leading to a roughly wavelike skull surface. The visible degenerative changes in the trabecular bone portions are accompanied by a general reduction of cortical bone as a consequence of trabecularization, as noted in a midrib section, discussed by Stout and Streeter in chapter 4 of this volume (figure 2.10).

The fact that osteopenia affects both cortical and spongy bone, coupled with the absence of visible vestiges of osteoclastic activity in the form of Howship's lacunae in Pakal's remains, hints at the chronicity of this process (Mosekilde 1999; Steiniche and Eriksen 1999). The advanced bone loss surely played an important role in the evolution of the dignitary's spinal changes. Marginal lipping was noted mostly in the upper spinal column without affecting much of the major and minor appendicular joints. Related spinal degenerative changes include porosis and osteophyte formation of the lower cervical vertebrae, coupled with interdiscal displacements (Schmorl's nodes) and deformation, resulting in wedge-shaped lower cervical vertebrae and a biconcave outline of those upper thoracic segments that could be analyzed (Mosekilde 1999; Ortner 2003)

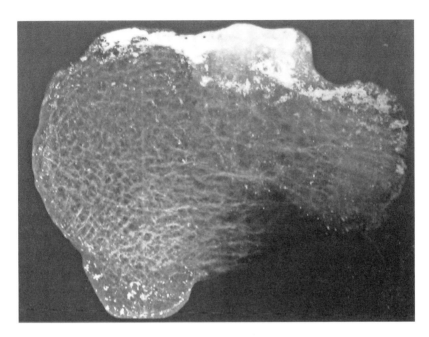

FIGURE 2.9 Mediolateral radiography of fragmented left talus, showing trabecular thinning and reinforcement lines

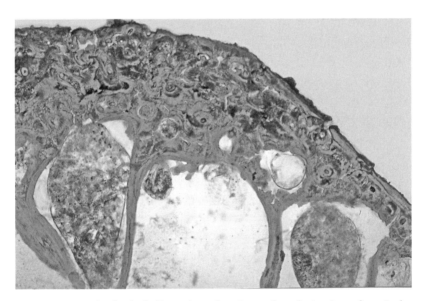

FIGURE 2.10 Histological rib section, showing trabecularization of cortical bone and trabecular thinning (20x microscope magnification) (photograph by Andrea Cucina)

(figure 2.11). As mentioned earlier, the observable joints of the superior extremities display only slight lipping of the humeral head, the margin of the glenoid surface, and the proximal joint of the ulna. The leg bones are almost free of arthritic changes, including the two kneecaps, which did not exhibit any surface anomaly. Again, the lack of positive evidence to indicate otherwise and the arguably mature age of the ruler speak for a sedentary lifestyle.

The appearance of Pakal's head was largely determined by artifice, which confirms the original conclusions made in the 1950s. His general head shape was distinguished by a pronounced tabular oblique modeling, which the young prince received during his early years of infancy. It was produced by a free head-compression device that apparently was used by the majority of the population of central Palenque, among them noticeably also the personage from Temple XIIIsub (Tiesler 1998, 1999; Tiesler, Cucina, and Romano 2002; see also Gómez 1999). The use of head devices, along with cradleboards, was a common practice among the Classic Maya, abandoned soon after the onset of the second millenium AD (Tiesler 1998, 1999). In Pakal's case, the compression device was probably complemented with bands that reduced the bilateral width of his head and accentuated its general backward orientation, although the bad preservation limits secure inferences on this matter. A pad was placed to mediate the pressure exerted on his forehead, leading to a slightly concave sagittal outline of his receding frontal bone, expressed also in his portraiture and mask (figure 2.12). I believe that the forced redirection of growth vectors during head compression should also have led to an out-thrusting outline of Pakal's face, as in other shaped skulls from the Maya area.

At some point after childhood, Pakal's two central upper frontal incisors and the left lateral incisor were filed. In his case, the operation produced an "Ik" shape (expressing B2, B4, B5, and B6 forms according to Romero) (see figure 2.13), as solar sign and visible emblem of social distinction in Classic Maya society (Tiesler 2001a; see also Buikstra et al. 2004). This pattern also matches the dental appearance on Pakal's mask, underscoring its symbolic importance and the individualized features of the king's portrait. Along with tooth inlays, "Ik" shapes are associated with high status on a regional scale (Tiesler 2001a) and figure prominently together with inlays and combined decoration techniques in Palenque central living spaces (López-Jiménez 1994; Gómez 1999; Tiesler 2001a).

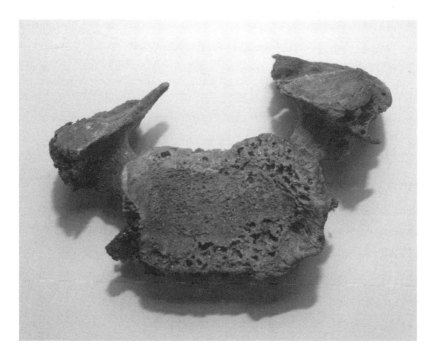

FIGURE 2.11 Lipping and wedging of the fifth cervical vertebra (photograph by Andrea Cucina)

Another noticeable feature is Pakal's remarkably low mandible. The original and new measurement of 30 and 31 millimeters, respectively, fall 5 millimeters below that of the male Maya average, well beyond 1.0 standard deviation (Tiesler 1999: N = 128, x = 35.48, s.d. = 3.64). We feel that this distinctive feature was originated in part by the above-mentioned degenerative processes that took place in the last decades of his life because it is not a characteristic feature of either Pakal's mask, recently restored by Laura Filloy and Sofía Martínez, or the stucco heads, which have been interpreted as early portraits of the king (Schele and Freidel 1990; Schele and Mathews 1998; Martin and Grube 2000). At the same time, the visual differences observed here underline the alleged functions that the ancient masks were serving: they were to immortalize the dignity, beauty, and power of the ancient paramounts, impersonating their eternal youth and the distinctive expressions of the divine (Garza 1992, 1998; Martínez and Filloy 2004; see also Grube, chapter 10, in this volume).

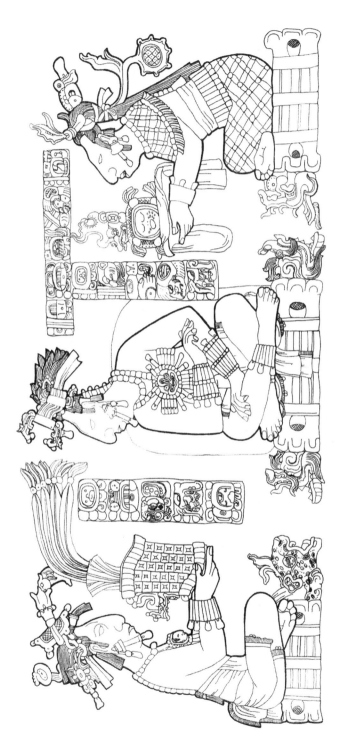

FIGURE 2.12 Portrait of Janaab' Pakal, his son K'an Joy Chitam II, and his wife, Lady Ix Tz'akb'u Ajaw, on the Palace Tablet (redrawn by Mirna Sánchez from Greene 1991)

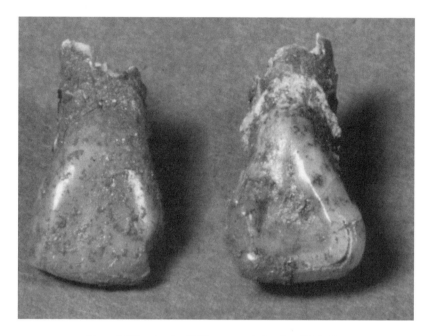

FIGURE 2.13 Dental filing in the "Ik" pattern in both of Pakal's upper-central incisors (photograph by Patricia Tamés)

Conclusion

Through a bioarchaeological lens half a century after the first analysis of Pakal's remains in the 1950s, this assessment was aimed at updating old controversies and addressing new questions on the life and death of this important ruler. To accomplish this goal, we put to service a set of new analytical tools and reference frames not at hand 50 years ago. Their joint application, interpreted and contrasted with other sources of information, is intended to advance the discussion on this historical personage's lifestyle and role in Palenque society. The results obtained by some of the other participants in this project, including a study on trace elements, have not been presented yet. An effort by Carney Matheson and his colleagues (2003; Matheson 2005) to extract and evaluate DNA samples from Pakal and three other individuals from the site, among them the Red Queen, has been fruitful only recently, after overcoming problems related to the poor preservation of the remains and the massive cinnabar covering. The preliminary results reject any genetic relationship between Pakal and the Red Queen.

Another pending line of research is the systematic bioarchaeological interpretation of Classic Maya aristocracy from a regional and social perspective. At present, the physical indicators point toward a distinction between the living style of the rulers' families and that of the rest of population in Palenque and in the region (see, for example, Haviland 1967; White 1997; Carrasco et al. 1998; Gómez 1999; Tiesler 1999; Tiesler, Cucina, and Romano 2002, 2003; Cucina and Tiesler 2003; Buikstra et al. 2004), as Grube indicates in chapter 10 from an epigraphically centered perspective. Pakal's life was no exception in that the present data point to adequate nutrition and a sedentary long life apparently not much exposed to the inclemencies of nature. However, we can only speculate on how extensive these privileges were in the upper spheres of society. In this sense, I hope that the aspects of this society touched on here and in the following chapters will inspire new studies along this line. They are necessary to put the enormous bulk of Maya skeletal data into regional perspective and social context and to create a new frame of interpretation of the ancient Maya—that of its people.

Apart from life history, this case study was intended to explore, through taphonomic signature, some crucial aspects of posthumous treatments of royal bodies. Present osteotaphonomic indications confirm that Pakal's body was not laid down shrouded, but was embalmed in several steps, leaving alternating layers of vermilion cinnabar and some blackish organic material. Practical factors related to the intent to slow the process of decay during the elaborate care of the body and to the prolonged rituals in preparation for an adequate dynastic interment have not been studied in depth yet. However, it seems likely that the highly toxic cinnabar components must have halted or slowed the biological decay process for some time. It is probably no coincidence that hair remains were found on two heavily pigmented skullcaps from another Classic period site of the central Lowlands. Both documented cases come from the epicenter of Calakmul and were studied recently as part of the two site projects (Tiesler 2003a, 2003b). On the ideological side, color combinations of black and red are laden with symbolism. Their mutual alternation stands for the perpetual solar cycle of demise and resurrection, represented by the daily sunrise and sunset (Hammond 1989). Based on the form and quantity that we witnessed on Pakal's dead body, it is easy to conceive that the red pigment covered the king completely, leading to several questions concerning shared elite funerary traditions. Was the coating a substitute for the wrappings found in other Maya elite tombs, such as the ones known from Copán or Calakmul (Buikstra et al. 2004; Carranco et al. 1998; García-Vierna and Renata Schneider 1996; Tiesler 2004)? Was the use of the vermilion coatings another form of bundling? A systematic investigation on the topic holds promise to provide novel insights on posthumous body manipulations and their ritual meaning.

Later re-entries of Pakal's tomb prior to the recent excavations cannot be confirmed because there are no indications of any secondary manipulation of his remains. The particular conditions of decay created inside the sealed cavity would speak against such an endeavor. The attributes and the distribution of pigmentation likewise strongly counterindicate assertions that his bones were painted once skeletal reduction was completed (see, for example, Schele and Mathews 1998:128).

Also noteworthy are the close similarities between the body treatment of the king and the arrangement of the remains of the Red Queen, who was laid to rest adjacent to Pakal's final resting place (Tiesler, Cucina, and Romano 2002, 2004). Several questions arise that are directly related to this enigmatic woman's role in the kingdom and her relationship to Pakal, as represented in the funerary treatment of her. What do the similarities in their burial arrangement mean? How many years apart from each other did the two paramounts die? What was the family relationship between them? At the moment, our recent results identify the personage from Temple XIIIsub as Tz'akb'u Ajaw, Pakal's wife and mother of Kan B'alam, the heir to his throne (Tiesler, Cucina, and Romano 2002, 2004). If the remains are of Tz'akb'u Ajaw, it would make sense that Pakal's future funerary shrine was located right next to her resting place 11 years later. It follows that important aspects of her funerary setup—such as the use of a monolithic vehicle, the complete cinnabar coating, and the placing of the mask—were the antecedent of the much more elaborate preparations for Pakal. Chapter 7 explores these and other issues concerning the ties between the two dignitaries from the point of view of individual provenance.

Regarding the funerary preparations after Pakal's demise, our present evidence is limited to his mortal remains in their monolithic coffin, so that we cannot make inferences about the possibly much protracted funerary ceremonies involving the vaulted chamber and the flight of stairs leading to it. The complete isolation of Pakal's remains inside the sarcophagus would have allowed for visits well after his death and burial, first as part of the preparations overseen by Kan B'alam and also afterward as a space of continuous worship and commemoration of the dead king in his sanctuary deep inside the Temple of the Inscriptions (figure 2.2). It is noteworthy that the photographs taken by Arturo Romano (personal archive) right after discovery of the tomb display clear signs of attrition on the calcite steps of the staircase. Does this accumulated wear indicate massive, most likely public visits to the shrine in the core of the Temple of the Inscriptions? After more than a millennium, we can only guess if and how long this central staircase was open to the public for the veneration of the deceased king. Put into a cultural perspective, the present results lead to broader questions pertaining to dynastic ancestor veneration and its place in public display of authority, all aspects addressed in chapter 8.

ACKNOWLEDGMENTS

I thank the following projects and colleagues for providing useful advice and information: Andrea Cucina (Universidad Autónoma de Yucatán), Arturo Romano (INAH), Jane Buikstra (Arizona State University), Sam Stout (Ohio State University), Margaret Streeter (Boise State University), Iván Oliva and Patricia Quintana (Centro de Investigaciones Avanzadas/ Politécnico Nacional, Unidad Mérida), and Marco Ramírez Salomón.

3

Janaab' Pakal

The Age-at-Death Controversy Revisited

Jane E. Buikstra, George R. Milner, and Jesper L. Boldsen

In this chapter, we address one of the key controversies about the human remains attributed to Janaab' Pakal: the age at which he died. We preface our analytical discussion with a brief history of the controversy, contextualized in terms of twentieth-century techniques for age estimation. We underscore the contrastive methodological trends for the two lines of evidence used to estimate age at death for Janaab' Pakal: inscriptions and skeletal anatomy. Glyph decipherments have become exquisitely precise following Berlin's (1958) and Proskouriakoff's (1960) seminal studies. By contrast, biological anthropologists have moved from formulations of rather narrow 5- or 10-year intervals, or even point estimates, to probabilistic statements and confidence intervals. Thus, paleodemography is shifting from apparent certainty, especially for age estimates in adults, to uncertainty. As illustrated here, probabilistic approaches do have the advantage of facilitating insights concerning the formerly inaccessible older adult years.

In 1955, Dávalos and Romano published the first (preliminary) report on the remains from the elaborate tomb within the Temple of the Inscriptions as an appendix to Ruz's archaeological report from the 1952 field season. Their account focuses on the preservation and location of specific bones, postdepositional treatment, estimation of stature from in-grave length, and masculine features: robusticity and pelvic morphology. The body, observed in situ, was described as being without notable pathology and of strong bone structure. The issue of age at death was not addressed explicitly, although alveolar resorption was noted in the region of both lower second molars.

Although the issue of age is not addressed in the appendix, Ruz's archaeological discussion includes an age-at-death estimate of 40–50 years, which is attributed to Dávalos and Romano. Ruz's presentation also includes Dávalos and Romano's sex diagnosis, stature estimate, and discussion of Pakal's robust physical condition.

Subsequent skeletal analysis, including laboratory study of the skull and a histological study by Mario Antonio Balcorta and Francisco Villalobos, continued to support the previous age estimate (Romano 1975, 1980, 1989; Ruz 1973, 1978). Influenced by the physical anthropologists' "scientific" study, Ruz further noted that archaeological samples seldom report advanced ages at death. His interpretation of glyphic evidence led him to conclude that Pakal would have been 39 years, 9 months, and a few days old at death (Ruz 1955, 1973, 1978).

Other translations by linguists and archaeologists did *not* support the physical anthropologist's assertions (Lounsbury 1974, 1991; Mathews and Schele 1974; Marcus 1976, 1992a, 1992b; Berlin 1977; Schele and Mathews 1998). Strategies for reconciling the conflicting lines of evidence vary, however. Some, such as Schele and Mathews (1998), have argued that Janaab' Pakal, son of Lady S'ak' K'uk' and her consort K'an-Mo'-Balam, was born on AD 26 March 603 and ascended the throne at the age of 12 on 29 July 615. He reigned for 68 years, dying on 28 August 683. Thus, the controversy centers on whether Pakal died at the age of approximately 40 years or twice that, at 80.4 years.

Mathews, Schele, and Lounsbury have asserted that the physical anthropologists are incorrect, but others have sought a middle ground. Berlin, for example, hints that the physical anthropologists might have erred, but prefers the possibility that the tomb contained a different royal personage who died at an age less advanced than Janaab' Pakal (1977:245). Marcus (1976, 1992a, 1992b) also accepts the translation, but cites the discrepancy as an example of revisionist history set in stone.

During the 1950s, when the Pakal skeleton was first studied, physical anthropologists typically used a variety of methods for estimating age at death, usually including cranial suture closure (Todd and Lyon 1924, 1925a, 1925b, 1925c) and metamorphosis of the pubic symphysis (Todd 1920, 1921a, 1921b). During the first third of the twentieth century, anatomists and the few anthropologists involved in medicolegal applications were those most interested in assigning chronological ages of death to human skeletal materials. In contrast, physical anthropologists working with archaeological materials were less concerned with refined divisions. For example, Hrdlička's influential handbooks, which were published in 1920 and 1939, stated that it was sufficient to categorize a skeleton simply as juvenile, adult, or senile. Anatomists such as Todd (1920, 1921a, 1921b), however, assigned relatively narrow age intervals. As comparative paleodemographic approaches became popular, influenced by Hooton's (1930) statistical and epidemiological methods, even point estimates were used.

It is worth emphasizing that Dávalos and Romano (1955) never explicitly reference either cranial suture closure or pubic symphyseal metamorphosis, and neither did the later reevaluations. There is some question, therefore, about the basis of their age estimate, though their 10-year interval would have followed standard practice for the time.

Somewhat neglected in studies of archaeological skeletons during earlier years, age estimation moved center stage in the second half of the twentieth century, as death profiles and age-specific disease patterns were increasingly used to estimate quality of life. During the past two decades, beginning with Bocquet-Appel and Masset's widely cited and highly critical article "Farewell to Paleodemography" (1982), paleodemographic approaches have received considerable scrutiny (see also Jackes 1992, 2000; Wood et al. 1992; Konigsberg and Frankenberg 1994; Molleson 1995; Milner, Wood, and Boldsen 2000; Hoppa and Vaupel 2002). Although the critique has been heated and painful at times, paleodemography has emerged a much stronger, statistically sophisticated field. One of the newly developed methods for estimating age at death, Transition Analysis (Boldsen et al. 2002), is applied here, along with a suite of more traditional techniques.

Before proceeding, we would like to underscore the significant contributions of Haydeé Orea-Magaña, national coordinator of restoration for the Instituo Nacional de Antropología e Historia (INAH), to the project. Despite the general fragmentation and poor preservation of Pakal's axial skeleton, Vera Tiesler and Jane Buikstra discovered during their in situ survey that the pubic symphyses were present. These portions of the bony pelvis had become obscured by collapse and subsequent application of a preservative and for this reason probably were not evaluated by Dávalos and Romano in their age estimate during the 1950s. Orea-Magaña managed to recover the pubic elements and to separate the two sides without further damage. Her skills were indeed vital to the success of these age-estimation efforts.

Sex Diagnosis

Because our comfort level in estimating age at death depends on accurate sex diagnosis, we emphasize that the Pakal skeleton is unambiguously male, thus reaffirming Dávalos and Romano's earlier observations. Morphological sex, based on the methods developed in Buikstra and Ubelaker (1994), clearly identifies the Pakal interment as a male. All features of the Phenice (1969) technique are uniformly masculine. Areas of muscle attachment in the skull are also robust, and the chin is bilateral, although this feature is somewhat obscured by alveolar resorption. In sum, these remains are unequivocally male.

Age at Death

Three sites of age-related morphological change were given priority: (1) pubic symphyses; (2) auricular surfaces; and (3) cranial sutures, which—with the exception of the Transition Analysis—were scored according to Buikstra and Ubelaker (1994). Three different systems for examining the pubic symphysis are considered here. The Todd (1920, 1921a, 1921b) and Suchey-Brooks (Suchey et al. 1984; Suchey and Katz 1997) systems are disadvantaged, however, in convincingly resolving the Pakal controversy because their resolution and reliability fade when we are dealing with older adult remains. The newly developed Transition Analysis method (Boldsen et al. 2002) has the advantage of permitting age estimation for the older adult years.

Pubic Symphyses

As illustrated in figure 3.1, the right pubic symphysis is virtually complete with slight postdepositional erosion of its superior aspect. The face is oval and flat, although a few residual billows remain. The dorsal aspect is lipped posteriorly, so that it appears that a newly developed articular element is present, pedestaled from the original face. The inferior extremity is fully defined, and the surface presents irregular ossifications, both sharp and rounded; macroporosity is present. A rim has formed and become eroded and lipped posteriorly.

The left pubic symphysis is complete and subrectangular (see figure 3.1c). An apparent bony nodule has formed at the superior extremity and subsequently become eroded. The surface texture is coarsened, granular, and porous. The face is well defined at its inferior extremity. A rim had been present, but has become irregular and lipped.

Both the right and left faces conform to Todd's Phase 10, which is described by Buikstra and Ubelaker as presenting a "ventral margin eroded at a greater or lesser extent of its length, continuing somewhat onto the symphyseal face. Rarefaction of face and irregular ossification. Disfigurements increase with age" (1994:22). This phase is associated with ages at death of 50 years or older. Considering the degree of "disfigurement," ages well beyond 50 must be entertained.

Similarly, both faces conform to Stage VI of the Suchey-Brooks system (Buikstra and Ubelaker 1994:24). Stage VI is described as "symphyseal face shows ongoing depression as the rim erodes. Ventral ligamentous attachments are marked. Pubic tubercle may appear as a separate bony knob [left side, in this example]. Face may be pitted or porous, giving an appearance of disfigurement as the ongoing process of erratic ossification proceeds. Crenelations may occur, with the shape of the face often irregular" (Buikstra and Ubelaker 1994:24). Although the age range for this phase extends across several decades of middle and old age, this observation is compatible with an advanced age at death for Pakal indicated by his remains.

As emphasized by Bocquet-Appel and Masset (1982), standard osteological methods for estimating age at death have little resolution for older adults and generally tend to underage older adults and to overage younger individuals. The Transition Analysis method being developed and refined by Milner and Boldsen (Boldsen et al. 2002) holds promise for resolving these issues.

The logic behind Transition Analysis and the development of this method have been outlined elsewhere (Milner, Wood, and Boldsen 2000; Boldsen et al. 2002). The probability of being a certain age is estimated from the particular mix of skeletal characteristics displayed by the pubic symphysis, sacroiliac joint, and cranial sutures. Each anatomical structure has several parts, or "components," that pass through a series of stages, ranked from young to old. The probability of being a certain age is estimated from the transition from one stage to the next. Overall age estimates are obtained by combining as many anatomical features as possible. For example, five separate components of the pubic symphysis are scored in Transition Analysis. The three anatomical units can be used singly or in combination to generate age estimates. Of the three parts of the skeleton—the pubis, the ilium, and the cranium—the pubic symphysis provides the most accurate estimates of age, consistent with the results of standard age-estimation techniques (Boldsen et al. 2002).

Transition Analysis age estimates are provided by a computer program that uses the particular combination of morphological features found on each skeleton. Milner and Boldsen scored and validated age transitions in the Terry collection, upon individuals with documented ages at death. African American and European American males and females were scored separately. The program estimates ages using a uniform distribution of age at death from 15 to 110 years (the upper limit is treated as the maximum human life span). Although the uniform distribution is unrealistic, we do not know the age-at-death distribution of the population from which Pakal was drawn, so it cannot serve as the basis for inference. We simply cannot "know" the true distribution for the ancient Maya through paleodemographic study. The program also allows ages to be estimated using a Siler mortality distribution (Gage 1988) based on seventeenth-century rural Danish parish register data. There is no reason to believe that the demographic characteristics of the ancient Maya and seventeenth-century Danes were identical. This approach, however, will produce estimates closer to the true age than those provided by a uniform distribution because problems with a uniform prior are particularly noticeable in the upper end of the human life span.

The full application of the Transition Analysis method to the auricular surface and cranial sutures was not possible for the Pakal remains due to poor preservation of the skull and sacroiliac articulation. Fortunately, it was suitable for the pubic symphyses and could be applied in a limited fashion to the auricular surfaces.

Another objective during the development of Transition Analysis was the definition of a replicable suite of skeletal features. Applying this method in the Pakal project, Buikstra received an e-mail attachment describing the scoring method the day before she left for Mexico and read it in transit. Therefore, neither was she directly trained in the technique by either Milner or Boldsen, nor did she have photographs of the various stages. While at Palenque, Buikstra ensured that high-quality photographs of Pakal's pubic symphyses were taken, which she forwarded to Milner

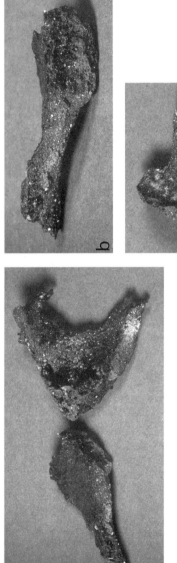

FIGURE 3.1 Janaab' Pakal's pubic symphyses: (a) anterior view; (b) right, medial view; (c) left, medial view; (d) right, posterior view (photographs by Patricia Tamés)

without revealing her scores or defining the nature of the age controversy (figure 3.1). Thus, Milner was not influenced by Buikstra as he scored the photographs. Boldsen, who did the computer analysis, was similarly not informed of the controversy, making their analysis a blind test of replicability and age estimation.

As illustrated in table 3.1, Buikstra and Milner produced very similar observations. Buikstra did not score the superior apex because of her unfamiliarity with the coding procedures. The observers occasionally provided two scores, such as Stage 5–6, for a particular morphological feature. Such scores were given when either the skeletal characteristic was deemed ambiguous or the photograph was not clear enough for a firm identification. Discrepancies between observers were never as great as a full stage.

Milner's scores were used to estimate age because observations were available for the superior apex. The Transition Analysis age estimates in figure 3.2 indicate that this skeleton was indeed from an older person. The lower and upper 95 percent confidence intervals and maximum likelihood estimate are provided here. The age estimates based on an early-modern (that is, preantibiotic-era) Danish prior distribution is the one we believe to be preferable in this example.

As illustrated in figure 3.2, when the Danish prior distribution is employed, the maximum likelihood estimate of 80.9 years is within one-half year of Pakal's age as recorded in the inscriptions. Keep in mind, however, that the estimates of most interest are the 95 percent confidence intervals, which show where Pakal might fall along the full adult life span. They indicate that there is a 95 percent probability that Pakal died between 67.5 and 90.7 years. Based on this work, we feel confident that Pakal did not die as a young or middle-aged man—he was, by any measure, old.

The results from the Danish sample appear more realistic than those from the uniform distribution. That is because the use of a "real" age-at-death distribution, whatever its origin, instead of a uniform prior distribution will lower estimates at the upper end of the human life span. In Transition Analysis, the "real" prior distribution—that is, the probability of dying at each age—is a function of the hazard of dying at that age and the probability of having survived to that point in the life span. For the Danish example, the distribution drops slightly during the early decades of adulthood to reach a minimum at 42 years, then rises sharply to reach a maximum at 76 years. From that point, it drops sharply, and there is

TABLE 3.1 Janaab' Pakal: Comparison of Buikstra's and Milner's Scores for the Pubic Symphysis

	Buikstra		Milner	
Feature	L	R	L	R
Relief	5–6	5–6	5–6	6
Texture	4	4	3–4	4
Superior Apex	—	—	4	4
Ventral Margin	7	7	7	7
Dorsal Margin	5	5	4–5	5

only an extremely small likelihood of anyone beyond 96 years old. The general shape of this distribution, including the old-age component, is likely to characterize viable human communities (that is, situations where the burial ground is not a result of catastrophic events). The old peak followed by a precipitous drop is why a "real" distribution and a uniform distribution depart from one another in the upper end of the human life span.

Auricular Surfaces

Unfortunately, neither auricular surface is well preserved. The right apical portion is present, including the apical one-third and the superior demi-face, and is more complete than the left. A portion of the middle third of the left auricular surface is also present. Following Lovejoy and cowork-ers' terminology (Lovejoy, Meindl, Mensforth et al. 1985; Lovejoy, Meindl, Pryzbeck et al. 1985; Meindl and Lovejoy 1989), the right surface shows well-defined apical change and is flat, eroded, and dense, with microporosity. The left surface also shows microporosity and is dense, with slight granularity. Both are consistent with Stages 7 to 8, but the absence of a retroauricular area severely limits our ability to estimate age at death during advanced age. Lovejoy's Stage 7 is listed as 50–59 years; Stage 8, as 60 and older.

The absence of a retroauricular area is also severely limiting to the Milner-Boldsen technique. The only systematic scoring occurs for the right face, wherein Buikstra judged the superior surface topography to be

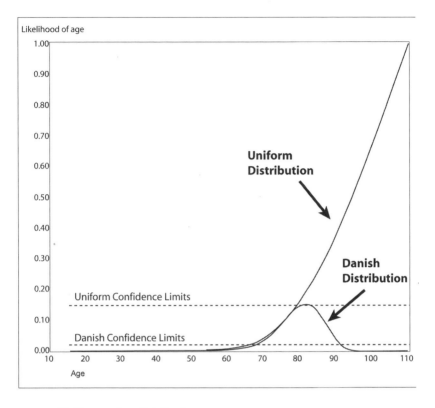

Likelihood of age

Uniform
Distribution

Danish
Distribution

Uniform Confidence Limits

Danish Confidence Limits

Age

Uniform prior distribution
    Lower 95% CI: 78.6 years
    Upper 95% CI: max. human
                     life expectancy

Danish 17th century prior distribution
    Lower 95% CI: 67.5 years
    MLE: 80.9 years
    Upper 95% CI: 90.7 years

FIGURE 3.2 Janaab' Pakal, Transition Analysis (CI = confidence interval)

flat (Stage 3 of the Milner-Boldsen technique), the superior surface morphology to be flat (Stage 4), and the apical morphology as Stages 4–5, showing elements of flattening and bumps. Milner did not have access to photographs of the auricular surface. In general, these characteristics represent the more advanced stages of morphological change. These limited data, although far from ideal, also produce age estimates consistent with advanced years. The uniform maximum likelihood estimate is 80.3 years with a 95 percent confidence interval from 30.5 to 110. Corresponding figures using the Danish prior distribution are: maximum likelihood 76.5 with 95 percent confidence limits from 49 to 88.4. Once again, Pakal's glyph age falls within the confidence intervals, which are wide because the data are limited, and the maximum likelihood ages are quite close to the reported age.

Pubic Symphyses and Auricular Surface Combined

Transition Analysis makes use of whatever information is available, even if it is rather limited, such as Pakal's auricular surface stages. Any additional data, however, add confidence to overall estimates. When the scores for the two anatomical features are combined, the estimates for the uniform prior age distribution are as follows: maximum likelihood 107.5, with confidence limits of 73.8 to 110. When the Danish prior distribution is used, corresponding estimates are: maximum likelihood 81.1, with confidence intervals of 68.2 to 90.5. The age estimates for the two anatomical features are not significantly different: chi-square = 1.26; degrees of freedom = 1; p = 0.26.

Cranial Sutures

Nearly all the observable cranial sutures are closed. The exceptions are the inferior sphenotemporal suture, which is open, but its configuration has been modified through postdepositional changes. The most inferior portion of the occipitomastoid suture is also minimally closed. In general, however, the degree of endo- and ectocranial suture closure are consistent with advanced age. Nonetheless, the artificial head shaping that Pakal underwent during his childhood may have affected the process of suture closure and the reliability of this indicator for age estimates (see Tiesler, chapter 2, in this volume).

Other

The facial skeleton shows extensive remodeling and considerable alveolar resorption, again suggesting advanced age. Osteoarthritic changes are not extensive, although there is some vertebral wedging (see Tiesler, chapter 2, this volume). There is, however, advanced temporomandibular joint disease and raised lipping at certain joint surfaces. An attempt was made to evaluate age at death through the study of dental histology. Unfortunately, the dental tissue was insufficiently well preserved for observations (Della C. Cook, personal communication, 22 December 2003).

Conclusion

This revisit of the Pakal remains in 1999 should convincingly resolve the age controversy. Our results point to an advanced age at death consistent with the record in the inscriptions, but not with the earlier bioarchaeological estimates. Although we cannot exclude the possibility that rulers' age from the epigraphic record may have been inflated by the dignitaries themselves to legitimate their authority (as discussed in chapters 5 and 10 in this volume), and we do not know with absolute certainty that Pakal was indeed 80 when he died, even our most conservative estimates indicate that he did not die during his fifth decade, but lived on well into his second half-century.

Other important results of this work include the demonstration that the newly developed Transition Analysis scoring procedures are replicable and are effective in resolving historical issues. We have also applied Transition Analysis at the site of Copán, including estimates of age at death for K'inich Yax K'uk Mo', Ruler 1 (Buikstra et al. 2004). In addition to being useful in examples of advanced age, Transition Analysis also produces estimates of uncertainty in age estimation, which are essential for future paleodemographic research.

In closing, we emphasize that the result here was *not* what Buikstra anticipated when she joined the Pakal Project. Furthermore, the morphological scoring and the age estimates by Milner and Boldsen were done in complete ignorance of the inscriptions and the controversy over Janaab' Pakal's life span. Thus, this estimate is truly the result of a blind test.

4

A Histomorphometric Analysis of the Cortical Bone of Janaab' Pakal's Rib

Sam D. Stout and Margaret Streeter

The remains of an individual believed to be the Maya ruler known as Janaab' Pakal are entombed in a sarcophagus in the Temple of the Inscriptions at the Classic Maya site of Palenque. This individual's age at death
is a topic of disagreement. Based on inscriptions, Pakal is documented to
have been some 80 years old at the time of death, but traditional osteological indicators estimate his age to have been 40–50 years. We undertook
a histomorphometric analysis of a rib sample from these remains in an
attempt to resolve this dispute.

For Pakal's remains, we determined several histomorphometric parameters of bone that exhibit clear age-associated changes. We then compared the results to data available for modern and other archaeological
samples, including a small sample of ribs from other individuals from the
site of Palenque. Although the findings are not entirely consistent, they
suggest overall that an age estimate as old as the ninth decade of life is not
unreasonable.

Osteon Population Density

It has been well established that the process of cortical bone remodeling
results in discrete histomorphological features called osteons or Haversian
systems. Because remodeling is continuous and lifelong, the number of
these structures per unit area of cortical bone increases with age. This fact
has led to the development of a number of histological age-estimating
methods based on cortical bone histomorphometry. Robling and Stout
(2000) provide a survey and evaluation of the major histomorphological
age-estimating methods that are currently available.

For this analysis, we employed the Stout and Paine (1992) histological age-estimating method for the rib, as modified by Cho and colleagues (2002). The predicting variables used in this method are osteon population density (OPD), osteon area (On.Ar), and relative cortical area (Ct. Ar/Tt.Ar). We estimated age using the equation:

$$\text{Age} = 29.524 + 1.560(\text{OPD}) + 4.786(\text{Ct.Ar/Tt.Ar}) - 592.899(\text{On.Ar})$$

OPD is the number of osteons per square millimeter determined for an entire cross-section of bone. It includes fragmentary osteons, which are osteons that have been partially obliterated by creation of new generations of osteons during subsequent remodeling activity. Osteon area is the mean area of osteons measured for the rib sample. Ct.Ar/Tt.Ar is determined by dividing the cortical area by the total cross-sectional area of the rib. OPD for the rib sample from Pakal's remains was determined to be 18.7 square millimeters; the average cross-sectional area of osteons (On.Ar) is .014 square millimeter, and Ct.Ar/Tt.Ar is 0.34. When inserted into the age-predicting formula, these data produce an age estimate of 52 years.

Although these findings support the relatively lower age-at-death estimate based on osteological analysis, there are several reasons why this histological age estimate by itself should not be weighted too heavily. First, continuous remodeling ultimately replaces all unremodeled primary cortical bone with secondary osteons or their fragments, and OPD reaches an asymptotic value (Frost 1987). The age at which the asymptote is reached varies for different bones and is dependent on factors such as cortical area and osteon size. Since OPD asymptote is estimated to occur by age 60 in the rib, histological age estimates from the rib are generally unreliable for individuals beyond 60 years of age. In addition, the state of histomorphological preservation was not ideal for this bone sample, making it difficult to identify all histomorphological features—that is, osteons—with great certainty. This would be especially true for the quantification of the number of osteon fragments, which become a more significant component of OPD for the bones of older individuals because they have undergone remodeling for a longer time period and usually exhibit thinner bone cortices. Finally, bone-remodeling rates and therefore the rate of increase in OPD varies among populations (Cho et al. 2002) and among past populations (Stout and Lueck 1995). Therefore, these results may be interpreted to mean that Pakal was in his fifties or older at the time of his death. We next examine some other aspects of cortical bone histomorphology that can provide additional evidence as to how old Pakal may have been when he died.

Cortical Area Measurements

Age-associated changes in the absolute and relative amount of cortical bone for the rib are well documented (Sedlin 1964; Epker, Kelin, and Frost 1965; Takahashi and Frost 1966). Once peak bone mass is achieved by around the third decade of life, both the absolute and relative amount of bone contained in the cortex of the rib declines with age. This decline is due primarily to the continued expansion of the marrow cavity and drastically reduced rate of periosteal apposition.

Total subperiosteal area (Tt.Ar), cortical area (Ct.Ar), and marrow cavity area (En.Ar) were determined for the rib sample from Pakal (table 4.1). We compared these results with data on age-associated changes for these parameters available for skeletal samples ranging in antiquity from the modern period to around 7,000 years ago and representing a number of subsistence strategies and cultures, including a small sample of ribs from the site of Palenque (table 4.1).

The overall size of ribs (Tt.Ar) increases slightly with age. Among the samples, rib size is greatest for the modern European American sample, but there is no clear pattern for rib size and antiquity (figure 4.1). Rib size for the Palenque sample, excluding Pakal's rib, does not differ significantly from any of the other rib samples. Pakal's rib size is more than 1.0 standard error below the mean for the comparative sample from Palenque. These results indicate that Pakal may have had smaller ribs. Rib size by itself, however, is not indicative of age.

A decrease in both the absolute (Ct.Ar) and relative (Ct.Ar/Tt.Ar) amount of cortical bone in the rib with age is well established. A comparison of these measures for Pakal with those for the other samples, especially for the rib samples from Palenque, suggests a very old age for Pakal. Ct.Ar does not differ significantly among any of the samples, but the value of 14.8 square millimeters for Pakal's rib is more than 2.0 standard deviations below and a Ct.Ar/Tt.Ar value of 0.34 is more than 1.5 standard deviations below the means for the other rib samples from Palenque (figures 4.2 and 4.3). It is interesting that this value for cortical area is most similar to those

TABLE 4.1 Descriptive Statistics of the Measurements of Transverse Areas

Sample	Tt.Ar	Ct.Ar	En.Ar	Ct.Ar/Tt.Ar
Pakal*	43.9 mm²	14.8 mm²	29.0 mm²	0.34
Archaeologic	53.5±23.88	20.6±8.36	33.0±18.4	0.42±0.130
Palenque**	52.9±18.47	28.3±5.56	24.7±14.3	0.57±0.144
Modern African American	63.4±18.07	20.5±7.17	43.0±16.2	0.34±0.115
Modern European American	72.0±20.75	21.8±5.74	50.9±18.9	0.32±0.094

Tt.Ar = total subperiosteal area
Ct.Ar = cortical area
En.Ar = marrow cavity area
*Values of transverse area are the average of measurements of two of Pakal's ribs.
**Statistics of ribs from Palenque, excluding Pakal.

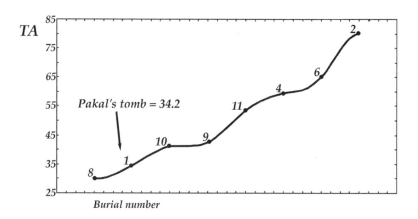

FIGURE 4.1 Scatterplot of distribution of total area of ribs, Palenque

reported by Jett, Wu, and Frost (1967) for a sample of post-osteoporotic females (10.7 ± 2 square millimeters). The mean age for these female osteoporotic ribs was 56 years, with an age range of 36–74 years. When senile osteoporosis occurs in males, it is usually at an older age (older than 70 years) than it occurs in females.

Much of the loss of cortical bone with age results from the continued expansion of the marrow cavity in the face of minimal cortical expan-

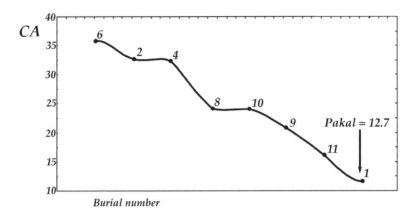

FIGURE 4.2 Scatterplot of distribution of cortical area of ribs, Palenque

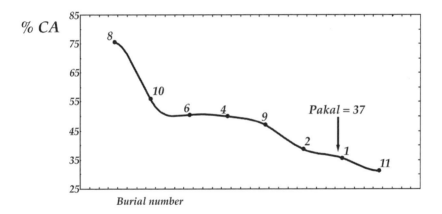

FIGURE 4.3 Scatterplot of distribution of relative cortical area of ribs (cortical area/total cross-sectional area), Palenque (percentage)

sion during adult life. Although Pakal's total subperiosteal, absolute, and relative cortical areas are all significantly below the means for the other Palenque samples, the size of his marrow cavity is almost 1.0 standard error above their mean (figure 4.4). This result is consistent with the typical loss of cortical bone with age due to expansion of the marrow cavity.

A sedentary lifestyle might result in earlier onset of osteoporosis. If

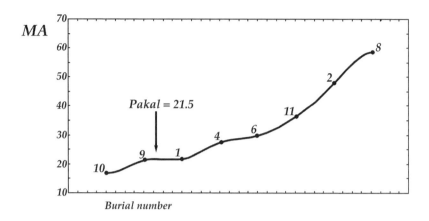

FIGURE 4.4. Scatterplot of distribution of marrow area), Palenque

higher status resulted in less physical activity during growth, then the bones would not reach their genetic potential peak bone mass. As they age in adulthood, there would be less cortical area, and it would be encroached on by marrow cavity expansion, producing osteoporosis sooner in that individual (Frost 1987; Jones et al. 1994). Nonetheless, it would probably take rather severe inactivity, bordering on immobilization, to produce a difference significant enough to be observable at a younger age, and it is known that Pakal was not inactive, which reinforces the hypothesis of his older age.

Osteon Size

The average size of the osteons observed in Pakal's rib also supports an older age at death. Osteon size decreases with age (Pirok et al. 1966). The mean cross-sectional area of Pakal's osteons is 0.014 square millimeters, which is well below the means determined for the other comparative samples (table 4.2). Subnormal osteon size is reported for osteoporosis (Wu et al. 1970).

TABLE 4.2 Skeletal Populations Included in the Sample of Comparison

1. Windover, Florida, an Early Archaic site dated to 7000–8000 BP.

    Paloma, Peru, a Middle Archaic site dated to 4600–7000 BP.

2. Koster, Illinois, an Early to Middle Archaic site dated to 4500–8000 BP.

3. Ajvide, Sweden, an Iron Age site dated around 2750 BC.

4. Gibson, Illinois, a Middle Woodland site dated to 1900–2100 BP.

5. Isola Sacra, Italy, an Imperial Roman site dated to the second to third centuries
    AD.

7. Ledders, Illinois, a Late Woodland site dated to 900–1000 BP (Cook 1976).

8. Campbell, Missouri, a Mississippian site dated to 500–800 BP.

Discussion and Conclusion

Pakal's age at death is an issue that has been addressed from different perspectives and using different techniques (see chapters 3, 5, and 10 in this volume). The state of preservation of Pakal's remains is poor, as underscored by all the scholars who have undertaken analyses of them. This condition limits the possibility of inferring his age accurately regardless of which technique is used, and histomorphology is not an exception, particularly in advanced age classes. Furthermore, the estimation of age in individuals older than 50 years of age is problematic even independent of the state of preservation (Hoppa and Vaupel 2002). Nonetheless, the application of this technique leads us to a general estimation of his age, at least with respect to the "less than 50" or "older than 50" debate.

The preponderance of the evidence from this histological analysis of a rib sample from the skeletal remains of Janaab' Pakal suggests that he was quite old when he died, consistent with his documented age of 80 years (see also Grube, chapter 10, in this volume). His small absolute and relative cortical area, especially when compared to ribs from other individuals from Palenque, is evidence of an elderly individual. Indeed, his extremely small cortical area and osteon size are consistent with modern clinical values reported for severe osteopenia or senile osteoporosis, which is associated with aged individuals. These histomorphometric results support an age estimate of the eighth or ninth decade of life for these remains, thereby confirming the results reported in the morphological study conducted by Buikstra, Milner, and Boldsen in chapter 3 of this volume. Senile osteopenia would also explain the severe degenerative changes of portions of Pakal's thoracic and cervical spine, which Tiesler explores in chapter 2. According to Tiesler, the vertebral bodies are reduced in size, being biconcave or wedge shaped, porotic, and lipped—all consistent with the present histological results obtained from a rib section. The comparison between Pakal's rib and those of other individuals from Palenque reveals that his bone is nearly 2.0 standard deviation values smaller than the other samples, which statistically indicates that he falls below the 2.5 percentile of the population approach used in chapter 5. In our case, the evidence permits us to state that he was well below the population mean, and by falling in the 2.5 percentile he was an outlier, at least with respect to the sample we could investigate. As Jett, Wu, and Frost (1967) reported, such values in males are characteristic of elderly individuals (older than 70).

Histomorphology thus indicates that Pakal was beyond his fifth decade when he died. All the biological parameters (osteon counts, cortical area and ratio, cortical/total area, and osteon size) are in agreement with an age much older than the one originally proposed in the 1950s. His senile age could be an exception for this population; Grube states that these long-living dynasts are clearly not the rule (chapter 10, this volume). However, speculating on the exceptionality of Pakal's age is not the purpose of this chapter.

ACKNOWLEDGMENTS

The samples of rib from Pakal and comparative samples from Palenque were provided by Jane Buikstra, Vera Tiesler, and physical anthropologist Enrique Serrano, who is in charge of the Headquarters of Physical Anthropology at the Instituto Nacional de Antropología e Historia (INAH). Cross-sectional area data for the various comparative archaeological samples were derived from Cho 2002 and Cho et al. 2002.

5

Pakal's Age in the Demographic Context of Late Classic Palenque Society

Lourdes Márquez, Patricia Hernández, and Carlos Serrano

The first study on Pakal's skeletal remains was carried out by Dávalos and Romano (1955, 1973), who identified a male aged between 40 and 50 years. Ruz's (1978) reading of the inscriptions concerning Pakal's age at death indicated that he had died at around 39 years of age, whereas other interpretations suggested that Pakal was a much older individual, exceeding 80 years (Mathews and Schele 1974; Schele and Freidel 1990:219). The latter interpretation markedly differed from the age determined at the osteological examination at the time of the tomb's discovery. The first age estimate of 40–50 years, contested by Mathews and Schele in a work published in 1974, led Ruz to perform an investigation of pre-Hispanic life spans, based on available data from pre-Hispanic populations in general and also from two ossuaries from the Potomac area (Ruz 1978). He also consulted historical documents on Postclassic rulers of known age. He called upon physical anthropologist Arturo Romano, who confirmed the first diagnosis. Ruz then added a histological assessment, which indicated an age of about 40 years (Ruz 1978:292–93).

New osteological and histological analysis by Buikstra and colleagues (chapter 3, this volume) and by Stout and Streeter (chapter 4, this volume) reevaluate the original assessments. In this chapter, we follow the approach used by Ruz (1978) in his comparison of the age-at-death distribution. Here, we wish to examine the demographic profile of Palenque's population during the end of the Classic, of which Pakal was a part, based on a recent paleodemographic and paleoepidemiological study (Márquez, Hernández, and Gómez 2002).

A special methodology was required because we were undertaking description and analysis of individuals who were extremely old. We also considered environmental indicators, which may reveal specific living conditions (Binford 1971; Peebles and Kus 1977; O'Shea 1984; Sempowski and Spence 1994). Finally, we made comparisons with other pre-Hispanic populations in which the percentage of individuals older than age 55 was in fact very small.

Skeletal Materials

The materials were excavated in several Palenque structures. Among them are Temple XV, the Temple of the Cross, and the Temple the Foliated Cross, all part of one building complex. All primary interments date mainly to the Late Classic and the beginning of the Terminal Classic (López-Bravo 1995). The excavations, carried out since 1993 by Arnoldo González Cruz, resulted in the recovery of at least 170 individuals.

We assume that the burials in the crypts contain members of the same lineage or otherwise related individuals (Haviland 2003:129–30). The burial locations, their dispositions, and their associated funerary contexts suggest that the individuals buried in the temples and in some nearby compounds, such as the ones in Group IV, likely belonged to both the high-status "primary and secondary elite" as defined by Chase (1992) and to a lower hierarchy of Palenque society. The latter includes not only noblemen and priests, but also specialized craftsmen, merchants, and architects, along with servants that probably inhabited the nobles' homes. These two units had a heterogeneous composition (Havilland 2003:133). Inhabitants of residential units of much lower ranks are not represented here.

Methodology

We assigned social position based on the burials' location, the buildings' type and function, the type of tomb or funerary deposit, and the quantity and quality of grave goods (Binford 1971; Peebles and Kus 1977; O'Shea 1984; Sempowski and Spence 1994).

We used standard osteological methods to determine sex, physical characteristics, signs of disease, and occupational markers (Buikstra and Ubelaker 1994). Because the most elderly decedents pose a unique problem to paleodemography, we used standard techniques; however, we employed them in a hierarchical fashion (Lovejoy 1985; Lovejoy, Meindl, Mensforth et al. 1985; Lovejoy, Meindl, Pryzbeck et al. 1985; Meindl and Lovejoy 1985; Iscan and Loth 1989; Ubelaker 1989; Brooks and Suchey 1990; Buikstra and

Ubelaker 1994): age-related changes in the pubic symphysis and in the cranial sutures played preliminary and minor roles; the degrees of osteophytosis in the cervical, thoracic, and lumbar regions and the metamorphosis of sternal rib extremities were next; proximal humeral and femoral epiphyseal changes were higher in importance; and dental attrition and especially changes in the auricular surface of the ilium were primary (see Meindl and Russell 1998 for issues in assessing extreme age).

As for entire demographic profiles, modern paleodemography broadly follows two main theory-methodology approaches. One line is based on formal principles of modern demography, whereas a second line of thought draws directly from actual cemetery analysis. The supporters of the first strategy use model tables or uniform mortality-distribution patterns that may or may not conform to the biological and sociocultural characteristics of the populations under analysis (e.g., see Coale and Demeny 1966; Weiss 1973; Coale, Demeny, and Vaughan 1983). These models are based on very selected experiences of modern and anthropological populations and tend to restrict the range of variations we suspect existed in prehistory (Konigsberg, Frankenberg, and Walker 1997; Paine 1997; Boldsen et al. 2002; Kemkes-Grotenthaler 2002; Konigsberg and Herrmann 2002; Wood et al. 2002). The other line of research considers population data from the analysis of osteological collections of well-documented archaeological sites. Such investigations see a supporting role in reference tables, but consider them to mask important biological and behavioral differences between populations. Instead, they employ observed cemetery distributions as primary data and as a basis for directly interpreting prehistoric demographic patterns (Lovejoy et al. 1977; Storey 1992; Storey and Hirth 1997; Camargo and Partida 1998; Civera and Márquez 1998; Camargo, Márquez, and Prado 1999; Hernández, Meindl, and Lourdes Márquez 2000; Meindl, Mensforth, and York 2001; Hernández 2002).

In some but not all archaeological instances, ages at death are measures that can be inferred through the detailed analysis of a representative osteological series. In the past 15 years, paleodemographic investigation has addressed the problem of bias in age-assessment standards (Buikstra 1997; Paine 1997; Meindl and Russell 1998; Konigsberg and Holman 1999; Meindl, Mensforth, and York 2001; Meindl 2003). In addition, modern paleodemography now borrows freely from ethnography for demographic reconstruction (Storey 1992, 1997; Storey and Hirth 1997; Saunders and

Barrans 1999; Meindl, Mensforth, and York 2001; Márquez, Hernández, and Gómez 2002).

Stable Theory and Demographic Growth in Palenque

Paleodemographic reconstruction has always rested on stable-population theory. A stable population is one in which birth and mortality were constant throughout the use of a cemetery (it is considered stationary when its growth is zero). However, "as in every theoretic construction, the theory in stable populations contains a fictional part. . . . [W]hen analyzed, no population is as stable as theory says" (Dumond 1997:175). Therefore, to draw inferences about the complete demographic dynamic of an ancient population, it is necessary to postulate the population's growth rate, a measure that is difficult to obtain directly from archaeological sources (but see Meindl and Russell 1998).

For various Classic pre-Hispanic populations, archaeologists have crudely estimated growth rates by means of settlement sizes and densities (Haviland 2003:111–43). In the case of Palenque, the archaeological data provided by Liendo (2002) suggest that during the Late Classic period the city experienced a moderate population growth, influenced by the weakening of the structures of power affecting the stability of food-distribution systems, which in turn effected some migration to peripheral sites. This situation surely had consequences for the health of its inhabitants and may have disturbed the levels of fertility even more than that of mortality (Márquez, Hernández, and Gómez 2002). Following these archaeological studies, we postulated an annual growth rate of 1.5 percent (0.015), and, with our adjustment of the cemetery age distribution (given later), we solved for the demographic parameters. Such a rate is representative of moderate growth for anthropological populations.

Demography of Palenque

Infant Underrepresentation

From our examination of the distribution of the Palenque series (table 5.1), we are convinced that individuals under the age of 5 are underrepresented. This underrepresentation may be due in small degree to poor preservation conditions, but it is certainly and primarily the result of differential burial practices (Márquez, Hernández, and Gómez 2002). That is, the reduced number of individuals under the age of 5 in the Palenque series is probably associated with social, cultural, ideological, and political factors. It is possible that at Palenque during the Late and Terminal Classic period young children did not acquire the same social position as the adults, until they reached an age by which the risk of death had considerably diminished. Perhaps young children who died were buried in spaces set apart, which have not been explored yet, given that buildings and temples were priorities during the excavations. The high mortality calculated for the birth-to-4 age group in other Maya populations supports this notion (Camargo and Partida 1998; Camargo, Márquez, and Prado 1999). Burial place is related to social position, which may explain the lack of infants younger than 5 years in the chambers, cysts, and tombs of the main buildings of Palenque. This lack may also be associated with cultural concepts of death in children. Within the Maya elite, particularly in the case of young heirs, there was a risk in naming as successor someone who did not have a great likelihood of survival. In our recent analysis of the remains of the tombs of Yaxchilán (with the collaboration of our colleague María Elena Salas, who studied these skeletons), we checked the bones in Burial 2 of Tomb 1, Structure 33, which corresponds to a child whose age at death we calculated to be between 5 and 9 years according to dental development. Tomb 4 in this same site housed the remains of a child between ages 4 and 5. The absence of younger infants might indicate that children were considered socially only after they had passed the ages of highest risk of death, and only then were they buried in special places of high rank.

According to Livi-Bacci (1990), the proportion of individuals younger than 15 years of age within preindustrial societies should be about 40 percent or more. The results obtained from the survey of Mesoamerican populations indicate that the age-at-death distributions for newborns to 4-year-olds vary from 35 percent to 53 percent of the cemeteries (Civera and Márquez 1996; Camargo and Partida 1998). To assess any underrepresentation of neonates and infants, we compared our sample to distributions obtained in two series that we consider the most adequate in terms of size and characteristics. The reference collection includes 411 skeletons from San Gregorio Atlapulco, Xochimilco (Hernández 2002) and 109 Classic Maya individuals excavated in the island of Jaina, Campeche, and studied by Storey, Márquez, and Schmidt (2002). In San Gregorio's skeletal sample, newborns represent 29.2 percent, the 1–4 age group totals 22.1 percent, and the 5–9 group is 5.4 percent (Hernández 2002). This collection allows us to quantify the important underrepresentation of newborns and infants between 1 and 4 years old in the Palenque series. In the collection, the proportion of children younger than 5 years are about half of the total population, whereas in Palenque the children of this age recovered are only 8.2 percent of the total sample (see table 5.1). It is clear that the underrepresentation of these ages, as argued, is due to their burial in smaller sites with little or no social or political importance, such as patios, plazas, in-between buildings, corridors, with no structure that allowed their preservation and posterior identification during the archaeological explorations. In addition to the aforementioned factors, the geochemical characteristics of the ground, especially in Palenque's hot and humid environment, must have disintegrated the infants' skeletal remains. However, the main cause of the lack of infants is burial patterns. This age segment must await additional archaeological excavation that focuses on areas away from the main structures where the funerary chambers, cysts, and under-the-floor burials have been found. Judging from the burials encountered, these places were reserved for individuals high in the hierarchy, mostly adult males, but also females (Márquez, Hernández, and Gómez 2002). In addition to the described sample, some skeletons, mainly those of adults, had been recovered during the excavations led by Arnoldo González Cruz outside the temples and in the plazas.

Table 5.1 lists the observed distributions of ages at death in the populations we used as reference and the adjustment made in the Palenque series. As shown, a rather conservative approach was pursued in the estimation of the number of infants 0 to 4 years old, which represent only around 28 percent of the overall Palenque population, different from both the populations of San Gregorio and Jaina, where their representation exceeds 50 percent. The distribution achieved after the adjustment resembles more what could be expected of an ancient population with moderate growth, with one-third of the population representing individuals less than 15 years old at death.

Figure 5.1 shows the distribution of the original and adjusted series. The only addition of individuals was newborns and the group between 1 and 4.9 years of age; that is, starting from the 5–9 group, the original distribution was retained.

TABLE 5.1 Distribution of Age at Death in Three Mesoamerican Pre-Hispanic Populations

Period	Classic		Postclassic		Classic			
Series	Jaina		San Gregorio		Palerque		Palenque	
Age	Observed	%	Observed	%	Observed	%	Adjusted	%
0	31	28.44	120	29.20	2	1.2	46	20.8
1–4	27	24.77	91	22.14	12	7.0	17	7.7
5–9	4	3.67	22	5.35	10	5.8	10	4.5
10–14	2	1.83	33	8.03	5	3.5	5	2.3
15–19	4	3.67	18	4.38	14	8.1	14	6.3
20–24	2	1.83	31	7.54	20	11.6	20	9.0
25–29	2	1.83	25	6.08	22	12.8	22	10.0
30–34	4	3.67	24	5.84	23	13.4	23	10.4
35–39	7	6.42	14	3.41	30	17.4	30	13.6
40–44	6	5.50	15	3.65	23	13.4	23	10.4
45–49	7	6.42	5	1.22	9	5.9	9	4.1
50–54	2	1.83	9	2.19	1	0.6	1	0.5
55–59	2	1.83	3	0.73	1	0.6	1	0.5
60–64	5	4.59	1	0.24	0	0.0	0	0.0
65–69	1	0.92	0	0.00	0	0.0	0	0.0
70–74	1	0.92	0	0.00	0	0.0	0	0.0
Adults	2	1.83	0	0.00	0	0.0	0	0.0
Total	109		411		172		221	

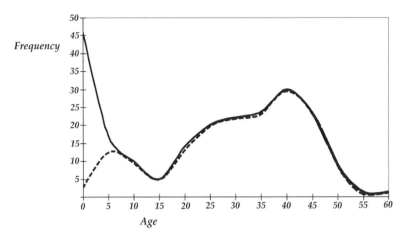

FIGURE 5.1 Palenque, Chiapas, Late-Terminal Classic mortality profile

Paleodemographic Indicators

For the purpose of this chapter, only those profiles related to the life span of the studied specimens are presented: total life average, life average in adults, survival, general and infant mortality, and life expectancy (table 5.2). According to Overfield, maximum life spans may very well be similar in every human population (1995:67); however, average life expectancies vary a great deal because they depend on multiple environmental factors.

The sample presents a somewhat young age profile: the mean for the whole population was 12.7 years. This indicator is greatly affected by our postulated level of infant mortality. The average age of the adults is 26.2 years. The survival of older adults at age 40 was 15.5 percent, whereas only 1 percent of the population older than 50 years survived. For Palenque, the proportion of individuals younger than 15 years at death was 35.3 percent; those between 15 and 49.9 years constitute 63.8 percent, and those older than 50 were another 1.0 percent of the overall population (table 5.3).

Studies on longevity of contemporary populations in the United States show that individuals older than age 60 are only 17 percent of the total living population, even with the development of medical science and the public-health services available (Overfield 1995:80).

TABLE 5.2 Palenque, Late and Terminal Classic Demographic Indicators

Mean age of the entire population	12.7 years
Adult mean age	26.2 years
Percentage of adults that survived to age 40	15.5
Life expectancy at birth	21.8 years
Infant mortality rate	208.1 deaths of infants under one year of age per 1,000 births
Crude mortality rate	57.9 deaths per 1,000 inhabitants

TABLE 5.3 Palenque, Chiapas, Late Classic Population Proportion According to the Three Age Groups

Age	Proportion within the Population
younger than 14.9	35.3%
15–50	63.8%
older than 50	1.0%

Figure 5.2 shows the population hypothetical census for Palenque, or the age structure of the once-living population, assuming the growth rate and the adjusted age-at-death distribution. Regardless of our adjustments, this population was certainly a young one. The first six adult groups representing individuals under the age of 40 predominate, with a very low proportion of adults older than 50.

Life expectancies at various ages imply health conditions (Overfield 1995:67–95). At Palenque, the estimated life expectancy at birth was 21.8 years, about the same as that obtained from the coeval sample from the Teotihuacán district of Tlajinga 33, which is 23 years (Storey 1992:157, 170–71); from Cholula, 23.2 years; and from Tenochtitlán, 23.6 years (Camargo and Partida 1998).

Total mortality in Palenque was as high as 57.9 for every thousand, which is higher than the values obtained from two series of Classic Monte

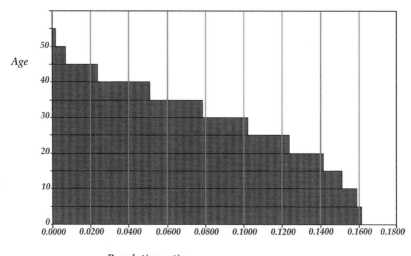

FIGURE 5.2 Palenque, Chiapas, Late-Terminal Classic hypothetical census

Alban, Oaxaca, and Tlajinga 33 (approximately 38.8 and 38.4, respectively), but similar to the value from San Gregorio, 57.2 per thousand, which had the highest infant mortality rate (212 dead per 1,000 born) (Storcy 1992; Hernández 2002). Lack of hygiene was one of the main problems suffered by ancient urban populations (Cohen and Armelagos 1984; Storey 1997; Glassman and Garber 1999; Saunders and Barrans 1999; Storey, Márquez, and Schmidt 2002).

The explanation we favor for Palenque is related to sanitary issues because even though drainage has been detected in some of the structures, such as the Palace, waste fluid was discharged in the Otulum River that crossed the city, so the drinking water often could have been contaminated. High population density and its accumulation of organic waste may have increased the spread of contagious diseases. Studies carried out by Márquez, Hernández, and González (2001) on this same sample have shown that the climatic and natural environmental conditions of the site affected the population's epidemiological profiles and its high mortality, despite the fact that most of the individuals supposedly belonged to governmental and managing groups with probably preferential access to food resources.

During the transitional period between the Late Classic and the Terminal Classic, socioeconomic problems arose that led to the fall of Palenque's political structure and the cultural decadence that characterizes the Terminal Classic. The quality of life was also affected. The noble groups were facing a situation of social and political conflict, coupled with the disintegration of the established systems of control. This situation must have been mirrored also in basic economical dynamics, such as food production and distribution as well as stable and sufficient access to resources.

Indicators of Health

We used Palenque's health indicators—among them cribra orbitalia, porotic hyperostosis, and periosteal reactions—to evaluate general health in this collection. The standardized methodology allows the comparison of data obtained from each indicator of Palenque's sample with other Mesoamerican series that might have shared similar lifestyles (Goodman and Martin 2002; Steckel and Rose 2002). We analyzed individuals by social rank, with archaeological indicators, but because the statistical results were not significant, we calculated frequencies for the whole urban sample within the same rank.

Pathological indicators such as cribra orbitalia and porotic hyperostosis present a frequency of about 80 percent, a relatively high incidence in the urban sample. Storey, Márquez, and Schmidt analyzed four Maya sites and obtained percentages of cribra orbitalia according to sex and age group (2002:294–95). They encountered the highest values (82 percent) in the rural population of Copán, a much higher percentage than that encountered at Palenque. Linear enamel hypoplasias (LEH) in Palenque is 51 percent for incisors and 70 percent for canines (see table 5.4). The incidence of this condition ranges between 40 and 60 percent in the Jaina, Xcaret, and Copán sample rural and urban populations (Storey, Márquez, and Schmidt 2002). The incidence of tibial periostitis is about 87 percent.

Analysis by sex shows no significant differences for LEH incisors, cribra orbitalia, and hyperostosis, but some differences for LEH canine and tibial periosteal reactions ($p < 0.05$). Comparing frequencies between adults and subadults, there was slight higher incidence in adult samples. Of the forty female observable cases, 97.5 percent present the indica-

TABLE 5.4 Palenque's Health Indicators

Indicator	n	%
LEH* incisor	24/47	51
LEH* canine	35/50	70
Cribra	23/28	82
Hyperostosis	62/69	89
Periostitis	106/121	87

*LEH = linear enamel hypoplasia

tor of periostitis; 100 percent of male cases present it, and 87 percent of subadults (see table 5.5). Periosteal reactions were common to the whole population. As in Palenque, the study carried out in Ambergris, Belize, by Glassman and Garber found no association between the incidence of periostitis and social strata (1999:128). Additional papers provide general information without distinction by social status (Storey, Márquez, and Schmidt 2002:294–95).

It is undeniable that individuals of higher social sectors had advantages over the remainder of the population, such as access to better or more stable food resources. Although results of paleodiet analyses are not yet available for Palenque, we assume that diet there was similar to that of other Maya sites such as Pacbitun, Belize (Coyston, White, and Schwarcz 1999:221–43). There, the diets of the commoners and the elite did not differ in the amount of carbohydrates. The protein intake of the high-status group was provided by animals used in rituals, such as turkeys and dogs, which when fed with maize provided a foodstuff rich in fat.

Pakal and the Elders of Palenque

The biological profile of an old individual can be outlined from the characteristics described in Overfield's (1995) book on longevity of contemporary North American and European groups. Aside from dental attrition and auricular surface metamorphosis, the most important changes that take place with extreme aging (that can be determined from a skeleton) are reduction of axial height and overall bone density. The loss of bone density occurs in the cortical areas at midshaft and in the trabeculae of

TABLE 5.5 Palenque's Health Indicators (Sex Differences at p > 0.05)

Indicators	Female	Male	Subadult	Unknown	Total	Pearson Chi^2
No LEH incisors	9	9	3	2	23	
	52.9%	50%	50%	33.3%	48.9%	
LEH incisors	8	9	3	4	24	
	47.1%	50%	50%	66.3%	51.1%	
Total	17	18	6	6	47	
	100%	100%	100%	100%	100%	
No LEH canine	3	9	2	1	15	
	18.8%	42.9%	28.6%	16.7	30%	
LEH canine	13	12	5	5	35	
	81.2%	57.1%	71.4%	83.3%	70%	0.048
Total	16	21	7	6	50	
	100%	100%	100%	100%	100%	
No Cribra	0	3	1	1	5	
	0%	23.1%	14.3%	100%	17.9%	
Cribra	7	10	6	0	23	
	100%	76.9%	85.7%	0%	82.1%	
Total	7	13	7	1	28	
	100%	100%	100%	100%	100%	
No Hyperostosis	1	2	3	1	7	
	4.8	8.0%	20.0%	12.5%	10.1%	
Hyperostosis	20	23	12	7	62	
	95.2%	92.%	80%	87.5%	89.9%	
Total	21	25	15	8	69	
	100%	100%	100%	100%	100%	
No Periostitis Tibia	1	0	2	0	3	
	2.5%	0%	13.3%	0%	2.5%	
Periostitis Tibia	39	48	13	18	118	
	97.5%	100%	86.7%	100%	97.5%	0.039
Total	40	48	15	18	121	
	100%	100%	100%	100%	100%	

the long-bone metaphyses. There is also an increase in the periosteal area, with enlargement of medullar spaces. Males tend to retain more of their bone density compared to females because females are more prone to osteoporosis, especially after menopause. Changes in the face and cranium are characterized by continuous expansion with age in both sexes. The mandible decreases in height (if edentulous), but gains width. Approximately one-quarter of people between 65 and 74 years old no longer have their own teeth, a rate that rises to about half the total among individuals older than 75, even with modern care. Aging is associated with the proliferation of vertebral osteophytes, a form of arthritis, identified on the rims of the vertebral bodies. In males after the sixth decade of life, there is noticeable bone loss in intervertebral bodies. Osteophytosis affects hands and feet in the great majority of males older than 75 years of age. The highest prevalence of osteoarthritis in elderly people is observed in the cervical region of the vertebral column, affecting 85 percent of men. Osteophytosis also increases dramatically in the phalanges of the hands after 60 years of age (Overfield 1995:79–80).

In the case of Palenque, osteoarthritis reaches high frequencies among the male adult population, specifically the 35–49 age group; the most affected region is the lumbar spine (17 out of 35 individuals, 49 percent), certainly related to aging and possibly to physical activity. The values presented for women (7 out of 35, 20 percent) were less than half of those for males, suggesting that their daily activities were not unusually strenuous (Gómez 1999).

In this series, out of 142 skeletons, 29 are of individuals older than age 40 when they died (8 females, 16 males, and 5 sex unknown). Some of the male adult skeletons present profoundly marked muscular insertions; two of them have mutilation and dental inlays, cultural traits associated with high-status individuals.

We identified only one individual older than age 50 when he died, found in Tomb 1 of Group IV. All archaeological indicators place this individual in the high-status group, implying that his life conditions, including diet, could have been adequate and similar to those of other members of the elite, including the rulers. The cervical portion of his spine exhibits severe osteophytosis with collapsing vertebral bodies, while in the thoracic spine osteophytes were moderate. The margins of his long-bone articulations had severe bony lipping similar to that of the phalanges of his hands. Strong alveolar resorption and marked dental attrition were seen in this individual. There was antemortem loss of only one tooth, and his teeth present an abundance of tartar. The dentition contained four carious teeth. Cavities are associated with the intake of carbohydrates, which when fermented with saliva produce bacterial plaques and dental caries. In the study of the Kichpanha, Magennis found a relation between the type of diet and dental pathology (1999:145).

Each of the changes observed in the individual from Tomb 1 (older than 50 years old at death) provides details for comparison to other elderly males within Palenque's society. The characteristics of the skeleton also have implications regarding the subject's everyday life in that his mobility was probably somewhat limited by the affliction in the cervical region of his spine. The arthritis in the hands remains one of the main forms of evidence of the aging process.

With respect to Pakal, the first study carried out by Dávalos and Romano describes the skeleton in a fragile state of preservation. The cranium was fragmented, and some portions were actually scattered outside the site. The facial portion was mostly preserved, with an intact mandible, which presented the following characteristics: robust, with a prominent chin, and quadrangular. "Teeth are well developed and scarcely worn out on the occlusal surface, were recovered in situ. . . . The sockets corresponding to the inferior second molars right and left were found reabsorbed" (Dávalos and Romano 1973:253).

The authors also describe the vertebral column from the seventh cervical vertebra downward, reporting that the dorsal, lumbar, and sacral portions were in situ, without mentioning any evidence of osteophytosis. In the report, they state that this skeleton did not present pathological alterations (Dávalos and Romano 1973). In a recent revised description of the Pakal skeleton, Tiesler (chapter 2, this volume) affirms the presence of osteophytosis and Schmorl nodes in the cervical vertebrae.

The description of the morphological changes related to the aging process in modern populations (Overfield 1995:79) and the description of an individual in Tomb 1 of Palenque's Group IV, whose age at death did not exceed 59 years, are consistent. Nonetheless, it is important to mention that the absence of individuals older than 59 in the Palenque sample does not mean that no one lived to older ages. It is difficult to infer from bony remains alone whether Pakal (or anyone) survived the fifth decade of his or her life. The decay the skeleton underwent after the discovery of the tomb is noteworthy, and the taphonomic process deeply affected the bony tissue, limiting the application of the criteria to estimate age at death. Nevertheless, if Pakal was indeed 80 years at the time of his death, his remains should carry the suite of aging characteristics described by Overfield.

Living conditions for the Maya elite and rulers have generally been considered favorable. Although they undoubtedly enjoyed better nutrition and freedom from strenuous work, they may not have escaped pathological conditions that could have shortened their lives, such as circulatory, gastrointestinal, and respiratory disorders. Maya rulers' lives were full of political and social confrontations as well as external warfare, as described in the epigraphic record. It is not difficult to infer that they underwent intense stress, health problems, and severe physical training, be it by military action or during the ball game, aspects that are rarely taken into consideration when tracking back their daily lives.

6

Did Pakal Suffer from Deforming Diseases?
True Facts and Iconographic Myths
Arturo Romano

This chapter reviews the skeletal evidence collected in 1952 on the potential congenital deforming diseases of the personage from the sarcophagus tomb of the Temple of the Inscriptions in Palenque. The original data are complemented with the results of the recent in situ reappraisal of the case in 1999. These joint results confront the allegations put forth in the 1970s that Janaab' Pakal suffered from potential body deformations, mainly founded on the iconographic record from the site (Greene, Rosenblum Scandizzo, and Scandizzo 1976).

Representations of physical anomalies at Palenque, as in Mesoamerican cultures in general, figure prominently in the pre-Hispanic pictorial and sculptural records. Physical defects or abnormal body proportions—such as dwarfism, hunchbacks, and polydactily—appear to be something desirable rather than imperfections in the ancient society. Persons afflicted by visual body malformations, conceived as signs of divinity, were considered to be provided with supernatural powers, as has been proposed by Greene, Rosenblum Scandizzo, and Scandizzo (1976); Miller and Taube (1993); and Prager (2002). The appropriation of these desirable physical attributes surely led to their public ostentation in the form of human curiosities in the ruler's court or malformations displayed personally by dignitaries.

Compared to the rich iconographic sources of information about physical deformities, considerably less is known from the skeletal record. No case of defects such as polydactily, cleft jaw, or dwarfism has been confirmed or proved in the literature on the Maya, and hunchbacks have only been inferred from vertebral body collapse and spinal displacement.

A potential match between the depictions of Janaab' Pakal's deformity and the skeletal evidence was established during the Second Palenque Round Table. In their work, Greene, Rosenblum Scandizzo, and Scandizzo

(1976:60–71) conclude from the sculptured portraits of the ruler that he suffered from a severe unilateral clubfoot. They argue that the full-figure portraits of Pakal on the Simojovel Plaque, on Piers B and D of House D in the Palace, and on the sarcophagus lid show a twisted foot (see also Greene 1985:61). In Pier D's portrait, the authors recognize the affected leg to be thinner and shorter than the other one and attribute this asymmetry to disuse atrophy from his equinovarus incapacity. They say a similarly "malformed" foot is displayed on the Dumbarton Oaks Panel 2, attributed to Pakal's grandson Hok (Greene, Rosenblum Scandizzo, and Scandizzo 1976:66, 71). In this case, however, the authors could not detect any associated shortening or thinning of the lower extremity.

Apart from clubfoot malformations, Greene and her colleagues propose from the broad nose, finger clubbings, elongated jaw, and large head in the portrait of Lady S'ak' K'uk' that Pakal's mother must have suffered from the disfiguring effects of advanced acromegaly. This disorder originates from a rare tumorous enlargement of the pituitary glands and the encapsulating sella turcica at the base of the brain (Greene, Rosenblum Scandizzo, and Scandizzo 1976; Ortner and Putschar 1981). Nor was the third dynastic generation in line spared from deforming disease. According to Greene, Rosenblum Scandizzo, and Scandizzo (1976), Kan B'alam, Pakal's son and follower to the throne, had a sixth toe and finger, as depicted in his Palace portrait (Pier D, House A) (see figure 6.1). Additional examples of polydactily come from the Temple of the Inscriptions, the Temple of the Foliated Cross, and the Temple of the Sun, all ascribed to Pakal's successor (Greene 1985:33). Pakal himself is proposed to have been affected by polydactily as well. Greene, Rosenblum Scandizzo, and Scandizzo encountered what they consider to be hints of his affliction on the sarcophagus lid, which they suggest depicts Pakal's split left fifth toe (1976:70).

The claims made by Greene and her colleagues regarding Pakal's disorders soon caused an outcry among Mexican scholars, who put into question their daring conclusions. The Mexican scholars cited negative skeletal and taphonomic evidence to underscore the absence of any malformation in Pakal's remains and publicly declared the allegations of deformation to be void of any scientific value (Ruz in Romano 1989:1421; see also Romano 1980). The present work intends to update the original arguments with the recently retrieved evidence from Pakal's tomb. In this

FIGURE 6.1 Portrait of Kan B'alam II's hand, displayed with six fingers, Pier D, House A, Palace, Palenque (redrawn by Mirna Sánchez from Greene 1985: fig. 70)

chapter, besides reviewing signs of general deformity, I address explicitly the possibility of the ruler's having suffered from polydactily or clubfoot defects, as has been suggested.

Analytical Procedures

This study is based on the original assessment of the remains performed in 1952 and on the recent graphic recordings of the skeleton provided by the project Conservación, Restauración y Estudio in Situ de los Restos Humanos de K'Inich Janaab' Pakal I, Personaje Hallado en el Recinto Funerario del Templo de las Inscripciones, Palenque, Chiapas. For this purpose, anatomical relationships between the skeletal elements of the feet and morphological properties of tibias, tarsals, and metatarsals were assessed along with the form of the finger bones. For the taphonomic interpretation of the processes that a body undergoes before, during, and after its deposition and that might hamper objective interpretation, a set of forensic concepts of decomposition of corpse and sequences of disarticulation was employed (Duday 1997; Tiesler 2004).

Apart from the general morphological evaluation, a number of osteological and radiologic indications of clubfoot deformities, synthesized from Brothwell 1967, Morse 1978 (cited in Aufderheide and Rodríguez

1998:75), and Murray and Jacobson 1982, were confronted with the evidence. The equinovarus is a rare disorder, defined by the dysfunctional rotation and inward movement of the foot (figure 6.2). One or both feet may be deformed, with men showing a higher incidence than women. Among the important morphological changes are the flat superior surface of the talus and its shortened neck, which appears fused to the body. Additional flattening is to be expected in the distal articular tibial facet, accompanied by formal changes in the malleolus. The talus exhibits adaptive shortening and widening in reaction to rotation, whereas metatarsals often appear flattened, the navicular bones reduced in size in the radiography. Dysfunctional locomotion in persons suffering from untreated equinovarus may engender general signs of reactive mechanical stress both in the affected and contralateral lower extremity.

Polydactily is commonly bilateral and accompanies syndromes and severe systemic body malformations. Supernumerary toes or fingers branch off the fifth proximal phalange or metacarpal/metatarsal. The sixth finger or toe is usually formed by three or two phalanges (Ortner and Putschar 1981:362–63; Aufderheide and Rodriguez 1998:76).

Results

The results obtained from the recent osteotaphonomic reevaluation confirm the original skeletal appraisal of the personage performed in 1952. Apart from Pakal's artificial head shape and dental appearance, both produced by artificial body modifications, no morphological changes were noted. Both axial skeleton and extremities appear as normally proportioned. There are no signs of supernumerary bone elements or malformations of tarsals or metatarsals.

As shown in figure 6.3 for the left side, the neck of the talus clearly separates the head from the body in both controlateral segments without any flattening in their superior parts. The navicular bones from both sides are likewise normally proportioned, as are the metatarsals, which exhibit a regular volume and shape. In consequence, no signs consistent with the clubfoot diagnostic criteria were detected. Further up, none of the right and left tibial, femoral, or patellar segments that could be evaluated showed signs of any abnormal loading or arthritis (see also Tiesler, chapter 2, in this volume).

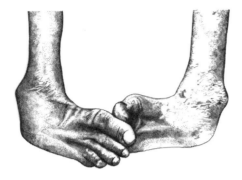

FIGURE 6.2 Clubfoot
in modern patient
(drawing by Mirna
Sánchez)

FIGURE 6.3 Left astragalus of the personage from the sarcophagus tomb:
(*left*) superior view and (*right*) lateral view (photograph by Andrea Cucina)

As concerns the decomposition process, the disarticulation sequence
during body decay displays a commonly observed pattern in free-space
decomposition (see figure 2.7 in chapter 2). Both complete legs collapsed
laterally down from the acetabular joints, originating a rotation of both
feet toward the sides. Their contact with and contention by the inner sarcophagus walls prompted the disintegrating foot bones to fall distally,
producing the bone assemblage recorded in 1952 and again in 1999. The
fact that the forefeet went down en bloc hints at the presence of some type

of footwear, such as sandals, which appear commonly in the sculptured portraiture of Palenque.

As regards polydactily in the lower extremities, no metatarsal or proximal phalanx showed any signs of malformation or branching. It is important to point out that all metatarsals and proximal phalanges were present in situ, denying in a compelling manner the possibility that this malformation was present. All metacarpals and proximal phalanges were preserved in the left hand (figure 6.4). The right hand was too destroyed to permit its complete assessment; nevertheless, the observable segments were physiologically proportioned. Again, no osteological signs reminiscent of polydactily could be detected, ruling out that the personage from the Temple of the Inscriptions had suffered from this rare disorder. An additional argument can be made from the five, not six, finger rings present on each hand of the ruler. As demonstrated by the participants of Alberto Ruz's team, the rings had been sized to fit each of the five fingers individually (Eusebio Dávalos, personal communication, 1952) (figure 6.4).

Concluding Remarks

The results obtained in the original and recent osteological and taphonomic study of Janaab' Pakal's mortal remains strongly dismiss the afflictions proposed from Palenque's sculptural record, demanding a reappraisal of iconographic evidence and a rethinking of the possible implications of that evidence. As for the suggested clubfoot depictions, I consider the regional stylistic consensus to express movements of the feet, as for instance during ceremonial dancing, rather than a static ostentation of a rare physical impairment. Grube (1996) provides this same interpretation in his pioneering epigraphic and iconographic work on the important ritual role of dancing in ancient Maya society. In the same work, he interprets the episode depicted in the Dumbarton Oaks Panel 2 as a dancing scene (1996:202).

Regarding the signs of polydactily of fingers and toes represented in the art of Palenque, we can now rule out definitely that they formed part of Pakal's anatomical features. Regarding other historical personages from Palenque, we do not have the skeletal evidence to be able to deny or confirm malformations, such as the case of the six fingers and toes of Pakal's son Kan B'alam. However, we are left to wonder why Kan B'alam should

FIGURE 6.4 Left hand of Pakal, in situ (photograph by Arturo Romano, 1952)

have been depicted with polydactylia in some portraits, but with just five digits in others. In either scenario, the anatomical correctness in the depictions of supernumerary toes and fingers in Palenque's sculptured imagery implies that the artists were aware of this rare physical anomaly. Its public exhibition in the main squares of Palenque, shown as a distinctive feature of Pakal's follower to the throne, underscores its role as a visible attribute of the extraordinary.

ACKNOWLEDGMENTS

I thank Vera Tiesler and Andrea Cucina for editing and translating this chapter.

Geographic Origin of Janaab' Pakal and the "Red Queen"

Evidence from Strontium Isotopes

T. Douglas Price, James H. Burton, Vera Tiesler,
Simon Martin, and Jane E. Buikstra

It is now possible to obtain direct evidence of human mobility from the chemistry of prehistoric human bone and dental enamel. Our investigations utilize the geographic variation of strontium isotope ratios preserved in ancient human bone and enamel to distinguish geographic provenience. This method for identifying migrants relies on differences in these ratios between human tooth enamel and the local strontium isotope signature of the place of burial.

This chapter examines the strontium signatures related to the residential histories of Janaab' Pakal and the so-called Red Queen, a female laid to rest in Temple XIIIsub, adjacent to Pakal's own burial place inside the Temple of the Inscriptions. Enamel samples obtained from two sacrificial victims accompanying her were included in this study to provide additional insights concerning individual movements and migration in Maya society, in the manner of previous studies at Copán and Teotihuacán (Price, Manzanilla, and Middleton 2000; White et al. 2000; White, Longstaffe, and Law 2001; Buikstra et al. 2004).

The summary of our investigations begins with a consideration of the existing epigraphic information regarding Janaab' Pakal and his wife. A brief description of the principles of strontium isotope analysis precedes presentation of the results of the instrumental measurements. A subsequent section considers the determination of the local (place of death) isotope signature, followed by a concluding section dealing with the geographic origins of the individuals considered in this study. Analytical procedures are detailed in appendix A of this volume.

Epigraphic Information

Ongoing debates surround the question of individual mobility among Maya rulers. Their travels likely were an integrated part of the pan-regional political and military strategies in which they participated, documented in the recent discussion of connections between the Maya and Teotihuacán (Braswell 2003) or the varied residential backgrounds of some of Copán's residents (Buikstra et al. 2004). As for Palenque, no documentation exists that hints at any foreign origin for its rulers, implying that all the kingdom's governors were from the area and that Palenque's ruling male elite did not suffer any subjugation from or impositions of foreign statesmen.

Female nobles most likely played a different, more passive role in the aristocratic network, with the exception of women rulers or interim throne holders (Martin and Grube 2000). The epigraphic coverage of women's residential histories is closely linked to royal marriage, whether celebrated within the local aristocracy or arranged between a local paramount and an incoming foreign woman. As in other societies, Maya ruling families carefully plotted marriage arrangements to nurture alliances with other political domains, to seek territorial expansion, and to strengthen their authority within the region. Maintaining family ties through marriages between high-standing noble lineages also helped to assure genealogical claims to succession and thus the continuity of dynastic reign.

Elite brides could be obtained from other polities to forge alliances or to cement unequal patron-client relationships. If their foreign origin enhanced political capital, it was lauded and reiterated wherever possible. But when less advantageous, it could almost escape mention. In consequence, it is unsafe to assume that a woman with no stated outside affiliation was necessarily local. A number of prominent women are mentioned in the inscriptions at Palenque, although only one, Ix Tz'akb'u Ajaw, Pakal's wife, is associated with another site. She is called a "Toktahn person." This place was apparently the first dynastic seat of the Palenque polity; the location is as yet unidentified. She came from a line of non-Palenque residents, with her father originating from Uxte'k'uh, another important site in the region that cannot be tied to a known locale.

Principles of Strontium Isotopes

The stable isotopes of strontium include ^{84}Sr (approximately 0.56 percent of total strontium), ^{86}Sr (approximately 9.87 percent), and ^{88}Sr (approximately 82.53 percent). A fourth isotope, ^{87}Sr, is formed over time by the radioactive decay of rubidium (^{87}Rb) and composes approximately 7.04 percent of total strontium (Faure and Powell 1972). Variations in strontium isotope compositions in natural materials are conventionally expressed as ^{87}Sr/^{86}Sr ratios (the abundance of ^{86}Sr is similar to that of ^{87}Sr). The naturally occurring average ratio of ^{87}Sr to ^{86}Sr thus is around 0.713, but this value is variable.

Strontium isotope ratios vary with the age and type of rock as a function of the original ^{87}Rb/^{86}Sr ratio of a source and its age (Faure and Powell 1972; Faure 1986). Geologic units that are very old (more than 100 million years) and have high Rb/Sr ratios will have high ^{87}Sr/^{86}Sr ratios today as well as in the recent past (less than 1 million years). Values may range to 0.730 or higher. In contrast, rocks that are geologically young (less than 1–10 million years) and that have low Rb/Sr ratios, such as Late Cenozoic volcanic areas, generally have ^{87}Sr/^{86}Sr ratios less than 0.706 (see, e.g., Rogers and Hawkesworth 1989). These variations may seem small, but they are exceptionally large from a geological standpoint and far in excess of the analytical error using a Thermal Ionization Mass Spectrometer (± 0.00001).

The basic principles of the method are straightforward. Strontium in bedrock moves into soil and groundwater and through the food chain (e.g., Comar, Russell, and Wasserman 1957; Elias, Hirao, and Patterson 1982). Virtually all strontium in vertebrate organisms is found in the skeleton. Strontium is incorporated into bone and enamel as a substitute for calcium in the mineral hydroxyapatite (e.g., Schroeder, Nason, and Tipton 1972; Rosenthal 1981). The strontium isotope composition of human bones and teeth, therefore, matches those of individuals' diets, which in turn reflect the strontium isotope compositions of the local geology.

Bone is a relatively plastic and reactive material, containing both an organic (mostly collagen) and inorganic (hydroxyapatite) phase. It is continually remodeled during an individual's life, so the elemental and isotopic composition of bone reflects the last years of life. Bone isotope ratios should then represent the place of death. Local strontium isotope ratios can also be measured in other modern or archaeological materials. The enamel in teeth, in contrast, forms during infancy and early childhood and undergoes relatively little subsequent change. The strontium isotope ratio in tooth enamel reflects the place of birth. Thus, differences in isotopic ratios between the local signal in bone (or other local material) and tooth enamel in the same individual document a change in residence (Price, Burton, and Bentley 2002).

Potential problems with diagenesis have been addressed in various investigations (e.g., Price et al. 1992; Sillen and Sealy 1995). Enamel has been shown to be highly resistant to contamination and a reliable indicator of biogenic isotope ratios even in samples hundreds of thousands of years old (e.g., Hillson 1986; Kohn 1996; Åberg, Fosse, and Stray 1998; Budd et al. 2000).

A number of studies have been published documenting the utility of strontium isotope analysis for a number of periods and places: the Anasazi period in Arizona (Price et al. 1994; Ezzo, Johnson, and Price 1997), the Neolithic Linearbandkeramik and Bell Beaker periods in southern Germany (Price, Grupe, and Schrorter 1994, 1998; Price et al. 2001), the historical period in South Africa (Sealy et al. 1991; Sealy, Armstrong, and Schrire 1995), and the Neolithic and medieval periods in Britain (Montgomery et al. 1999; Montgomery, Budd, and Evans 2000), among others (Montgomery, Evans, and Neighbour 2003; Montgomery, Evans, and Roberts 2003).

In addition, a series of investigations in Mesoamerica is using strontium and oxygen isotopes. The basic principle of enamel versus bone applies to both isotopes, but oxygen isotopes vary geographically with differences in sources of rainwater. Strontium isotope studies have examined residence and migration at Teotihuacán (Price, Manzanilla, and Middleton 2000); the origin of the ruler and other buried individuals under the central acropolis at Copán (Buikstra et al. 2004); and individuals and populations from Kaminaljuyu and Tikal (Wright 1999b). Several papers on the oxygen isotopic provenience of individuals from various contexts at Teotihuacán, at Monte Alban, and in the Maya region have appeared (Stuart-Williams et al. 1996; White et al. 1998, 2000, 2002, 2004; Wright 1999b; White, Longstaffe, and Law 2001; Spence et al. 2004).

Results of the Isotope Analyses

We measured strontium isotope ratios in the six samples from Palenque and present these values in table 7.1. We analyzed three samples from Pakal—one enamel from a third molar and two bone samples from a tibia and a rib—along with first molar enamel from the three individuals buried in a tomb adjacent to Pakal's, including the Red Queen and her two companions. The measured values range between 0.708081 and 0.708669. Interpretation of these values requires consideration of the local geology of the Palenque area.

Palenque is located at the contact between sedimentary rocks of Paleocene age (the hills upon which the site itself is built) and rocks of Miocene age (the broad plain immediately to the north) (figure 7.1). These calcium-rich (and hence strontium-rich) sedimentary rocks are of marine origin and have been shown to exhibit the $^{87}Sr/^{86}Sr$ ratio characteristic of the ocean at the time of their deposition (Hoddell et al. 2004).

Because the seawater values are well known over time (e.g., Veizer and Compston 1974; Burke et al. 1982; Richter, Rowley, and DePaolo 1992; McArthur, Howarth, and Bailey 2001), we can use these data (figure 7.2) to infer the ratios for the rocks of each age: 0.7078 to 0.7080 for the Paleocene sediments (Hodell and colleagues [2004] measured a Palenque limestone $^{87}Sr/^{86}Sr$ of 0.70783) and 0.7083 to 0.7090 for the younger Miocene sediments. Depending on the relative contribution of food from each rock type to the total strontium of the diet, we can estimate a local value for the Palenque area of 0.7078 to 0.7090, with little likelihood of either extreme; we expect the local $^{87}Sr/^{86}Sr$ ratio to be biased toward the north (around 0.7085), where agricultural fields were likely placed.

The available sample data that represent the "local" Palenque signature are the two $^{87}Sr/^{86}Sr$ ratios from the bones of Pakal himself. As long as Pakal did not move into the area as an elderly adult (within the last few years of his life), his bone values should represent the local $^{87}Sr/^{86}Sr$ ratio regardless of his place of death. These two bone measurements range between 0.70818 to 0.70862, which are well within the estimates derived from the ancient seawater values and are close to our expectation of 0.7085. Although the actual range for Palenque $^{87}Sr/^{86}Sr$ is likely to be somewhat greater than the values obtained from only two samples, we accept the bone data from Pakal (0.7084) as a measure of the local $^{87}Sr/^{86}Sr$ signature for residence at Palenque.

TABLE 7.1 Results of Strontium Isotope Analysis of Bone and Enamel Samples from the Temple of the Inscriptions and Temple XIIIsub at Palenque

Individual	Material	$^{87}Sr/^{86}Sr$ Ratio
Pakal	M3	0.708612
Pakal	proximal left tibia	0.708620
Pakal	rib	0.708184
Red Queen	M1	0.708081
Female companion of the Red Queen	M1	0.708669
Child companion of the Red Queen	M1	0.708286

For the Red Queen and for the woman and the child associated with the Red Queen, the $^{87}Sr/^{86}Sr$ rations are 0.7081, 0.7087, and 0.7083, respectively. These values slightly expand the range of ratios measured in Pakal but are still within the range of the Miocene and Paleocene carbonates described earlier.

The isotope ratios of the dental enamel—reflecting childhood residence—of Pakal, and the Red Queen's two companions are all within the local range estimated from the seawater curve for local rock types and are close to or within the range exhibited by the two bone measurements from Pakal. Thus, we cannot conclude from this evidence that any of these individuals were immigrants. The results differ slightly in the enamel sample of the Red Queen, which shows a lower isotopic ratio than the remainder of the series, although still within the range of expected paleocone isotope signatures. This observation is of interest, more so if we consider her potential identification as Lady Ix Tz'akb'u Ajaw, Pakal's wife, who is epigraphically associated with another, unidentified site in the area. The local provenience of her sacrificial companions argues against their foreign recruitment, as documented in some colonial sources for the Yucatán peninsula (Scholes and Adams 1938; Landa 1982) or as suggested by the isotopic signatures seen in other sacrificial contexts in Mesoamerica (White et al. 2000, 2002; Buikstra et al. 2004; Spence et al. 2004).

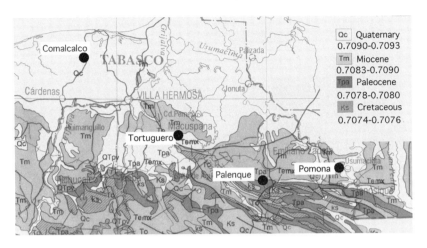

FIGURE 7.1 Geological map of the Palenque region showing major geological units and the location of the site on a boundary between sedimentary rocks of Paleocene and Miocene age. These geological units should have differing strontium isotope signatures. Map from Ortega et al. 1992

Although we cannot rule out origins in places that are isotopically similar, much of Mesoamerica is isotopically distinct and can be excluded from consideration (figure 7.3). For example, the lowlands of the northern Yucatán are more recent marine sediments and are isotopically higher (greater than 0.7090); older sediments to the south are isotopically lower (less than 0.7075); and the volcanic terrain farther south is lower still (less than 0.706). We parsimoniously accept the enamel isotope ratios as indicating a local origin, but we cannot rule out the possibility of origin in a region of similar geology and isotope ratios. The only nearby region of similar geology is the western part of Veracruz, which has the same Miocene sedimentary bedrock.

With regard to the residential history of Pakal as a historical individual, whose life was described in both contemporary and retrospective inscriptions, an epigraphic approach to the question of origin provides crucial additional insight. Because a local birth was the norm for members of a city's ruling elite, it is frequently unspecified in the texts. A foreigner, by contrast, is typically marked with the nominal component "he/she of . . . ," joined to an appropriate toponym (Stuart and Houston 1994). Similarly, the introduction of a foreign ruler or returned local exile is signaled by the

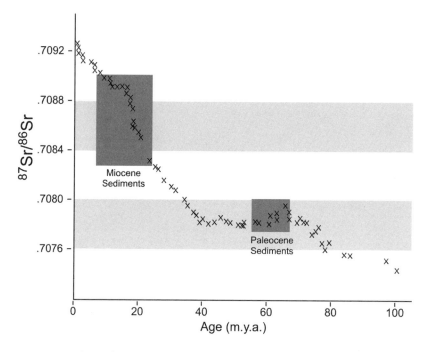

FIGURE 7.2 Strontium isotope ratios for seawater for the past 100 million years (Richter, Rowley, and DePaolo 1992). Of particular relevance for the Palenque area are values for marine sediments dating from the Miocene and Paleocene (shaded)

formulaic phrase "he/she arrived (here)" (MacLeod 1990; Schele and Freidel 1990). Neither of these phrases is used for Pakal, and so, in rhetorical terms at least, he is presented to us as a Palenque native—that is, having been born and raised in the region and residing there during adulthood.

This information is consistent with the local isotopic signatures, as we have seen. The chemistry of the ruler's bone samples reflects the place of residence during his last years of life. As documented in the inscriptions, Pakal lived most likely in or around Lakanhá, capital of the B'aakal kingdom. The enamel analyzed comes from his third molar, which mineralizes substantially later than the other teeth, at approximately 8 or 9 years of age (Logan and Kronfeld 1933). Whereas the enamel of other teeth indicate the $^{87}Sr/^{86}Sr$ ratio of the diet of an individual's first years of life, the third molar reflects late childhood and early adolescence. The epigraphic data for

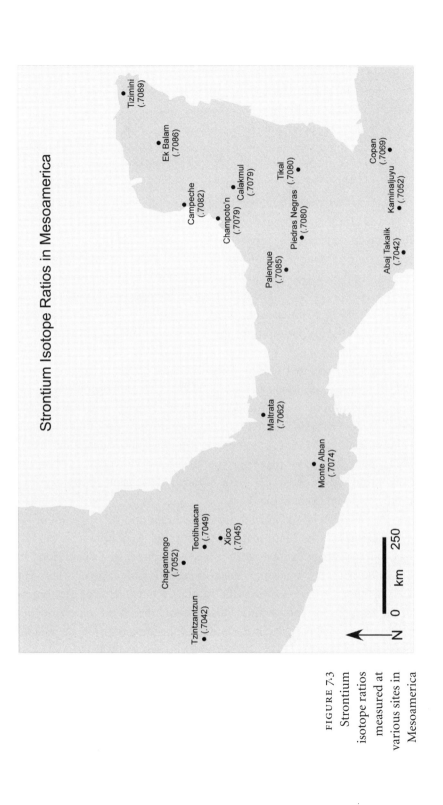

Strontium Isotope Ratios in Mesoamerica

Tizimini
(.7089)

Ek Balam
(.7086)

Campeche
(.7082)

Champoto'n
(.7079)

Calakmul
(.7079)

Tikal
(.7080)

Piedras Negras
(.7080)

Copan
(.7069)

Kaminaljuyu
(.7052)

Abaj Takalik
(.7042)

Palenque
(.7085)

Maltrata
(.7062)

Monte Alban
(.7074)

Chapantongo
(.7052)

Teotihuacan
(.7049)

Xico
(.7045)

Tzintzantzun
(.7042)

N

0   250
km

FIGURE 7.3
Strontium
isotope ratios
measured at
various sites in
Mesoamerica

Pakal do not specifically document Palenque as a place of birth, but they do indicate that he lived at Palenque or in its surrounding areas during his formative years and likely also at the time when he took the insignias of power from his mother S'ak' K'uk' at the young age of 12.

The isotopic signature of the Red Queen points toward a local or nearby origin on the east-west fringes of the Chiapanec Mountains (figure 7.1). Unlike the samples from Pakal, her isotopic value was derived from a first molar, which reflects the geology of her very early infancy and probably also that of her nativity. Although it appears unlikely that the Red Queen originated in a place with a different isotopic profile as the range around Palenque, we cannot determine if she was born specifically in or around the city. We cannot rule out, for example, that she spent her first years of life in neighboring Pomoná or Tortuguero or any other place in the area with a similar isotopic signature. As with Pakal, the isotopic signature in the Red Queen is for the region around Palenque, not for the site itself.

Regarding the Red Queen's probable match with Ix Tz'akb'u Ajaw, Pakal's wife, her isotopic signature is relevant for determining the geographic location of the still unidentified Toktahn site, which the inscriptions acknowledge as the first dynastic seat of the Palenque polity. The comparison of the ratios shown by the Red Queen provides valuable evidence, for example, for decreasing the likelihood that Tz'akb'u Ajaw was born in the Tabascan coastal plains around Macuspana, as has been recently proposed (Bernal 2005).

Our analyses of the inhabitants of Palenque and investigation of local signatures in the Maya region will continue. In addition, we plan to incorporate oxygen isotope ratios as a second dimension of variation in our studies in order to improve the discrimination of places of origin. For the moment, it seems clear that the entombed inhabitants of the Temple of the Inscriptions and Temple XIIIsub were born in the general region around Palenque, perhaps at the site itself. In these remains, there is no indication of a place of origin outside the Miocene and Paleocene carbonate deposits that characterize the local environment. Isotopic studies such as this one will continue to reveal the nature and extent of human movement in the Maya area.

ACKNOWLEDGMENTS

Thanks are due to the National Science Foundation for funding the analyses of these samples and to Paul Fullagar at the University of North Carolina at Chapel Hill for instrumental analyses. Samples were prepared in Madison, Wisconsin, by Bernadette Cap. The samples of the individuals from Temple XIIIsub—from the Proyecto Arqueológico Palenque, Instituto Nacional de Antropología e Historia, in the charge of A. Arnoldo González Cruz—were provided by Arturo Romano, whose collaboration we gratefully acknowledge.

The Companions of Janaab' Pakal and the "Red Queen" from Palenque, Chiapas

Meanings of Human Companion Sacrifice in Classic Maya Society

Andrea Cucina and Vera Tiesler

This chapter addresses the formation processes, circumstances, and ritual meanings of two multiple human deposits encountered in two well-known funerary precincts at Palenque. One is Pakal's funerary chamber in the Temple of the Inscriptions, and the other is the tomb of the "Red Queen" from Temple XIIIsub (López-Jiménez and González-Cruz 1995). The latter personage, whose true identity has yet to be totally unveiled, has been identified as Lady Ix Tz'akb'u Ajaw (Ahpo Hel), wife of Pakal and mother of Kan B'alam, on the basis of a profile facial reconstruction and its comparison with local portraits (Tiesler, Cucina, and Romano 2004; see also Tiesler, chapter 2, this volume). The two case studies document the cultural marks encountered in the bones of the associated individuals and interpret them together with the contextual archaeological and taphonomic evidence. We discuss the results in terms of archaeological signatures of ritual violence and human exegy (companion) sacrifice during the Classic period. The ritual setting, acknowledgment, and differentiation of companion sacrifice from other funerary rituals, sensu stricto, are heavily debated in regional research (McAnany 1995:61–63; Weiss-Krejci 2001:778–79, 2003). Here we aim to participate in the discussion by contributing some new conceptual elements and data.

Attendant Sacrifice in Ancient Maya Society

Maya human sacrifice is well documented historically and iconographically, with the former including many pre-Hispanic references (Boone 1984). Ritual killing played an important role as a supreme religious expression that allowed for direct communication with and petitioning of the life-sustaining forces. This expression was achieved by the destruction and offering of life itself, materialized in the victim's blood and its vital organs (Nájera 1987; Garza 1998). Judging from the early colonial records, victims of human sacrifice were not restricted as to age, sex, or social standing. Nevertheless, individuals were often recruited from the fringe sectors of society or brought in from outside (Tiesler and Cucina 2004). Some historical accounts refer to slaves, whereas others mention war captives, foreigners, orphans, and delinquents as candidates for ritual death. Quite different from the victims' status, practitioners were strongly identified with the ruling elite and religious authorities (Scholes and Adams 1938; Schele 1984a; Nájera 1987; Anda, Tiesler, and Zabala 2004). Regarding the age and sex profile of sacrifice-prone individuals, Anda, Tiesler, and Zabala (2004) have recently compiled colonial data from northern Yucatán. Their results underscore the heavy predominance of (mostly male) children and adolescents in the recruitment for ritual death.

Like other ritual acts, Maya human immolation followed a set of strict rules and a sequence of predetermined steps to ensure its effectiveness—including extensive preparation for bloodletting; the placement of the victims; and the violent and fierce, but not malicious, immolation itself. The offering of the bodies' vital essences represented the time for supernatural invocation and petitioning. Ritual killings were performed mainly through heart excision and decapitation. The climax act was occasionally followed by visual destruction of the life-symbolizing body in the form of body mutilation (Nájera 1987). Posthumous body processing included skinning, bleeding, dismembering, and burning. These procedures are also documented for other cultural areas of Mesoamerica, mostly for the Postclassic period (Robicsek and Hales 1984; Schele 1984a; González-Torres 1985). Alternatively, the dead body could be discarded in dry wells, caves, or *cenotes* (underground water deposits or ponds) without receiving any further attention.

We are bound to imagine that ritual killings, acted out in public, soon were to become apt means of ostentation by political and religious authority. The male-dominated public scenes of kneeling, bound, and tortured war captives ready to undergo ritual death, which are amply depicted in Classic monumental sculpture, powerfully display patterns of institutionalized violence, foreshadowing the depersonalized mass executions known from Postclassic times (Demarest 1984; Schele 1984a).

Sacrifice of attendants deserves a separate mention. As Bourdillon pointedly emphasizes, "prestigious killings do dramatically express the relative values of the people performing them. They communicate the idea that, compared with the person being honored, even human life is trivial" (1980:13). This acknowledgment of absolute personal superiority and power is demonstrated poignantly by Maya exegy sacrifice, which was practiced by members of the elite and was directed toward them as part of dynastic mourning and ancestral commemoration (McAnany 1995).

Considering the purposes of companion sacrifice, one is left to wonder, however, to whom these ritual executions were directed. Was sacrifice intended to honor the divine forces in order to intercede for the nobles' afterlife? Or was the offering of human life meant to worship the defunct noble himself? The latter possibility gains strength when one considers the divine or semidivine power attributed to some ruling members already during their life (Houston and Stuart 1996). From the historical information, Nájera infers that the purposes of attendant sacrifice could have been essentially threefold (1987:201–4). Ritual companion killings performed right after the noble person's death might have been motivated to help the dignitary in his or her transition to the Xibalbá (Underworld), whereas human sacrifice during the later postmortem stages of the dignitary's death must have turned into a powerful means of direct ancestral invocation. Finally, the human companions were included with other goods to serve as offerings and donations on occasion of the periodical commemorative ceremonies for the deceased (Nájera 1987; see also Eberl 2005). In both early and late postmortem rituals, the victims were likely to become "nonpersons." Once life was removed from their bodies and their vital essences were donated, their bodies remained as empty containers or ritual artifacts at best.

From these details, we conclude that the motivations for attendant sacrifice and the placement of the victims most likely responded to the specific demands during each phase of the funerary preparation and ancestor commemoration. Markus Eberl recently contributed important information on the sequence of death paraphernalia for the elite, as drawn from the epigraphic record (2005:53–57). Starting from the day of the dignitary's death, the timing of different mourning and commemoration rituals can be grouped into three subsequent periods, identified by the type of expressions used in the inscriptions. The so-called *muhkaj* events, which refer to the initial interment, are limited to the first ten days after death.

References indicate a second period of time, between one hundred and four hundred days, which is devoted mainly to setting up the final resting place and consecrating it through smoke ceremonies. *El naah* smoke ceremonies and secondary treatments of the now skeletonized body are recorded as taking place years after death. This proposed schedule of events likely corresponds to the obligations of the living toward the defunct and at the same time reflects the dead individual's gradual metamorphosis according to the pre-Hispanic views on death. The timing and motivation of attendant sacrifice should follow the ritual needs during each postmortem stage, an idea that we address later in this chapter.

In Maya mortuary archaeology, scholars have identified sacrificial victims mainly on the grounds of contextual evidence, for lack of direct skeletal indicators revealing the form of death and mortuary treatment. It is for this reason that the sacrifice of attendants has been inferred from evidence such as irregular and ventral positioning, entangled primary multiple interments arranged around one central skeleton, particular age profiles in multiple burials, and the negative or reduced evidence of associated funerary objects (Tozzer 1941; Schele 1984a; Welsh 1988; Ruz 1991; R. Carrasco 2000). The lack of further indication as to the form of death has recently led to an academic dispute over the presence of companion sacrifice in royal tombs from several Maya sites, including Palenque (McAnany 1995; Weiss-Krejci 2003). The debate mainly challenges the often arbitrary inferences of companion sacrifice from multiple interments—inferences that are perceived as missing scientific foundation (such as the ones proposed by Ruz [1991] and Welsh [1988]). The very concept of the "funerary attendants" has been put into question and reinterpreted as the potential result of alternative cultural practices. Interment of these individuals inside or next to rulers' tombs has been interpreted as merely an opportunistic placement within "sacred" locations, with no direct cultural relationship between these individuals and the tombs' main occupant, aside from a few exceptions cited by Weiss-Krejci (2001, 2003).

Compared to the bulk of published resources on funerary architecture and offerings, relatively little bioarchaeological and taphonomic mortuary assessment has been done, despite the rich information that these data sets provide for the interpretation of mortuary treatments (Tiesler 2004). Such analysis is based mainly on the interpretation of the disarticulation sequences in primary and secondary burials.[1] This information can provide important indications of unnatural death and posthumous body processing, going far beyond the reconstruction of living conditions and basic biographic information. Skeletal analysis can also document direct marks of manipulation in the form of blunt-force impacts and cut marks, inflicted between the time of death and the body's primary and secondary deposition. Thus, the detection of specific patterns in the osteotaphonomical assessment of human skeletal elements is of paramount importance to determine their timing with regard to death and to reconstruct contexts of perimortem violence and posthumous body processing. In primary mortuary depositions, direct skeletal marks may permit one to differentiate between various groups of lesions inflicted at the time of death from those patterns probably originating well afterward. The potential of osteotaphonomical assessment in the general reconstruction of perimortem violence in Maya society has already been demonstrated by the work conducted in Colha (Massey and Steele 1982, 1997; Massey 1994; Mock 1994), Tikal (Laporte 1988, 1999), Calakmul (Carrasco et al. 1998; R. Carrasco 2000; Tiesler 2002, 2004), Copán (Buikstra et al. 2004), Topoxté (Wurster 2000), and recently Palenque (Tiesler, Cucina, and Romano 2002) (see also Welsh 1988 for a general review).

One of the main purposes of this chapter is to contribute to the ongoing discussion on Classic Maya companion sacrifice with new analytical elements and with recent osteological and taphonomic information on body treatments in the companion contexts of the tombs of Janaab' Pakal and of the Red Queen. In both cases, the remains of more than one individual were encountered inside or immediately outside the funerary chambers. In the Temple of the Inscriptions, the remains of five or six individuals were discovered in front of the huge triangular stone door closing the access to Pakal's funerary chamber (Ruz 1973). The two individuals encountered in Temple XIII rested at each side of a monolithic sarcophagus inside a vaulted chamber (López-Jiménez and González-Cruz 1995; González-Cruz 1998, 2001; Tiesler, Cucina, and Romano 2002).

General Procedures

The study of the remains of the multiple deposit from the Temple of the Inscriptions was conducted during 2002 and 2003 at the Headquarters of Physical Anthropology at the Instituto Nacional de Antropología e Historia (INAH). The two attendants from Temple XIII were analyzed in June 2001 at the Claustro de Sor Juana, Mexico City, as part of the "Red Queen" Archaeological Project, Palenque (INAH). The general osteological techniques were based on osteometry and macroscopic observation, supported by optical microscopy. Cut marks were scrutinized using 4x and 10x magnifiers and tangential illumination. Thin sections were taken from the midrib portions of the individuals from Temple XIII for diagenetic assessment.

The taphonomic evaluation of the remains was based on the available photographic record of Temple XIII's companions, made by Arturo Romano, and the drawings by Alberto Ruz (1973) helped us figure out the multiple burial outside Pakal's funerary chamber. Our interpretation of anatomical disposition and articulation patterns follows the principles put forth by the French *anthropologie du terrain* (Duday 1987, 1997; Duday and Sellier 1990; Duday et al. 1990; Leclerc and Duday 1990). Additional input comes from the results obtained during previous regional taphonomic research.

The Attendants of Janaab' Pakal

In 1952, during the excavation of the Temple of the Inscriptions in Palenque, Chiapas, Ruz encountered a sealed "box" at the base of a staircase in front of what was to be recognized as the entrance to Janaab' Pakal's funerary chamber (Ruz 1955, 1973). The north and east walls of the small corridor and the external side of the chamber's immense triangle-shaped stone door formed three sides of the case. Its fourth side consisted of a 36-centimeter-tall stone box. A lid, which collapsed at some point afterward, originally sealed the container. The box, 1.00 meter long and 1.40 meters wide, contained the deteriorated skeletal remains of five (or maybe six) individuals identified as primary interments (Ruz 1955) (figure 8.1). Due to the restricted room available, the remains were adjusted inside the box by force, which made the preliminary investigation difficult, more so because of the presence of dried and hardened quicklime that filled the space and surrounded all the remains. Despite this condition, Ruz stated that the box was an unquestionably primary deposition: "pero puede asegurarse que se trata de un entierro primario compuesto de probablemente cinco o

FIGURE 8.1 Multiple deposit in the Temple of the Inscriptions, Palenque, and hypothetical reconstruction of four bodies (redrawn and interpreted by Mirna Sánchez from Ruz 1991:334, fig. 30)

quizá seis cuerpos" (but we can be sure that it is a primary burial consisting of five or maybe six bodies) (1973:55).

Miguel Dominguez, a physician in Palenque, performed in situ the preliminary analysis of the skeletal remains, and physical anthropologist Felipe Montemayor later analyzed the bones (Ruz 1973). Both studies confirmed the presence of an adult female and a small and gracile individual (presumably a subadult) among the five. Their placement had resulted in an irregular arrangement of entangled skeletons, as shown in the hypothetical reconstruction of four of the five bodies in figure 8.1. Three individuals had been laid down oriented toward the north, and one oriented toward the south. Two bodies rested on their right side, and two others on their left; an additional skeleton was considered to have been interred in a sitting position. The sixth body, if present, was extremely poorly preserved, and the description of it does not provide information on its placement (Ruz 1955).

The recent study confirms some of the original results and at the same time sheds new light on the findings. A minimum number of five individuals was positively identified in the assemblage, but was not confirmed as the total number present, inasmuch as the poor state of preservation did not permit a complete evaluation of the remains. The individuals include one infant around 3 years of age, one subadult aged around 15 years, and three adults. Among the latter, one was determined as probably female, another one as probably male, whereas the third adult individual could not be sexed.

Heavy calcite deposits were still covering most of the bone fragments and were not removed during the study. These deposits obviously limited the investigation of direct cultural marks, the manner of death, and potential postmortem body treatments. At the same time, the calcite provided important clues on the primary status of the interment because it preserved some of the anatomical configurations. The articulation of axial and limb skeletal segments reveals the assemblage's primary deposition (figure 8.2) and hints at the faithfulness of the original drawing, which emphasizes the tight simultaneous packing of corpses.

Weiss-Krejci (2003) has recently argued that the available space (1.0 by 1.4 by 0.36 meters) was not sufficient to host the volume of six fleshed individuals. She follows from this argument that the individuals' interment in the cyst in front of the monolithic chamber cannot be the result of a single event. Quoting Ruz's (1955) doubts about the bodies' fitting in a "box" of less than a cubic meter, she concludes that the remains must have been in fact the final result of separate interments through time, with the decomposition of the previous individuals' soft tissues providing space for additional corpses. Weiss-Krejci (2003) follows from this statement that Janaab' Pakal's "attendants" were not intended as "sacrificial" victims, but possibly had been laid to rest to take advantage of an "energy-rich" place.

FIGURE 8.2 Calcite block with lumbar vertebrae shown in anatomical position, multiple deposit in the Temple of the Inscriptions, Palenque (photograph by Andrea Cucina)

However, Ruz's statements are not contradictory (Ruz 1955) and do not leave much room for reinterpretation. He explains that the bodies were forcedly piled up due to the small volume of the "cyst." He never refers to the impossibility that they were deposited simultaneously, but rather to the difficulty of doing that. He never confirmed the presence of six individuals, but remained conservative by naming five or *maybe six* individuals (Ruz 1973), with important implications for the total volume occupied by the bodies.

Based on the considerations derived from the present study, and trusting in principle the faithfulness of the original drawings made in the 1950s, we have concluded that the primary deposition of five (or maybe six) individuals could take place in such a reduced space. The presence of a 3-year-old infant, a 15-year-old subadult, and a gracile female adult, even in full flesh, do not occupy a large volume. Furthermore, the average stature of pre-Hispanic Maya individuals was around 1.6 meters for adult males and 1.5 meters for adult females (Tiesler 1999). Flexed individuals of such stature may be accommodated easily in a 1.4-meter-wide cyst, invalidating the argument that the space was not large enough. At the same time, the tight packing of several corpses offers an explanation for the irregular position they present in Ruz's drawing and mirrored in our hypothetical one (figure 8.1).

From an analysis of the original drawing, it is evident that the bodies were not piled up irregularly, but that each corpse appears to have been adjusted to the limited space and the volume of the other bodies. All of the determined postures appear flexed with irregular limb arrangement; two bodies were clearly placed face down (figure 8.1). The individual labeled as "1" in the original drawing is definitely a primary deposition and likely the last body to be fitted in. The pelvic bone underwent a taphonomic rotation and collapse as a consequence of the decomposition of the soft tissues of the skeleton underneath (Specimen 2). Such collapse would not have occurred had the second body already been skeletonized. Skeleton 2 and particularly Skeleton 4 seem to have been laid down ventrally. The latter still preserves its right arm in anatomical connection, an improbable condition had it been disturbed during subsequent interments (see anatomical reconstruction in figure 8.1).

Additional hints come from insights obtained during the recent re-evaluation of vertebrae, ribs, and long bones because some blocks of lime concretions contained anatomically articulated portions of a spine, hand, and forearm. Vertebral anatomical configuration, for example, is important in differentiating the decomposition patterns of assemblages in simultaneous multiple interments from those expected in subsequent deposits. In the latter case, burial reopening to lay down additional bodies implies a rearrangement of the previous remains, be it intentional or unintentional. Vertebrae (as well as ribs, hands, and the mandible) easily dislocate under such conditions (Duday 1997). This aspect, again, puts into question the possibility of a secondary or successive deposition in the cyst in the Pakal tomb. Bone dislocation in this situation would be highly likely, in particular in the spinal column and the other labile articulations, and especially in consideration of such a reduced space (Duday 1997). The taphonomic signature encountered in the cyst of the Temple of the Inscriptions is therefore consistent with a simultaneous fitting of at least five individuals,

a determination that in turn leads to questions as to the motivations behind their placement in such a specific place.

The skeletal evidence contributes additional taphonomic information to the general interpretation of the mortuary assemblage. As shown
in figure 8.3, a cut mark was documented on the ventral side of a tenth
thoracic vertebra. The cut runs vertically, and its distal narrow portion is
still covered by concretions, indicating that its presence was prior to lime
apposition; in contrast, the broken upper edge of the vertebral body that
occurred recently in time does not reveal any presence of lime concretions. The size and shape of the vertebra indicate that it belongs to an
adult individual, even though it is not possible to assess to which of the
three adults it once pertained. The presence of concretions in one part
of the mark shows that the body did suffer from a direct blow inflicted
with a cutting implement. The ventral location is similar to the position
of marks of perimortem violence in other Lowland Maya sites (Tiesler
and Cucina 2006). That pattern has been associated with heart removal
through a subthoracic opening of the trunk, a detail to be discussed later
in this chapter.

Other body treatments consist of exposure to fire, noted in two adult
iliac fragments and possibly one tarsal. The fire marks are circumscribed
to small blackened areas, which are associated with hardened spongy
bone. The observed changes are consistent with charring below 600°C
(Mayne 1997). At the moment, we are not able to deduce any particular
treatment that might account for the marks. The same holds for the isolated dots of red pigment displayed on the surfaces of one adult humerus
and fibula.

The Attendants of the "Red Queen"

The second companion context was discovered inside Temple XIII, next
to the Temple of the Inscriptions. At the time of discovery, the skeletal
remains of two individuals, labeled XIIIsub-1 (a child 8 to 10 years old,
probably male) and XIIIsub-2 (a female 20 to 30 years old), were encountered in the narrow space between the sarcophagus and the chamber walls.
According to recent results (see chapter 7), both individuals were from
the area of or around Palenque. Each was placed face down directly on
the floor on each side of the monolith. The female individual was found

FIGURE 8.3 Tenth thoracic vertebra with cut mark on superior edge of vertebral body, multiple deposit in the Temple of the Inscriptions, Palenque (photograph by Andrea Cucina)

with her arms crossed behind the back. The taphonomic analysis of the two skeletons and the archaeological context suggest that their placement was not performed in a careful manner. As in the cyst from the Temple of the Inscriptions, the ventral and irregular position of their limb segments rather suggest that the funerary ritual was not directed to them, but that their bodies were instead discarded, fitted in the reduced space between the walls and the monolith.

Upon analysis, both individuals bear clear evidence of skeletal indications of perimortem violence. The child's third cervical vertebra (C3) displays a flat, continuous cut mark running sagittally over its whole body (figure 8.4). The cut left the posterior portion of the spinous process practically unaltered, but removed a large part of the body and the transverse processes. The vertebral body's anterior rims are slightly irregular due to the outward pressure discharged by the exiting tool, which removed minor flecks from the bone. The pattern exhibited in the child's third cervical

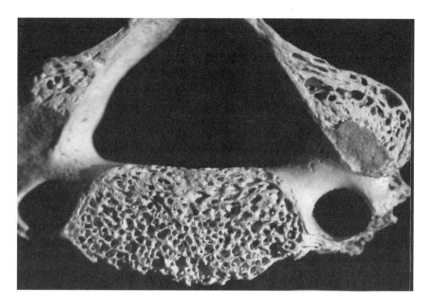

FIGURE 8.4 Cut mark on third cervical vertebra; distal view, Burial XIIIsub-2, Palenque (photograph by Andrea Cucina)

vertebra can be achieved only by violently impacting an individual's neck from behind with a sharp tool. The neck had to be flexed down, which explains why the spinous process of C3 was not affected and the body was largely removed. The impact vector is postero-anterior with a downward component. In this case, the mandible should not be in the way. Nonetheless, a mark on the mandible's lower ridge may indicate that this segment was also affected. Such a violent action can be performed when the body is fleshed, although it is hard to infer from the skeletal evidence whether the action was lethally inflicted when the child was still alive or after death was achieved through other means.

The adult female shows various cut and stab marks on two ribs and several thoracic and lumbar vertebrae. In the ribs, stab impacts were located in the vertebral portion, probably stemming from a complex stabbing and cutting action (figure 8.5). The eleventh thoracic vertebra was the most severely affected skeletal segment (figure 8.6). It was hit antero-posteriorly and laterally by a profound stroke that removed almost all the left transverse process and part of the body, while another stroke sliced the proximal portion of the body. It also shows a vertical mark on the left side

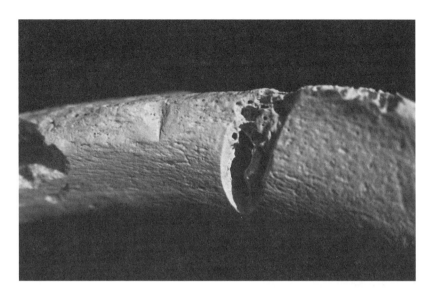

FIGURE 8.5 Cut marks on the neck of rib numbers 7 to 9; Burial XIIIsub-2, Palenque (photograph by Vera Tiesler)

FIGURE 8.6 Cut marks on the eleventh thoracic vertebra from upper left side, Burial XIIIsub-2, Palenque (photograph by Andrea Cucina)

FIGURE 8.7 Chop mark on the spinous process of the third lumbar vertebra, Burial XIIIsub-2, Palenque (photograph by Andrea Cucina)

of its body. The mark is in the shape of an L, with the long branch diverging backward. This pattern, particularly the anatomical position, seems to share some common features with the previously discussed mark encountered in one of Pakal's attendants. The severe strokes were not limited to the eleventh thoracic vertebra. They also involved the tenth thoracic and the third lumbar vertebrae. The latter manifests a 3-millimeter-deep sharp mark, running on top of the spinous process, inflicted from behind from the left side of the body and witnessing the violent perimortem treatment of the body (figure 8.7). Some of the marks on the eleventh vertebra also may have affected the twelfth thoracic vertebra, but this segment of the spine is missing, which precludes a reconstruction of the complete pattern of the cut marks.

Considered together, the multiple, deep, and multidirectional marks indicate a complex pattern of violence. Interestingly, the affected area is relatively delimited, inasmuch as only the lower thoracic vertebrae down to the third lumbar one show multiple lesions. Such a concentration could have been motivated by the separation of the body in two halves or by simply butchering as part of a ritual body mutilation possibly following sacrificial death by heart removal (Tiesler, Cucina, and Romano 2002).

The taphonomic disposition of Burial XIIIsub-2 supports the osteological assessment of such body treatment. The skeletal remains were in a primary deposition, still in an almost complete state of articulation despite some damage by rodents and water filtration. The vertebral elements forming the upper trunk were in anatomical sequence, as were the ones forming the lower trunk. Nonetheless, the two sections (upper and lower) did not seem to be in sequence but shifted aside. Although postdepositional taphonomic factors may have contributed to the separation between the skeletal segments, the signature encountered may also indicate that the upper and lower portions of the trunk were deposited as separate entities.

Patterns and Meanings of Exegy Sacrifice

The patterning and interpretation of specific indicators around ritual killing and body discard assume the existence of a set of underlying social correlates and ritual norms that are essentially different from funerary treatment. In the case of companion contexts, the association is established through definition by the presence of a highly furnished tomb. Both processes—that is, funerary treatment and sacrifice—are spatially correlated (see figure 8.8). The remains belong to the same chronological frame; they share the same physical space; and the bodies are sometimes even in physical contact. In archaeological reconstruction, this situation is prone to hamper a clear-cut distinction, demanding explicit differentiation criteria.

Here, we discuss the evidence from Palenque according to a set of expected osteotaphonomic, archaeological, and demographic indicators (table 8.1). This discussion intends to reconstruct the historical circum-

FIGURE 8.8 Scene of dead dignitary, showing heart extraction and headless body (redrawn in parts from a polychrome vase painting K1377, by Vera Tiesler from Robicsek and Hales 1981:fig. 31)

stances surrounding the death and placement of Janaab' Pakal's and the Red Queen's attendants with direct skeletal evidence and the taphonomic and archaeological signature of regional human exegy sacrifice.

The categories presented in table 8.1 intend to disentangle the possible or potential array of individual correlates produced by each case, which have been documented jointly or separately in the region's archaeological, historical, and iconographic record from the Classic and Postclassic periods (see Robicsek and Hales 1984; Schele 1984a; Anda, Tiesler, and Zabala 2004). The classification is intended to facilitate the correlation between ritual behavior and its skeletal traces and to assist in the distinction of these traces from the patterns left by subsequent posthumous body treatment. The general signature is patterned for the Classic Lowland Maya and has to be considered wholly. In fact, only a joint osteological, taphonomic, and archaeological analysis permits us to understand the complex sacrificial pattern and its archaeological expression. Arbitrary interpretations based on one single condition are discouraged, in particular when restricted to indirect archaeological or demographic evidence (Ruz 1973; Welsh 1988; Weiss-Krejci 2003).

The first two aspects to be considered are the number of individuals

TABLE 8.1 Evidence of Ritual Killing versus Natural Death
(Processes Related to Funerary Treatment) and Expected Pattern of
Associated Archaeological Variables

Archaeological Variables	Evidence of Potential Ritual Killing and Expected or Possible Skeletal Indication	Evidence of Funerary Treatment in Elite Contexts and Expected or Possible Skeletal Indication
1. Number of individuals	One to several bodies, laid down simultaneously	Usually one individual or several bodies laid down at different moments
2. Demographic profile	Mostly subadults (infants, adolescents) and young adults	All adult ages, both sexes, but predominantly mature males
3. Cause of death	Intentional, violent	Natural
4. Form of death	Heart sacrifice, decapitation with possible vertebral marks	Various; skeletal evidence physiopathological, not cultural
5. Predepositional body treatment	Body processing in the form of butchering, stabbing, dismembering, flaying, exposing to heat	Applying cinnabar, embalming, dressing, and adding objects and personal attire
6. Placing and body arrangement	Discharge and abandonment of the body followed by irregular placing, ventral positioning	Careful arrangement of the body in an organized, central, inner space
7. Grave architecture	None or functional. Bodies can be found in antechambers or in the periphery.	Elaborated grave preparation in chamber, crypt contexts
8. Grave goods	Mostly none	Presence of prestige objects

and their demographic profile. In both contexts under study, the associated primary assemblages are composed of more than one individual. In Pakal's case, the multiple interment has all the prerogatives to be simultaneous. The interment of several fresh corpses at the same time is, by itself, an indication of intentional, accidental, or catastrophic death, given the low probability of various persons dying at the same time from natural causes. Although simultaneity cannot be confirmed in the case of the Red Queen companions, the mortuary complex as a whole (i.e., the funerary chamber) can be considered a multiple interment.

Apart from numerical considerations, the particular demographic profile of associated individuals has induced scholars to consider them "sacrificial victims" (Welsh 1988). Some investigators note that infants, children, and young adults (among whom are females) are in the majority and that the representation of their age and death does not correspond to that of the normal population (Ruz 1973; Welsh 1988). There is no doubt that the infant and the subadult segments of the common population are underrepresented in archaeological samples (see Marquez, Hernández, and Serrano, chapter 5, in this volume). This aspect is prone to hamper any comparison, so we cannot discard other possible explanations. Nonetheless, although this variable by itself does not support the hypothesis that the skeletons were the product of ritual killings, it is clearly biased toward specific age classes and is sustained by evidence suggesting that victims were not taken randomly, but were selected according to specific needs and availability. The biased mortality profile should exclude older individuals, as opposed to the prevalence of older adults among the main tomb occupants. The latter holds true also in the case of Palenque. Of the seven (possibly eight) individuals encountered in Temple XIII (two) and in the Temple of the Inscriptions (five or six), three are subadults (younger than 15 years old), and the others are young adults, at least two of them being females. If this pattern were representative of the mortality profile of the population in Palenque, as well as of the other sites where "attendants" have been found, it would indicate that life expectancy at birth was well below that of any other contemporary Mesoamerican population (Civera and Márquez 1996; Márquez, Hernández, and Gómez 2002; see also Márquez, Hernández, and Serrano, chapter 5, in this volume).

As for the third parameter under consideration, the skeletal evidence does not leave much doubt as to the violent circumstances of death in both contexts. Perimortem violence is strongly suggested in the two attendants of the Red Queen. Both the osteological and taphonomic data permit a joint interpretation of the events that led to the deposition of these individuals. The mark on the third cervical vertebra of Burial XIIIsub-1 might have resulted from killing by decapitation, and the eleventh thoracic vertebra of Burial XIIIsub-2 bears one lesion (figure 8.9) that shares many coincidences with two other primary interments from the region. A similar cutting location is displayed in one companion context from Calakmul and one problematic primary deposit positioned during the seal-

FIGURE 8.9 Anatomical distribution of cut marks on the lower thoracic vertebras from (a) E-1003, Becán; (b) II-6a, Calakmul; and (c) XIII-2, Palenque; left lateral view (photographs by Andrea Cucina)

ing of rooms from Becán's Structure X (figure 8.9) (Tiesler and Cucina 2003, 2006). The anatomical position and impact type follow a common pattern: the lesion is situated ventrally or on the left side of the lower vertebral bodies, usually the eleventh and twelfth. The explanation we have proposed (Tiesler and Cucina 2006) intends to acknowledge, from an anatomical perspective, the probable procedure involved in heart removal, a sacrificial ritual that has been studied so far only from the ethnohistorical and iconographic evidence (Tozzer 1941; Moser 1973; Landa 1982; Boone 1984; Schele 1984a; Schele and Miller 1986; Nájera 1987). In detail, the proposed procedure considers that the heart was accessed from underneath the rib cage by opening the trunk immediately below the twelfth rib at mediastinum level, which corresponds to the lower thoracic vertebrae. From there, the experienced hand could be inserted in between the lungs without the interference of the abdomen's internal organs, and the heart grasped and pulled out. The cut marks left on the vertebral bodies might be the incidental result of the vehement sectioning of the heart's vessels and ligaments in an overexcited ritual atmosphere. Notably, the mark we found on the tenth thoracic vertebra of one of the individuals attending Pakal (figure 8.3) fits into this pattern.

Unfortunately, the poor state of preservation and the calcite embedding the bones do not allow a thorough investigation of the remains. We can only hypothesize about the relationship between this mark and sacrifice, without being able to rule out the possibility that it might have been produced by other means. Regardless of the mark's origin, it stands out as a direct skeletal indicator of perimortem violence.

Additional indications of violence appear to be related more to post-mortem body processing than to killing. The exposure to fire and the traces of red pigment that some of the bones from the cyst in the Temple of the Inscriptions display are in fact related to posthumous body treatments. Although pigment scattering was a widespread Classic tradition, very scarce documentation exists on funerary charring or cremation in the Classic period Lowlands, a different situation from what is known for the Postclassic and colonial times (Iglesias 2003; Ruz 1973; Welsh 1988). During the first millennium AD, exposition to fire was probably associated with ritual nonfunerary treatments rather than with the ancestral cult. In fact, it is found mainly in "offerings" or "problematic" contexts, as has been recently reported for Becán and Calakmul (Campeche) and for Kohunlich (Quintana Roo) (Tiesler and Cucina 2003; see also Ruz 1991).

More difficult to interpret in this sense is the evidence of stabbing and butchering, encountered in the Red Queen's female attendant, which might relate either to her death or to ritual violence enacted soon afterward, as referred to by ethnohistorical sources or hinted at from the iconographic record (see Robicsek and Hales 1984; Schele 1984a).

Regarding the ulterior correlates, the one that draws major attention is the placement and arrangement of the bodies. Both multiples from Palenque show irregular axial and limb placing; the forearms crossed at the female victim's back indicate that they were still bound. Such primary interments do not appear to express funerary treatments after natural death, especially considering the regional mortuary traditions of the times (Ruz 1973). Face-down placing, as discussed earlier, was not a probable treatment of an individual who died naturally, unless it was meant to disrespect or throw infamy onto the individual. Therefore, it is reasonable to think that the way the bodies were discarded is instead related to their function within a funerary or commemorative ritual: as ritual vehicles rather than as the object of it. Being part of the offering explains the bodies' particular disposition and the absence of personal attire and offerings.

There are no individual containers for the attendants in Temple XIII. The two bodies were discarded outside the sarcophagus, with no burial space reserved for them or associated goods placed with them. The form of the multiple interment right outside Pakal's chamber, designated by Ruz as "a small box," equally emphasizes a lack of attention to the bodies.

Recent analysis confirms that these bodies were fitted into the small container, which was sealed directly above. If they were primary depositions from natural death, one has to wonder why they had to be piled up in such a small volume inside a corridor sealing the main chamber of a dignitary's tomb, instead of being buried along the corridor or laid to rest in crypts and niches along it.

Considering jointly the variables relevant to our case, we feel reasonably certain that the individuals accompanying the two dignitaries in Palenque were victims of sacrificial rituals. In the case of the Red Queen, the archaeological context does not permit assessment of the timing of their interments in relation to the dignitary's death and her deposition. Were the woman and the child sacrificed and offered jointly, or one after the other? Were they placed during the funerary preparations, before these preparations, or on the occasion of the woman's interment? Or were they united with her remains at some point after that? Though we have no direct clues on the simultaneity of the events, we do have some evidence on the timing. The two attendants might have been sacrificed soon after the Red Queen's demise or on the occasion of a so-called muhkaj event, as indicated also by the mentions of Pakal's death in the inscriptions (Eberl 2005). Although we cannot rule out the possibility that their deposition did take place at some point after initial interment, maybe during one of the commemorative "smoke rituals" (Eberl 1999), no signs of reopening of the inner chamber have been documented by either past or present archaeological teams (López-Jimenez and González-Cruz 1995; González-Crúz 1998, 2001). A postdepositional chamber reentry is also improbable, at least during the first few postmortem years, if we take into account that the female dignitary's sarcophagus was not hermetically sealed as was Pakal's monolithic resting place.

The contextual information of Janaab' Pakal's attendants provides more crucial insights into the meanings and timing of attendant sacrifice in the mourning and commemoration schedule that followed his death. According to the inscriptions, K'inich Janaab' Pakal, divine ruler of Palenque, died on 29 August 683 to unite with his ancestors at an altar place in the House of the Nine Figures. Pakal's son Kan B'alam prepared the funerary precinct in the interregnum period before his accession to the throne in January of the following year (Schele and Mathews 1998; Eberl 2005:43, 54, 66; Martin and Grube 2000). These preparations must have been carried out inside the chamber before it was sealed, the arrangements met by Kan B'alam. The activities in the funerary chamber were thus bound to precede the placement of the attendants, but were probably carried out after Pakal had already died. Although we suppose that the king was laid to rest relatively shortly after his death, the unique design of the monolithic grave allowed for additional time. Because the decomposing body was hermetically sealed off inside the sarcophagus, the interior design of the vaulted chamber could quietly take its course (also see Tiesler, chapter 2, in this volume).

Several weeks or, more likely, months must have passed before the time the big triangular door was closed, long after the muhkaj event and the semidivine ruler's passage to the Underworld had been concluded (Eberl 2005). The sequence of funerary events thus implies that the sacrificial killing, preceding the placing of several individuals outside the sealed inner chamber, was not motivated by the desire to seek supernatural intervention on the king's behalf during his last passage. Instead, the ceremony seems to have marked a commemoration event to worship an ancestor now joined with the divine and granted a new status and ancestral powers. The fact that the arrangements were commissioned by Pakal's son and successor to the throne links this sacrifice with Kan B'alam's ritual obligations toward his dead predecessor. During the interregnum period, this welcomed occasion surely reinforced publicly Kan B'alam's genealogical ties to the great king and thus strengthened his new authority and claims to the throne (Schele and Freidel 1990; McAnany 1998; see also Tiesler, chapter 2, and Grube, chapter 10, in this volume).

Conclusions

The direct and indirect evidence encountered in the remains of Pakal's and the Red Queen's attendants, like that in other sites, supports the idea that companion sacrifice was among the rituals performed during the Classic period. In evaluating both contexts, we considered jointly a series of criteria that would help us to avoid simplistic interpretations. The skeletal and taphonomical evidence from the Temple of the Inscriptions and Temple XIIIsub argues against some scholars' tendency to consider the lack of direct skeletal marks of sacrifice as an indication that such rituals were not performed. The existence of Classic Maya companion sacrifice does not seem to be questioned among art historians and epigraphers, however, and we hope that the present results may settle some of the doubts about it exerted by other segments of the academic community.

Although we cannot determine the exact timing of the companions' placement in the mortuary ritual calendar of the Red Queen, we infer in Pakal's case that a single deposition occurred once the sealing of the inner chamber was completed. A probable occasion was a commemoration ritual dedicated to the now semidivine ancestor. The ceremony offered to the royal woman from the sarcophagus tomb inside Temple XIIIsub likely was performed in a different moment, possibly on the occasion of her interment. Regardless of timing, the present results underscore the power and high social standing of both individuals, especially Pakal, now venerated as a semidivine ancestor. The different meanings associated with both contexts at the same time manifest the differentiated expressions of the veneration of royal ancestors, an integral part of a selective dynastic cult exclusively directed by and toward the ruling families in Palenque.

ACKNOWLEDGMENTS

We thank the following projects and colleagues for providing information, assistance, and valuable comments: Arnoldo González-Cruz (Proyecto Arqueológico Palenque), Proyecto Arqueológica Becán (directed by Luz Evelia Campaña), Proyecto Arqueológico Calakmul (directed by Ramón Carrasco), Francisco Ortíz Pedraza (Dirección de Antropología Física, INAH); Margaret Streeter (University of Missouri at Columbia), Iván Oliva, and Patricia Quintana (Centro de Investigaciones Avanzadas/Politécnico Nacional, Unidad Mérida).

Longevity of Maya Rulers of Yaxchilán

The Reigns of Shield Jaguar and Bird Jaguar

Patricia Hernándcz and Lourdes Márquez

> Our problem in answering these questions underscores the fact that the ancient
> Maya put on their monuments only what each ruler wanted future nobles to
> believe, sometimes deliberately altering his true age and genealogy.
>
> Joyce Marcus, *Mesoamerican Writing Systems*

For decades, epigraphic work has shed light on aspects of the history of Classic period Maya rulers, thcir gcncalogy, and events through which they lived. The registration of births, rise to power, capture of enemies, and the moment of death are all part of the information decoded from the inscriptions (Ruz 1958, 1973; Proskouriakoff 1963, 1964; Berlin 1977; Schele 1979; Schele and Miller 1986; Schele and Freidel 1990; Mathcws 1997; Martin and Grube 2002).

It has been demonstrated that the inscriptions narrate the information the rulers wanted to pass on (Marcus 1992a, 1992b). Very often dates and events do not match, or personages are represented in events that occurred after they had already passed away. The discussion regarding age at death has caught physical anthropologists' and archaeologists' attention, for the biological estimation from the osteological standards determines, in some cases, younger ages than those reported by epigraphers. The cases of Janaab' Pakal, lord of Palenque during the Late Classic period; Yukno'm the Great, lord of Calakmul (born in 600, deceased in AD 686) (Martin and Grube 2002:108); and Jaguar Shield, the lord of Yaxchilán, are clear examples of this issue. On this matter, Joyce Marcus (1992b) suggests that the date of birth of some Maya rulers, in particular Sun Shield or Propeller Shield (Pakal) from Palenque and Shield Jaguar I from Yaxchilán, were "moved back" with political aims so that these rulers would be recognized as the legitimate heirs to the throne. She states that rulers who ordered the inscriptions manipulated some dates of birth and rise to power in order to guarantee their legitimate succession because the inscriptions were crafted at a time when they were already in power (Marcus 1992a:345). In Pakal's case, the first inscription where he is mentioned was manufactured 24 years before his death, which, according to Marcus, gave more than enough time to move back in time his dates of birth and rise to power. She asserts that

> his supposed birth date on A.D. March 6th, 603. . . is around a date that may have been selected many years after the actual event, perhaps at the time of his rise to the throne. The first text that records this ruler was actually carved when he was already supposed to be 57 years old and there are no earlier monuments to verify his date of birth. Propeller Shield like many other Maya rulers had an opportunity to backdate his birth, either to pretend that he was born before other candidates for succession or to make himself older in wisdom and experience. . . . [It] seems like Propeller Shield deliberately exaggerated his age. (1992a:235–36)

For Berlin (1977; cf. Marcus 1992a:345), Pakal's intention was to settle his kingdom as a key moment in the history of Palenque rather than to keep an exact track of his age. It is probable that the date of demise carved on the inscriptions corresponds to the "social death," a moment that is represented with a ritual called *muknal.*[1] This ritual was addressed officially to an individual's death; Gillespie (2000) makes a distinction between biological death and "social death." McAnany interprets this ritual as the lapse of time that goes from the moment the person passes away until his mortal remains are placed on a site destined for that purpose, finding that this period could last from 482 days up to 24 years (1998:289). In Pakal's case, recent investigations have backed up the supposition that the tomb was manufactured before his death and that he began the construction of his own tomb in the Temple of the Inscriptions 10 years before he passed away (Schele and Freidel 1990:225). According to Marcus (1992b), Pakal's 48-year-old son "took office"[2] 132 days after his father's death, but did not rise to the throne until the age of 57, a full 9 years later. Kan B'alam II was the one in charge of finishing the construction of the temple and of the Group of the Cross, where he is represented (Martin and Grube 2002:168–69). Schele and Freidel register Kan B'alam's date of birth in May 635 and his death in February 702 at the age of 67 (1990:219) (see table 9.1). The tomb with this ruler's skeletal remains has not been found yet; however, it has been proposed that he must be buried with the Group of the Cross.

TABLE 9.1 Age at Death of Several Palenque Rulers

Ruler	Date of Birth	Date of Death	Age at Death
Ahkal Mo' Naab' I	5 July 465	29 November 524	59 years
K'an Joy Chitam I	4 May 490	6 February 565	74 years
Ahkal Mo' Naab' II	5 September 523	21 July 570	46 years
Kan B'alam I	20 September 524	3 February 583	58 years
K'inich Janaab' Pakal I	26 March 603	31 August 683	80 years
Kan B'alam II	May 635	16 February 702	67 years

Sources: Schele and Freidel 1990:219; Martin and Grube 2002:156–75.

The case of the rulers of Yaxchilán is similar; however, a clear date for the birth of Itzamnaaj B'alam II, or Shield Jaguar, has not been decoded yet. Inscriptions report the date of his rise to the throne as the year 681 and the date of his death as 742 (see Martin and Grube 2002:122–24). Mathews identifies him as Shield Jaguar I and confirms that "he passed away in 9.15.10.7.14 (AD 742) at an approximate age of 96" (1997:360). The purpose of moving back the date of birth of many Maya rulers may have been political. In the absence of a direct heir, the rulers sometimes changed their genealogy to claim the right to the throne (Marcus 1992a:345, 1992b:236–37).

In our current investigation, we have estimated the biological age of the skeletal remains found in several tombs of some of the main structures built under the reign of Shield Jaguar II (AD 681–742) and of his son Bird Jaguar IV (AD 752–68), located in Structures 23 and 33 (García Moll 1996).

Schele and Freidel (1990) and Mathews (1997:360) report that Shield Jaguar I died when he was about 96 years old. Data are also presented on his wife, Lady K'ab'al Xook, and on his son Bird Jaguar IV. According to the epigraphic references, Lady K'ab'al Xook, who was older than Shield Jaguar, attended her husband's funeral. In the case of the son, Bird Jaguar IV, one epigraphic register claims his birth in the year 709 of this era; his rise to throne in 752, when he was 43; and his death in 768. Therefore, he lasted in power for 16 years. Epigraphers state that he was an old adult of about 59 years old when he died (Martin and Grube 2002:128–33).

We have approached this investigation from an ecological perspective, weighing the lifestyle and living conditions of the inhabitants of the Maya society and their rulers because these factors determine life expectancy (Márquez et al. 1982; Storey 1997; Márquez, Hernández, and González 2001; Márquez, Hernández, and Gómez 2002; Storey, Márquez, and Schmidt 2002). In the past few decades, paleodiet has become a major research topic, and investigators have focused on the analysis of trace elements and isotopes to determine diet (see Whittington and Reed 1997; Wright 1997; White 1999; Brito 2000; Almaguer 2002) and on the study of ancient DNA in molecular biology (Merriwether et al. 1997:208–21; González-Olivier et al. 2001:208–21). Nutritional status is inferred by health indicators of nourishment disturbances, by signs of the incidence of specific diseases, and by specific markers that show growth disruption or the individual's degree of adaptation (see Márquez et al. 1982a; Márquez, Benavides, and Schmidt 1982; Cohen et al. 1997; Márquez and del Angel 1997; Saul and Saul 1997; Márquez, Hernández, and Gómez 2002; Márquez, Jaén, and Jiménez 2002; Storey, Márquez, and Schmidt 2002).

Studies on demographic profiles and health conditions of one sector of Palenque's population have also been performed by estimating age and sex of the skeletal archaeological remains. The joint results of all these investigations about the Palenque population permit a thorough interpretation of the relationship between lifestyle and general health status, as well as of the impact these elements had on life expectancy (Márquez, Hernández, and González 2001; Hernández 2002; Márquez, Hernández, and Gómez 2002; Hernández and Márquez 2004). The role of men, women, and children; the age at which they joined the workforce; the activities carried out during each age; lifestyle; and nutrition—all constitute factors that have to be understood in order to interpret past societies and the individual's relationship with society (Goodman and Leatherman 1998; Márquez and Hernández 2001; Goodman and Martin 2002).

In this chapter, our interest is in the individuals who ruled the sites of Palenque and Yaxchilán in the lower Maya region during the closing of the Classic period.

Methodology for Age Assessment

The correct estimation of age at death by means of skeletal analysis has been one of anthropology's main research interests, in particular for paleodemography and forensic analyses. The identification of the age and sex of the skeletons recovered during archaeological explorations is essential for any anthropological study. Recent reviews on methods for estimating age at death from skeletons (see Meindl and Russell 1998; Kemkes-Grotenthaler 2002) show the development of techniques for determining morphoanatomical changes of pubic symphysis, the auricular surface of the ilium, the sternal end of the ribs, and the dental occlusal surface; for identifying structural changes in the trabecular tissue of the long bones epiphyses, in particular femur and humerus; for studying differential closure of cranial sutures; and for analyzing the remodeling of the bone tissue.

Age-estimation techniques formerly studied only one trait—for example, the suture closure method, based on craneometric studies and on observations of cranial intentional modification. Soon studies of this trait were supplemented by studies of the modifications of the pubic symphysis, made from reference series by Todd (1920), which was thought to be more reliable. Ubelaker's work (1989:80–81) and papers by Gilbert and McKern (1973) list the different techniques for age determination. Doubtlessly, the development of the forensic disciplines has contributed to the improvement of the old techniques and the incorporation of new ones, which are continuously being tested, modified, and calibrated. The approach shifted from the study of a single trait to the study of multiple traits, a change that, by means of complex statistical elaborations, permits researchers to estimate the degree of reliability of each indicator (Ferembach, Schwidetzky, and Stloukal 1979; Lovejoy, Meindl, Pryzbeck et al. 1985).

As a matter of fact, the past two decades have witnessed the proliferation of critiques to particular age-estimation techniques (Bocquet-Appel and Masset 1982), but also the effort to renew methods (Lovejoy, Meindl, Pryzbeck et al. 1985). For example, according to Meindl and Mensforth (1985), the study of the modification of the auricular surface of the ilium grants more accuracy in the estimation of age at death, even more so if the sample is part of a series. The Transition method of analysis by Boldsen and colleagues (2002) apparently offers a new approach. It takes into consideration three body segments. In the case of the pubic symphysis, it scores the morphological changes that occur in specific sectors: the surface of the symphysis, the texture, the superior apex, the ventral and dorsal margins—each with specific features that have to be registered. The method considers three possibilities: that only one segment is available, that two are available, or that all three are available. Regardless of how precise this new methodology may be in its application of mathematical techniques, the results depend also on the state of preservation of the anatomical segments, such as cranial sutures, pubic symphysis, and auricular surface of the ilium.

In the case of the Maya skeletal remains, their significant deterioration and poor preservation are well known. Taphonomic processes due to the climate and type of soil profoundly affect the preservation of the remains. Even when new methodologies appear more reliable, the age evaluation of the ancient Maya depends on the state of preservation and fragmentation of the skeletal elements available and on the standards developed for analyzing them.

Teeth are easily preserved due to the hardness of their structure and are often recovered. For subadults, the estimation of age rests on the degree of development and eruption of each tooth. For adults, the degree of wear or dental attrition is observed on the occlusal surface. However, dental wear is the result of the type of diet, whether soft or abrasive, so this indicator should take into account the individual's lifestyle as well as the food ingested. Meindl and Russell (1998), however, have proposed dental wear as a good age indicator for old adults.

The trabecular tissue of the long bones' epiphyses is another readily observable indicator, although the epiphyses are fragmented in most of the Maya remains. Regarding suture closure, it is important to recognize that it is not feasible to use this indicator on skulls altered on purpose, wherein the phases of regular obliteration suffered severe modifications, as is the case for the Maya skulls, most of which underwent this process. It is also possible to observe modifications in the auricular surfaces of the ilium. However, because correct assessment of them depends mostly on the identification of changes on the surface, taphonomic processes can impede the correct observation. In addition, for diagnosis, the segment must preserve every area, in particular both the superior and inferior auricular surfaces and the retroauricular area, because the majority of the changes that are the bases of this age criterion occur in this region (Lovejoy, Meindl, Pryzbeck et al. 1985). Therefore, the better preserved the surface, the more reliable the evaluation will be. This research depends on the state of preservation of the skeleton, anticipating that in most cases it is possible to use only a few indicators.

The Rulers of Yaxchilán

Yaxchilán is a Classic period Maya site of great attraction and fame because of its architecture and the great amount of inscriptions in the form of glyphs carved in stone or paintings on pottery and other elements, describing the histories of their rulers and events. From these carved monuments, epigraphers have been able to reconstruct part of the dynastic history of Yaxchilán (see Mathews 1997; Drew 1999; Martin and Grube 2002). The ancient site is located on a bend of the Usumacinta River. The first inscriptions from Yaxchilán date to the year AD 320, and the last references were recorded at the onset of the 800s. Most of the history of Yaxchilán refers to Shield Jaguar I and Bird Jaguar IV, who ruled from 681 to 771. The history of their dynastic ancestry is described in lintels and carved stones that mention the first ten rulers, starting with Yoaat-B'alam I in Temples XII and XXII, apparently the main legitimization strategy, according to Marcus (1992b; see also Schele and Freidel 1990:264). Yaxchilán exhibits a very elaborate architectural plan formed by imposing building structures. In some of these structures, the tombs of important personages have been encountered (García-Moll 1996).

The most outstanding findings have been those in Structures 33 and 23: the burial places of two of the site's most important rulers, Shield Jaguar I and his son Bird Jaguar IV, along with several burials of women and children. Of the latter, the most important finding was that of Lady Fist-Fish or Lady Xook, wife of Shield Jaguar and one of Yaxchilán's most interesting dignitaries. Table 9.2 shows data on these personages and their tombs, the archaeological and anthropological data not having been published yet.

Epigraphers have studied Structure 23 thoroughly, given the great number of lintels with important inscriptions on the personages who ruled this place during the Late Classic period and on their consorts. In particular, the inscriptions make references to the life of Itzamnaaj B'alam

TABLE 9.2 Localization of Skeletal Remains at Yaxchilán, Chiapas.
Sex and Biological Age Estimates

Tomb	Burial Number	Location	Ruler	Sex	Biological Age
Tomb I	Burial 1	Structure 33	Bird Jaguar IV	Male	30–40 years
	Burial 2	Structure 33	Child	?	5–7 years**
Tomb II		Structure 23, room 3	Shield Jaguar	Male	50–60 years
Tomb III		Structure 23, room 2	Lady Xook Fist-Fish*	Female	45–55 years
Tomb IV		Structure 24	child	?	4–5 years**
Tomb V		Structure 24	Lady Ik' Skull* ?	Female	40–50 years
Tomb VI		Structure 16A	?	Male	40–50 years

*Stela 35 located inside Structure 21 registers a ceremony carried out by Lady Ik' Skull
(Tate 1992:123–24), which might suggest that the skeleton discovered by García-Moll
corresponds to that of this woman, but this connection is just speculation. Biological data
were analyzed by María Elena Salas with the authors' collaboration.
**We include age analysis of these two children in accordance with our discussion on
funerary practices.

II, or Shield Jaguar II (Martin and Grube 2002:122); to his spouses—Lady
Fist-Fish (Lady Xook), Lady Ik' Skull of Calakmul, and Lady Sak B'iyaan,
or White Serpent; and to his son Yaxun B'alam, or Bird Jaguar IV, along
with his wives, Lady Mut Balam, Lady Great Skull and Lady Wak Tuun of
Motul de San José, and Lady Wak Jalam, Chan Ajauw, of Motul de San
José (Mathews 1997: 361; Martin and Grube 2002:131). According to Schele
and Freidel (1990), epigraphic data evidencing Bird Jaguar's legitimacy as
ruler of Yaxchilán lie inside Structure 23. This structure is located to the
northeast of the Great Staircase in the first platform. It is formed by two
big vaulted halls divided into rooms (Tate 1992:203), which Roberto García-Moll explored in 1980. Several graves with skeletal remains thought to
belong to some of the dignitaries are located there. This information has
not been published yet.

Shield Jaguar II

In the second grave excavated in Structure 23, García-Moll discovered the
skeleton of an individual whom he associated with ruler Shield Jaguar

II (see García-Moll 1996). In the osteological study carried out for this chapter, we examined each of this skeleton's bony segments, which unfortunately were poorly preserved. We used several of the appropriate standards to calculate age at death; we observed remodeling in the auricular surface of the ilium, dental wear, osteophytic processes on articulations, and the physiological state of deterioration and loss in the bones.

Osteological Analysis of Shield Jaguar II

Auricular surface of the ilium. We noted the following changes on the auricular surface of the ilium. The surface is irregular; there are signs of destruction of the subcondral tissue. Topography shows no transverse organization. No striae or billows are present. The tissue is dense, with severe macroporosity and loss of bony density. The margins are irregular, with changes along the apical region and osteophytic borders.

This morphoanatomic appearance corresponds to the fifth decade of age (50 to 60 years) (Lovejoy, Meindl, Pryzbeck, et al. 1985:26). Meindl and Lovejoy (1989) claimed this criterion to be one of the most precise for age determination in adults.

Osteophytic processes. The degenerative processes of the joints are also associated with age, especially because they reflect the damage ascribed to physical activity. Ubelaker describes the age-related phases of osteophytic development (1989:84–87). In Shield Jaguar's case, a grade 3 of osteophytic lipping could be detected on a lumbar vertebra. The patellas present strong, grade 4, osteophytic processes, corresponding to an individual between ages 51 and 60.

Dental wear. Teeth analyzed show asymmetric wear. Upper molars have marked attrition, showing dentine exposure. According to the most widely used attrition aging system (Brothwell 1987; see also Hillson 2002:239–40), this range of dentine exposure corresponds to an age of about 45 years old. Thus, we assess an age at death between 40 and 50. It is worth mentioning that after this age group, there is no description of the changes associated with wear.

The different standards used to estimate this individual's age—especially changes on the auricular surface of the ilium, osteophitic process, and dental wear—indicate that Shield Jaguar died at 50 to 60 years of age.

Occupational markers. Osteology has developed several techniques that allow researchers to draw inferences about physical activity. Changes in muscular insertions and their degree are registered, as well as lesions at the point of insertion of muscles and tendons. Robusticity is measured by osteometrics. Changes in the joints and the appearance of different degrees of osteophytes can also be used as indicators of activity. From several bony segments of Shield Jaguar's skeleton, we could infer physical characteristics as well as possible level of activity. Muscular insertions are well developed. Noteworthy is the knee joint, with the margins of both patellas presenting strong osteophytic processes, suggesting he was in his late fifties. In all humans, the knee joint is affected by the flexion and extension movements and by the stress of the body weight. For Shield Jaguar, enthesopathies could be observed on the anterior surface of both patellas[3] in a comb shape. This pathological condition may have also been triggered by a severe traumatic lesion that affected the right foot and that could have limited the individual's locomotion. The metatarsals of the right foot present a process of synostosis that María Elena Salas believes was a trauma that might have immobilized this individual's foot (personal communication, 2003). The second, third, and fourth metatarsals are collapsed and joined. Salas identified an infectious process in these segments.

Lady K'ab'al Xook

Tomb II (García-Moll's numbering) in Structure 23 belongs to Shield Jaguar. This grave is the richest in offerings, containing nine carved bones with hieroglyphic texts, six of them mentioning Lady K'ab'al Xook. On this matter, Mathews states:

> The text can be partly read *u-ba-ki* of lady Fist Fish'. *u-ba-ki* is composed of *u-bak,* which means "the bone of his or hers." In other words, the bones were "name tagged" and say that actually this is a bone that belongs to lady Fist Fish. . . . [T]hese bones therefore belonged to lady Fist-Fish and it is possible that the objects were the same ones she used for piercing her tongue in the bleeding ceremony observed in lintel 24. I think it is clear that this tomb houses the mortal remains of Shield Jaguar's queen, Lady Fist-Fish. (1997:276)

Lintels 23, 24, and 25, harbored in Structure 23, represent scenes in which Lady Fist-Fish participates in a ritual together with Shield Jaguar II.

Lintel 23, located on the west side and discovered in 1979 by García-Moll, bears scenes important for our interpretation as well. Its inscriptions were first deciphered by Schele. The date AD 22 June 726 was associated with a "fire" event dedicated to Lady Xook.

McAnany and Plank (2001) attempt to unveil the nature of feminine spaces and the role of women in the Classic Maya. By analyzing the iconography in Structure 23 at Yaxchilán, they state in agreement with Mathews (1997) and with Schele and Freidel (1990) that this building was Lady Xook's (or Fist-Fish's) residence. The inscription specifically states that "Lady Xook's house is the hearth of Tan-ha' Yaxchilán." Stuart (1998) claims that the frontal portion of Lintel 23 offers an extended genealogy of Lady Xook (cf. McAnany and Plank 2001:104).

Mathews presents some data of the age at death and information on Lady Xook's life:[4] "She surely lived in 9.13.17.15, the date on lintel 24, which indicates that she lived for at least two *katunes*. It is likely that when she died she was in her sixties or seventies" (1997:161). It is important to point out that all consulted publications (Schele and Freidel 1990; Tate 1992; McAnany and Plank 2001) corroborate that Structure 23 was Lady Xook's residence. On this, Martin and Grube comment:

> Roberto García-Moll's excavation of Temple 23 revealed a series of burials. Tomb 2, the richest one, was behind the western door of the facade, and it contained the body of a mature woman, a great collection of ceramic vessels and about 20 thousand obsidian knives. It also included a set of nine bleeders made of carved bone, out of which six have the name of Lady K'ab'al Xook. Even though this could mean it was the queen's tomb, in the adjacent temple 24, there is a record of her death in year 749 and a fire ritual practiced in her *muknal*, "place of burial," that probably identifies this structure as a commemorative sepulcher. (2002:126)

According to this evidence, epigraphists assumed that the skeleton found in this tomb is that of Shield Jaguar's main spouse, Lady K'ab'al Xook. María Elena Salas's first osteological analysis stated it belongs to a man. As there is a debate around the identity of the remains, we checked skeletal indicators for sex, confirming her diagnosis.

As regards Lady Xook and offspring, it has been speculated for a long time that she never had any children, and for this reason it was the son of

Shield Jaguar's second wife who rose to the throne. Josserand identified a record on the corner of Lintel 23 that refers to Lady Xook as "the mother of" a personage Josserand named "Ah Tzic," Lord Number or the Count. Owing to the lack of any further reference to this individual, his social and political identity at Yaxchilán is unknown. However, Josserand asserts that "[t]he existence of a son by Shield Jaguar's primary wife would explain what was going on during the ten-year inter-regnum between the ruler-ship of the king and his eventual heir Bird Jaguar, who was the son of a secondary wife" (2002:123).

Other authors, such as Martin and Grube (2002:127), agree that Lady Xook gave birth to at least one male heir. However, it is evident that this heir never rose to the throne, be it from premature death or for political reasons.

Osteological Analysis of Lady K'ab'al Xook

The analysis of one of the poorly preserved skeletal remains in Structure 23 allowed the identification of a female individual. In order to assess this female's age at death, we checked every one of the available skeletal elements. In this case, however, we were able to apply only two of the ad-equate methods.

Osteoarticular degenerative processes. There are osteophytes in the observable margins of the joints, in particular the elbow, which show osteophy-tosis in the margins of the distal epiphysis of the humerus, with tiny pores and lipping. Estimated as Ubelaker's Stage 3 (1989:84-86), this element corresponds to a range between 41 and 50 years of age. The hand pha-langes present moderately expressed osteophytes, which agrees with the estimated age.

Dental wear. Dental wear was visible only in a mandible central incisor showing dentine exposure. According to Brothwell's attrition aging sys-tem (1987:105–8; Hillson 2002), the range of dentine exposure corresponds to an age period of about 45 to 55 years old. Thus, we can assess an age at death of between 40 and 50.

Because the skeletal remains are in such poor preservation, we could apply only these two criteria, so it was difficult to assess an age at death for Lady Xook. We think she had completed her fifties when she passed away.

Occupational markers. We know osteophytes in hands are influenced by the kind of physical activity. Resting on this evidence, we infer that this woman, like others in the Maya royalty, such as those of Copán, could have been involved in textile activities. Some of them were masters in the prestigious activity of weaving high-quality textiles. The case of K'inich Yax K'uk' Mo's probable wife, buried in the Margarita tomb (Bell 2002:97), stands out.

Cultural practices. Moreover, it was possible to observe cultural practices in these remains—for example, the custom of covering the corpse with cinnabar, already identified in other noble Maya burials such as Janaab' Pakal and the Red Queen in Palenque. This pigment was found on some of the phalanges in Lady Xook's hands.

Pathology. We could detect the presence of periostitis in several long bones. This lesion is identifiable as a thickening of bone surface. Its unspecific etiology does not permit relating it to any particular source. However, it is commonly associated with infectious problems because the periosteum is usually affected. When several bony elements are involved, systemic infection is a potential etiology, along with other pathological conditions that may produce these kinds of marks on the bones.[5] The presence of infections in these populations was quite common, given the ecological characteristics and the sanitary conditions in urban centers, including garbage contamination, fast decomposition of organic matters due to the heat and humidity, and the abundance of parasites—all being part of everyday life (Márquez, Hernández, and González 2001; Márquez, Hernández, and Gómez 2002).

Yaxun B'alam or Bird Jaguar IV

Structure 33 is one of the most important in the architectural complex of the city. The tomb with the skeleton of one of the most important Maya rulers, Bird Jaguar IV, was discovered inside this building (García-Moll 1996). On Stelae 10 and 11, Bird Jaguar IV refers to Shield Jaguar I and Lady Ik' Skull as his parents, and his birth is registered on Lintels 29 and 30 as 9.13.17.12.10 (Mathews 1997:173). According to Martin and Grube, he was born on 23 August 709 and rose to the throne during April 752 at the age of 43 (2002:128). Marcus argues that this ruler's birthday, as in the case of other rulers, was backdated, perhaps for political reasons. As she says, after Shield Jaguar I's death, there was a 10-year lapse before the new ruler could rise to power (1992b:235–37). Suppositions have been made regarding possible rulers or regents during this time. It is suggested from one record of Piedras Negras that during the interregnum the king's power was held by Yoat B'alam II, and it is argued that he was excluded from the record in Yaxchilán for obvious reasons (Martin and Grube 2002:127). It is speculated that perhaps Bird Jaguar was not the direct heir to throne, for he was the son of a lower-ranked queen, Lady Ik' Skull (Martin and Grube 2002:128), and this is why there was a regent for 10 years. The uncertainty about who was to rule the kingdom resolved in a supposed political instability. Tate (1992) suggests that Bird Jaguar's mother acted as the regent. Another question posed by Marcus is whether Bird Jaguar was too young to rule, even though the interpretation of the epigraphic data indicates he would have been 33 years old at the beginning of the interrugnum, which discards this argument. The most adequate interpretation, however, is that his date of birth was actually "pushed back," as Marcus asserts, and when Shield Jaguar I passed away, his son was just a boy not ready to rule, thus giving way to regency. Marcus's interpretation appears to be the most likely; our osteological evaluation of the skeletal remains attributed to Bird Jaguar indicates that he would have been between 30 and 40 years old at death. If he was in his late thirties when he died, and he ruled for 16 years, this would indicate that he rose to throne at age 19. Therefore, he was only a 9-year-old boy when his father passed away, too young to rule, which would explain the 10-year interregnum.

Nevertheless, epigraphic data indicate that Bird Jaguar IV rose to throne at age 43 and lasted in power for 16 years. According to this evidence, he should have been at least 59 when he died and was born when his father was 60. The epigraphic estimate of Shield Jaguar's age is supported by the fact that he was named *ahaw* (lord) for three K'atuns.[6] However, the date of Bird Jaguar IV's death has not been found yet, but it can be placed between 9.16.17.6.12 and 9.16.17.12.9 (Martin and Grube 2002:130).

Unfortunately, the ruler's skeletal material is very fragmented and incomplete because part of the building collapsed on top of the skeleton. Nonetheless, we were able to analyze part of the surface of the ilium, with which we obtained a reliable age at death. During the osteological analysis, we could identify that it was a male individual.

Osteological Analysis of Bird Jaguar IV

Auricular surface of the ilium. There was only one available fragment of the apical portion of the left auricular surface, with changes that correspond to Stage 3 of Lovejoy's method (Lovejoy, Meindl, Pryzbeck et al. 1985:15–28), characterized by the loss of the tissue's traverse organization, which is replaced by striae marks and rough granulation on the bony surface. The apical segment does not show meaningful changes. There are small areas of microporosity and reduced retroauricular activity. Because the ilium is fragmented, we assess a wider range of 10 years and identify this individual as being in his late thirties.

Osteoarticular degenerative processes. A complete lumbar vertebra was observed with phase 3 osteophytes in the margins of the body. The fragments of four dorsal vertebrae show osteophytes in phase 2. Stewart (1979; cf. Ubelaker 1989:85) ranked these structures between phases 0 and 4. The first indicates absence of osteophytes, and the last the maximum presence of osteophytes. After age 30, the percentage of individuals in phase 2 starts to increase. Because the degree of variability is very wide, this indicator is not recommended for use as a single age indicator and demands a wider calculated age range when it is the only standard available. The distal epiphyses of the humerus as well as the radius and the ulna also have light osteophytes in phase 2. The carpal and metacarpal bones and the phalanges show no signs of osteophytosis. After this analysis, we assessed an age at death of 30 to 40 years old.

Dental wear. Eight molars and four premolars show slight dental attrition, corresponding to an age of 25–35 years old, according to Brothwell's attrition aging system (1987:105–8).

Resting on the aforementioned age indicators, mainly the auricular surface, we suggest that Bird Jaguar IV died between 30 and 40 years of age.

Occupational markers. According to the marks of muscle insertions identified in fragments of humerus and femur, this individual must have been a muscular person. Mathews indicates that the sons of rulers were initiated to the art of war at early ages (1997:240). Schele and Freidel (1990) mention that Bird Jaguar IV, son of Shield Jaguar I, engaged in warfare when he was 14 years old. They also acknowledge a warlike event in which Bird

Jaguar participated at the young age of 11 (1990:265). For Martin and Grube, "Bird Jaguar's mystique is closely related to his image of the untamable warrior" (2002:130). The military achievement of "twenty captives" was usually associated with his name for several campaigns, although the majority of the victims were of low rank. Nonetheless, Martin and Grube mention that he amassed a great fortune from numerous victories and provided Yaxchilán with the reputation of a "conqueror state."

Lady Ik' Skull

García-Moll also explored Structure 21. In its interior, he encountered Stela 35, where Lady Ik' Skull, Bird Jaguar's mother, is depicted taking part in a bleeding ceremony. On this stela, she is referred to as "Lady Mah K'ina," identifying her as a ruler. According to Tate, this title suggests the possibility that Bird Jaguar's mother took over the regency (1992:124–25, 130).

Inside one of the rooms of Structure 21, García-Moll explored Tomb V, in which a very fragmented and poorly preserved skeleton was laid to rest. Given the record of Lady Ik' Skull in Stela 35, it can be suggested that this is her skeleton.

A complete mandible, analyzed during our osteological investigation, stands out for its strong muscular insertions. The chin is particularly squared, a masculine attribute. However, the long bones are quite gracile, and the muscular insertions are weak. The poor preservation of the skeleton and the few diagnostic elements available impeded us from defining the sex of this individual, though it might be a female. As for age, we applied two of the available standards for the segments analyzed.

Dental wear. All the cusps of the mandible molars present a moderate degree of attrition, consistent with an age of 35 to 45 in Brothwell's system for age estimation from attrition (1987:105–8).

Osteoarticular degenerative processes. Only one complete vertebra was recovered, along with several diverse fragments of the spine. They show lipping and flattening of the vertebral body. Four fragments of dorsal vertebrae showed slight borders, which makes us infer that there was more activity in the neck area. The degree of osteophytosis corresponds to an age range between 45 and 49. According to these standards, we assessed a range of age at death between 40 and 50 years old.

Occupational markers. The right clavicle is complete and presents an enthesopathies in the shape of a well in the place of insertion of the costoclavicular ligament and angulations of its mesial end. These characteristics are associated with intense physical activity of the superior region of the thorax. These marks might be related to textile manufacture—as noted earlier, an activity carried out by elite Maya women (Bell 2002:97).

Elite Member Not Identified

Tomb VI was discovered inside Structure 16A. Tate states that it could have been a habitational unit and that perhaps "the chamber with no outlet held burials" (1992:177). This building has several lintels with inscriptions of personages and dates. According to Schele (1982; cf. Tate 1992:177), the dates on Lintel 38 suggest that it was carved during the reign of Bird Jaguar IV.

Inside the tomb, a skeleton was found. Our osteological analysis was based only on dental wear, identifying a man between 40 and 50 years of age. We lacked any archaeological information to identify this person within the society of Yaxchilán, but hope that epigraphic data may shed light on this matter.

Dental wear. Two complete mandible incisors could be inspected, along with one canine and six molars with occlusal wear consistent with an age at death of 35–45 years (Brothwell 1987:105–8).

Occupational markers. We also checked the physical features related to robusticity and activity and looked for evidence of health-related problems. The long bones of the lower limbs, the femur in particular, present a robust femoral crest, indicating physical activity. At the level of inion in the posterior region of the cranium, it is possible to observe marked occipital insertions, which might be associated with intense activity of the neck muscles.

Health indicators. Marks of healed porotic hyperostosis are displayed on the skull. This affliction is commonly related to iron deficiency and parasitism that provokes diarrhea and inhibits regular iron absorption. The presence of lesions in the periosteum is associated with nonspecific ailments, given that such lesions can be caused by an endless number of diseases (Steinbock 1976; Ortner and Putschar 1981; Márquez, Hernández, and Gómez 2002; Storey, Márquez, and Schmidt 2002).

Osteology and Epigraphy

The paleodemographic data in this volume show that the sociocultural and rain forest contexts in which Janaab' Pakal lived in the ancient city of Palenque are associated with high percentages of chronic infections and other diseases that cannot be diagnosed with precision because the marks they leave on the bone can correspond to several health problems. Such diseases likely affected life expectancy significantly (Márquez, Hernández, and González 2001), as is clear from the low percentage of Palenque's population who survived beyond age 50.

As for the lords of Yaxchilán, the skeleton of Shield Jaguar II, which is better preserved in terms of skeletal elements, shows an athletic structure underscored by the prominent muscle-insertion areas. It is known that the individuals of his rank received military training from young ages or were instructed in the ball game. Schele comments that "when Shield Jaguar was eleven, one of his relatives participated in a war lead by king Pakal, the ruler of Palenque" (1990:265). An event like this would have given the royal house of Yaxchilán a great deal of prestige; however, public monuments do not make any mention of it, and we know of the existence of this event only from the inscriptions of the staircase of House C in Palenque.

Shield Jaguar's date of birth, according to the epigraphic record (see table 9.3), is around the year AD 647, and his death was around 19 June 742 (Martin and Grube 2002:123); if the record is correct, his age at death would have been about 95. Mathews mentions that the last date registered on Lintel 23 places Shield Jaguar II as an ahaw of four K'atuns, with an age between 94.8 and 98.5 years. Dates might be incorrect in some cases because they were recorded posthumously, as noted earlier. According to Mathews, some records were carved many years after an actual event occurred and might refer to the ruler's age at the moment of carving rather than to his age at the moment of the event (1997:140).[7]

As for the osteological analysis, we estimated Shield Jaguar's biological age at death according to the aforementioned standards, in particular the changes in auricular surface of the ilium. This technique has proved its reliability with adults older than 50, and our estimation for Shield Jaguar is that he was in his late fifties. The discrepancy between our estimation and the epigraphic date is very wide, but we know that it is very difficult to determine age in old adults. Most of the osteological techniques so far

TABLE 9.3 Important Dates and Events of Yaxchilán's Rulers

Ruler	Event	Date
Shield Jaguar	Birth	ca. AD 647
Shield Jaguar	Rise to the throne of Yaxchilán	23 October 681
Bird Jaguar	Birth	24 August 709
Bird Jaguar	Rise to the throne of Yaxchilán	27 June 736
Shield Jaguar	Death	19 June 742
Lady Xook	Death	3 April 749
Lady Evening Star	Death	13 March 751

have not been able to provide precise differences after age 60 because skeletal changes are hard to distinguish and highly variable. We find it unlikely, however, that the characteristics of a 60-year-old man can be confused with those of a man 95 years old.

Lady Xook's case is even more difficult to understand. According to Schele and Freidel, Lady Xook was middle-aged by the time Bird Jaguar IV was born, whose mother was Evening Star. Twenty-eight years earlier, during her husband Shield Jaguar's rise to throne, she was already represented as an adult, denoting that she was older than he and perhaps even in her postreproductive stage when the last ritual bleeding occurred, barely before Shield Jaguar passed away. According to the epigraphy, Shield Jaguar died on AD 19 June 742, 7 years before Lady Xook, who passed away on 3 April 749. If this holds true, the question is, What was her age at death? The skeletal analysis corresponds to that of a woman around fifty. Epigraphic data indicate an older age.

Epigraphic interpretation indicates that Bird Jaguar IV was born on 24 August 709; that at age 43 he rose to the throne, 10 years after his father passed away; and that his death occurred on 768, which would have made him about 59 years old. Some authors suggest, however, that Bird Jaguar fabricated the genealogical documentation inscribed in his documents.

Bird Jaguar's age at death no doubt marks an important disparity between the data calculated by epigraphers (59 years old at death) and the biological age of death estimated from the skeleton (between 30 and

40 years old). We agree with Joyce Marcus's hypothesis that inscriptions backdated the age at birth in cases of political crises in order to establish legitimacy to the throne. The osteological standards developed for ages younger than 50 are quite reliable, which makes us believe that the age estimated for Bird Jaguar is correct and that he was not older than age 40 when he died.

ACKNOWLEDGMENTS

We thank our colleagues Roberto García-Moll and María Elena Salas, who allowed us to examine these important skeletal remains, even when García-Moll's study on the funerary pattern and the osteological analysis directed by Salas are still in preparation. We are in debt to Richard Meindl, colleague and friend, for his permanent tutoring on age-assessment criteria and on the applications of the standards for the auricular surface. His help has been invaluable for this investigation. We also thank Joyce Marcus, who kindly reviewed and corrected this article. Her support and encouragement have been fundamental in our work.

Ancient Maya Royal Biographies in a Comparative Perspective

Nikolai Grube

K'inich Janaab' Pakal I of Palenque can easily be regarded as the most famous Classic Maya king. His fame is associated not only with his spectacular burial place—the Temple of the Inscriptions, the subterranean vault, and the sarcophagus resting in it—but also with his extraordinary life, distinguished by remarkable longevity. Pakal ruled the kingdom of B'aakal, as the realm of Palenque was called in Classic times, for 68 years before he died at the advanced age of 80 (Mathews and Schele 1974). Pakal's age as recorded in the hieroglyphic inscriptions has given rise to a great deal of controversy, especially because early investigators of Pakal's skeleton did not find evidence for his age at death. The conflict between the osteological and epigraphic evidence in this particular case has resulted in a broader dispute over the reliability of age assessment from skeletal material and the credibility of the recent advances in the decipherment of Maya writing (Dávalos and Romano 1955, 1973; Fastlicht 1971; Ruz 1973, 1978; Marcus 1976, 1992a; Romano 1989; Urcid 1993; Hammond and Molleson 1994).

More recent studies have shed doubt on the reliability of the original age-at-death assessment by Dávalos and Romano and have finally even confirmed that Pakal was an individual of old age when he died. As initially advanced by Schele and Mathews (1974) and Lounsbury (1974), the decipherment of the hieroglyphic texts recording Pakal's biography has been almost universally accepted, including the birth of Pakal in AD 603 on 9.8.9.13.0 and his death in 683 on 9.12.11.5.18. These dates and Pakal's biography are inextricably tied into a dynastic history of Palenque recorded in a great number of inscriptions, reaching far into the past and forward to the succeeding reigns of his sons Kan B'alam and K'an Joy Chitam, so that any modification of the dates would involve an implausible and impossible rearrangement of the entire epigraphic basis of Palenque's history, if not of the entire foundations of Maya epigraphy.

In 1999, Pakal's bones were reexamined by a team of international scholars coordinated by Vera Tiesler, now at the Universidad Autónoma de Yucatán. In early 2003, the project came to the conclusion that Pakal indeed was at an advanced age when he died, certainly older than 60 (55). Like many other members of the Maya aristocracy, he enjoyed better alimentation than the majority of individuals at Palenque. Although he suffered from osteoporosis and arthritis, he was in relatively good health. These data now lend support to the reconstruction of Pakal's life history as based on the reading of the inscriptions.

Pakal's reign is often considered a showcase for unusual longevity and disagreement between written sources and physical anthropology. A closer look at other reigns and Classic Maya dynasties shows that his long life is not an isolated and extreme case. Pakal was not the only Maya monarch who reached the fifth K'atun of life, nor was he the king with the longest reign. Longevity and better health than the rest of the population seem to have characterized the Maya nobility and especially Maya kings in general. Healthier physical conditions may even have been an aspect of elite identity, a distinguishing feature along with the use or knowledge of Classic Mayan as a "high language" and the claim of a different, sacred origin.

It is important, therefore, to compare Pakal's biography with that of other Maya kings and queens in order to learn that his life was not totally unusual. But even more important than contextualizing Pakal's life is understanding what Maya kings expected of their biographies and how they planned their lives and made decisions regarding succession and the continuation of their dynasties. A comparative biographic approach to Maya dynasties has no precedent, but it will certainly help to reach a more sophisticated understanding about the nature of Maya kingship and the sources of authority in the center of Maya states.

This chapter is not about Pakal's biography or about new decipherments of the dynastic history of Palenque. It aims at a broader understanding of Maya reigns and the functioning of dynastic succession in the Maya Lowlands. The approach taken here is to study the relationship between life expectancy, length of reign, and dynastic succession. The continuity of dynastic succession through the patriline is one of the key issues for the legitimization of royal power. Through the comparison of biographies and reigns, I attempt to discover patterns in life histories and finally to unravel how Maya nobles assured proper dynastic succession. Both long reigns and short reigns would threaten the continuity of a lineage. The claim of continuity and connection to a dynastic founder is one of the central issues of Maya inscriptions. This study will help us to gain a better understanding of the rhetoric of Maya inscriptions and their highly selective record of history. If we learn more about the life histories of Maya kings and queens, we will be able to uncover more of the problematic episodes in royal biographies that were deemed not fit for the written record.

Given the limited information that can be obtained from Classic period sources, my investigation focuses on Maya kings' age at accession and on the little we know about preaccession events and rituals. Two related issues concern the length of reign and the age at death. I ask the question, How were Maya dynasties able to cope with extremely long and unusually short reigns? An associated question is, Did old kings expect their death and undertake steps to secure succession? Very little is known about interregnum periods. Because interregnums always constitute a threat to the survival of dynasties, I devote one section of this chapter to the average length of these periods. A final observation concerns the age at which Maya kings had offspring. This analysis shows that primogeniture perhaps was not practiced at all, at least not in those cases where the father reached an old age. Finally, I discuss the patterns observed in the nature of Maya kingship and the broader question of the veracity of Maya inscriptions.

The Sample

The sample as represented in appendix B of this volume includes sixty-seven biographies from Classic Maya individuals. The word *biographies* may be misleading because the events recorded include only birth, accession, and death. The reason for this brevity simply is the extremely selective nature of the written record. It used to be stated that Maya inscriptions provide detailed information about the life of Maya rulers. David Stuart has corrected this view, however, which was mostly stimulated by the enthusiasm generated after Proskouriakoff's historical breakthroughs describing Maya inscriptions as predominantly dealing with ritual and only occasionally with royal lives, if these events were significant for the maintenance of ritual practice.

The most significant event in the life of a Maya king was his accession, which explains why it is by far the most commonly described event in the written sources. Accessions and the related ceremonies provided the foundation for a king's power. In the course of these rituals, individuals would transform their personality and go through a rite of passage, emerging as a sacred being far removed from the common populace. Accession statements therefore show up very early in Maya inscriptions. The earliest accessions recorded in the entire corpus of Maya inscriptions are found on monuments from Balakbal, Campeche, from the so-called Marcador from Tikal, and from the "Hombre de Tikal"—all being roughly contemporary from 8.18.10.0.0 (AD 406). In comparison, birth was not given so much prominence in Maya texts because childhood in general was not regarded as important, unless a monarch wanted to stress the fact that he was already singled out as a future successor during his early years. Kings always recorded their own births retroactively; there is not a single instance of parents announcing the birth of their offspring. Records of birth therefore were quite uncommon in the Early Classic, becoming more prominent at the beginning of the Late Classic period.[1] The death of a previous king is recorded on the monuments of a successor usually in the context of ritual obligations by the latter to the former, or because the new king wanted to stress the continuity of the dynasty. Several early stelae record death and burial of rulers, such as Stela 5 from Balakbal, Campeche (8.18.10.0.0), and the even earlier (though not precisely dated) Stela 1 from Corozal, Petén.

In the Terminal Classic period, a surprising change occurred in the narrative of Maya monuments: a shift away from the interest in royal lives. After 9.18.10.0.0, there was hardly any inscription recording biographic events. The last account of a birth is from Piedras Negras Stela 12, dated at 9.18.5.0.0. Accessions are not recorded later than on Naranjo Stela 32 (9.19.10.0.0), and the last time the death of an individual was commemorated on a monument is on the so-called Walter Randel Stela dated to 10.1.15.0.0. Although the subjects of Terminal Classic inscriptions are still kings and their families, the focus of these texts has shifted to a greater emphasis on ritual. There are no life-historical dates for the last hundred years of Classic Maya civilization. This explains why not a single birth or accession date for any of the lords is depicted on the monuments of Seibal, a city that had its second florescence in the Terminal Classic period. This tendency to focus on ritual rather than on the glorification of kings also is a feature of Yucatec inscriptions (Grube 2003:342–43) and certainly is an indicator of significant social and political change in the Terminal Classic period, an internal change that was both a symptom and a driving force of the Maya Collapse.

The Age at Accession

Out of the sample of sixty-seven biographies, we have both the date of birth and the date of the accession to the throne in forty-one of them. According to this sample, the average age at accession was at 28.43 years (figure 10.1). It may be more than a coincidence that this age is significantly above the average life expectancy at birth calculated for skeletal samples at various Maya sites, such as 26.9 years at Palenque and 26.3 years at Xcaret, Quintana Roo (Márquez, Hernández, and Gómez 2002:30), and 15 to 18 years in seventeenth-century Tipu, Belize[2] (Cohen et al. 1997:80; see also Márquez, Hernández, and Serrano, chapter 5, in this volume). Diane Chase provides an estimate for the majority of adults in the skeletal sample of Caracol, who lived to somewhere between 25 and 35 years of age (1997:23). At Altar de Sacrificios, the mean age at death of sixty-three adults from both sexes is 39 years (Saul 1972:table 7) and thus higher than the mean age at accession of Maya lords. Most Maya lords thus took power when average people would have expected their death.

The main rationale for a late accession may have been the fact that after the age of 20, selection has got rid of all the "unfit" individuals. Subadults in the first decade of life were more vulnerable to the aggressions of their surroundings than were individuals in their second decade of life (Márquez, Hernández, and Gómez 2002:20). With a late accession, the Maya escaped the danger of placing on the throne a successor whose life would still be under the threat of high childhood mortality. Acceding to power in the late third decade also must have been a visible sign of the successor's exalted position and membership in a privileged social group.

The other reason why most Maya kings acceded in the third decade of their lives is entirely political. Pages used the years before they acceded to power to build up alliances and networks of support. Before accession, Maya lords were considered *ch'ok*, a word that translates as "young," "sprout," and "child" in Maya languages. This status probably corresponded to the Aztec *pilli* "child," a terminus that was employed for all members of the nobility (R. Carrasco 1970). In fact, any member of the Maya nobility who did not advance into the state of kingship was labeled *ch'ok*. Rather

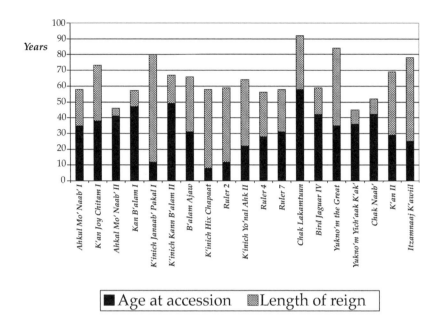

FIGURE 10.1 Maya rulers' age at accession and length of reign

than referring to a state of age, the term *ch'ok* established a metaphorical child–parent relationship between the king and all other members of the nobility.

It is unknown at what age the future successor was selected among the current king's offspring. Elite childhood among the Maya as a subject is still dramatically understudied, certainly because all the texts recording childhood events are retrospective, written by kings who already had been in office for many years (Houston and Stuart 2001:66–67). An important, yet unresolved question is whether there were many different junior claimants to the throne—perhaps sets of brothers and half-brothers—who received instruction and acquired special knowledge in preparation for accession. Was there a process of selection among several potential candidates? When was a successor elected?

Inscriptions from various sites record first bloodlettings and other childhood initiation rites. These rites were usually performed at the age of 5 or 6. Dos Pilas Panel 19 shows Ruler 3 presiding over a ritual bloodletting of a young boy referred to as *ch'ok mutal ajaw*, "Prince of Dos Pilas," in the presence of other courtiers and noble visitors (Houston 1993:fig. 4-19; Houston and Stuart 2001:67). It may reflect Ruler 3's special concern for his eventual succession. Caracol's greatest lord, K'an II, conducted a "first bloodletting" at the tender age of 5 years, which was supervised by his father and predecessor, Yajaw Te' K'inich II. This passage, written on the back of Stela 3, is important because it represents a claim to rightful inheritance—perhaps as a retrospective reply to the fact that it was an older half-brother who became king before K'an II could accede to the royal throne.

The most explicit preaccession rituals are described at Palenque, where childhood events and initiation rites are recorded for various kings. K'an Joy Chitam I was 6 years old when he entered the office of *oktel,* a term that still remains opaque, although there is no doubt that it is associated with heir apparency (Schele 1984b). The Tablet of the Sun at Palenque, which provides the information about the heir apparency of K'an Joy Chitam I, connects this statement with a record of the accession of Kan B'alam II into the state of *okte k'in* at the same age of 6. This latter event was of such importance that not only is it repeated in the glyphic captions of the Temple of the Cross and Temple of the Foliated Cross, but we also see two images of Kan B'alam displayed on these panels: one as a mature king, the other as a 6-year-old child (Bassie Sweet 1991). Another panel from Palenque, the so-called Palace Tablet, records the birth of K'an Joy Chitam II on 2.11.644[3] and tells of a first offering in the company of the patron gods of the city on 16.10.651, when he was almost 7. When Kan B'alam, his older brother, became ruler in 684, K'an Joy Chitam II took the title of *b'aah ch'ok,* "head prince" or heir apparent. By this time, K'an Joy Chitam was already 40, so there can be no doubt that *ch'ok* here means "noble" or "prince" rather than "child." In the time before their accession to throne, Maya kings would continue to use their preaccession name *(ch'ok k'aba')* (Grube 2002:324–25). Part of the accession ritual required the adaptation of a new identity that included a change of name. The new name very often would stress the new king's intimate connection to one of the principal Maya divinities.

There can be no doubt that initiation rites played an important role in the life of future kings. What we do not know is whether these rites were exclusive to heirs to the throne or were part of the initiation of all (male?) members of the nobility, but recorded only by kings who wanted to highlight their juvenile compliance with their ritual obligations.

Although the average age at accession was 28.43 years, there are extreme deviations from this calculated mean (figure 10.1). At least four kings and a queen acceded to the throne at ages younger than 10 years. In all cases, there were secondary lords in the background who would be in charge of state affairs.

The youngest accession is that of Toniná's Ruler 4, who became king at the age of 2. There is no doubt that this baby was installed only in order to secure dynastic succession, while real power rested in the hands of prominent nobles, two powerful lords with the title Aj K'uhu'n: K'el Ne Hix and Aj Ch'anaah. After the death of K'el Ne Hix, he was replaced by another Aj K'uhu'n, a lord named Bird Jaguar. A woman, Lady K'awiil Chan, also seemed to have played a major role during the reign of the child king. A very similar case at Toniná is the accession of K'inich Hix Chapat, who took power in AD 615 at the age of 8. Monument 154, the largest text commissioned during Hix Chapat's tenure, focuses on the accession of several Aj K'uhu'ns and other nobles, a strong indication that these figures were in charge of state affairs while the actual occupant of the throne was still too young.

Another case of a child king is K'ak' Tiliw Chan Chaak of Naranjo. Born on 3.1.688, he became ruler on 28.5.693 as an infant of barely 5 years. His rule was overseen for many years by his mother, Lady Six Sky. Although she was never invested as a Naranjo ruler, she assumed every other prerogative of kingship in representation of her infant son. K'ak' Tiliw started acting as a ruler on his own account at the age of 18 with a series of military campaigns.

The only child queen known is the so-called Lady of Tikal. According to Tikal Stela 23, she was elevated to the rank of queen at the age of 6 in 511. Her reign was overseen by a male co-ruler, an individual named Kaloomte' B'alam, who must have been a high-ranking military leader before he became associated with the Lady of Tikal. All cases of child kings or queens occurred in situations of dynastic crisis, when for some reason no other elder successor was available. In all instances, infant rulers were accompanied and supervised by adult nobles who acted in their behalf, even performing important period-ending rituals. These troubled times therefore permit rare insights into the structure of nonroyal nobility at Classic Maya courts. In his discussion of the mechanisms of succession, Jack Goody (1996) emphasizes the need for stakeholders during an interregnum. Based on the comparison of several traditional societies, he proposes that such officials are most effectively recruited from among the priesthood, for they are caretakers of the emblems of sacred authority so important to both popular religion and kinship. They are ideally suited because they may be members of the royal line with a vested interest in the social order, yet, because of their membership in junior descent groups, lack strong claims to the paramount position.

The opposite of child kings were "old" kings, those accessions that took place extremely late in the successors' lives. Extremely late accessions might be the consequence of an unusually long reign of the preceding king (figure 10.2). This was, for example, the case of Pakal's two sons, K'inich Kan B'alam II, who was 49 at the time of his accession, and K'an Joy Chitam II, who was 57 on taking power. Other instances of late-accession dates very likely are actually reconfirmations of sublords and officials who seem to have occupied other elevated positions previously. At Los Alacranes, for example, the 56-year-old lord Sak B'aah Witzil was confirmed in power by Sky Witness of Calakmul, and El Cayo's Sajal Chak Lakamtuun was placed in his position by the king of Piedras Negras at the age of 58.

Length of Reign

In the sample of biographies included in appendix B, there are forty-two individuals for which both the date of accession and the date of death are known (figure 10.1). These two parameters define the length of reign. The average length of reign of these forty-two individuals is 30.64 years. This is considerably longer than the average reign of 16.5 years for the nine Aztec Tla'toanis before the arrival of the Spaniards (Gillespie 1989). It is also longer than the mean length of reign in other preindustrial societies with hereditary kingship. The average reign in the old Babylonian dynasty was 25 years; in the Middle Assyrian Empire it was 21.85 years; and in Pharaonic Egypt it was 23.79 years.[4] There is a simple explanation for the seemingly extraordinary length of Maya reigns. The sample on which this calculation is based simply is biased toward long reigns. Kings with short reigns neither assembled enough power and wealth to commission their own monuments, nor were their dates of death recorded by their successors. The true average length of reign can be calculated only if kings with short

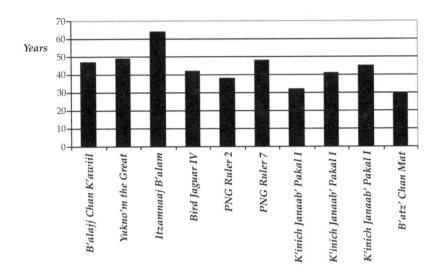

FIGURE 10.2 Maya rulers' age at birth of successor (in years)

life spans and reigns are included in the calculation even though they lack hieroglyphic inscriptions recording the major events of their reign and sometimes not even their names are known. An adjustment is possible if all reigns within a given period are taken into account. We can do this with the "count of ruler" statements found at many sites (Riese 1984; Grube 1988). These counts specify the position that a current ruler takes in the succession of the founder of the particular dynasty. If the precise number of reigns within a dynasty is known, as well as the beginning and end of the first and last reign, the average length of reign for a particular dynasty can be reconstructed.

TIKAL

Chak Tok Ich'aak I (fourteenth successor)   Accession AD 360
Yax Nuun Ayiin II (twenty-ninth successor)   Death ca. 794

Sixteen reigns in 434 years: average length of reign 27.12 years

NARANJO

Aj Wosal (thirty-fifth successor)   Accession 546
K'ak' Tiliw Chan Chaak (thirty-eighth successor)   Death ca. 728

Five reigns in 182 years: average length of reign 36.4 years (the count of reigns excludes Lady Six Sky, who acted as a queen with all prerogatives of kingship [Martin and Grube 2000:74])

YAXCHILÁN

Yoaat B'alam I (founder)   Accession 359
Itzamnaaj B'alam II (sixteenth king)   Death 742

Sixteen reigns in 383 years: average length of reign 23.93 years

PALENQUE

K'uk' B'alam (founder)   Accession 431
K'inich Kan B'alam II (tenth in the line)   Death 702

Twelve reigns in 271 years: average length of reign 22.58 years (the count of ruler title attributed to K'inich Kan B'alam in two Palenque inscriptions excludes two problematic reigns)

COPÁN

K'inich Yax K'uk' Mo' (founder)   Accession 426
Yax Pasaj Chan Yoaat (sixteenth king)   Death ca. 810

Sixteen reigns in 384 years: average length of reign 24 years

Taken together, this overview of dynastic successions in five large Maya cities represents sixty-five reigns in 1,654 years and yields an average duration of a reign as being 25.44 years. This average now includes short reigns such as that of the twenty-third and twenty-fourth ruler of Tikal, who did not leave any monuments to themselves, and the tenures of the short-reigning Early Classic rulers of Copán, who are equally opaque, having left no significant traces in the epigraphic record or in the city's architectonic programs.

The most powerful and successful rulers, however, were those who had particularly expanded periods of reign. Eight kings in the sample had tenures more than twice as long as the average 25 years. They are, in order of their length of reign: K'inich Janaab' Pakal of Palenque (68 years); Smoke Imix of Copán (67 years); Spearthrower Owl (65 years), who was a ruler associated with Teotihuacán, if not actually a Teotihuacán king (see Martin and Grube 2000:29–31; Stuart 2000); K'ak' Tiliw Chan Yoaat of Quirigua (61 years); Itzamnaaj B'alam II of Yaxchilán (60 years); Yax Pasaj of Copán (57 years); Itzamnaaj K'awiil of Dos Pilas (53 years); and K'inich Hix Chapat of Toniná (50 years). Not included here is Naranjo's Aj Wosal, but only because his death date is not recorded. However, Aj Wosal's accession was in 546, and the last event that can be associated with him is a three and one-half K'atun anniversary of his accession in 615. This detail implies that his tenure lasted more than 69 years, turning it into the longest Maya reign known so far.

Most of the kings with long reigns started late during their tenure with the erection of their own monuments. K'inich Janaab' Pakal was in the thirty-second year of his reign when he built the Olvidado, his first major construction. Smoke Imix from Copán acceded in 628, but did not set up any stelae until 652, when he was in the twenty-fourth year of his reign. K'ak' Tiliw of Quirigua acceded to power in 724 under the auspices of Copán's Waxaklajun Ub'aah K'awiil, but his first securely dated monument is from 746, many years after he freed himself from Copán's dominance. Itzamnaaj B'alam II from Yaxchilán waited until the forty-second year of his reign for the creation of his own record. It seems that the majority of Maya kings delayed the commission of their own inscriptions until they were well established. There is no clear pattern regarding the years of reign that had to be completed, but dynasties such as Piedras Negras, where there is an uninterrupted sequence of stelae and where even rulers with short tenures created their own record, are certainly an exception. It is much more common for Maya kings to wait 10, 15, or more years until a first monument to them is carved. This delay is almost always a sign of reigns that started in contexts of political unrest and foreign domination, indicating that new kings needed a long time to build up their power or to free themselves from the dominance of foreign overlords, which prevented them from writing their particular history. Even in those cases where succession was not disputed and no foreign domination was apparent, new kings may have needed years to establish and confirm the political networks on which their power lasted. The new evidence for "multiple accessions" shows that the transfer of political allegiance from one overlord to the next required new crowning ceremonies (Martin 2003b). A newly installed king may have spent considerable time in his early reign reconfirming his vassal lords in their office and reassuring their loyalty. A king who died only a few years after his accession may never have finished this task, which was a prerogative for a successful reign and for the creation of glorifying monuments.

The Age of Death of Maya Kings

Out of a total of sixty-seven biographies, only seventeen give a record of both the date of birth and the date of death. Not included among these seventeen are two cases wherein a king disappeared or was killed in connection with a war event (Piedras Negras Ruler 7 and Calakmul's Yukno'm Yich'aak K'ak'). The average age of death of these seventeen lords is 64.7 years. This average at first seems to be unexpectedly high, and, indeed, it needs to be adjusted because the sample is biased toward long and influential reigns. A very simple way to correct this average is to add the average age of accession (28.43 years) to the average length of reign (25.44 years), which yields 53.87 years as an average age of death. Although from the perspective of a nonelite this average life expectancy of a Maya king (and probably also of his kinsmen and members of the court) must have appeared incredibly long, several Maya kings were even significantly older than this average when they died. The oldest individual recorded in Maya inscriptions is Calakmul's king Yukno'm the Great, who was 85 when he died. Other individuals with extremely long lives are Sajal Chak Lakamtuun from El Cayo (82 years), Janaab' Pakal from Palenque (80 years), and one of the latter's ancestors, K'an Joy Chitam I (74 years).

Other Maya kings also had particularly long lives, but their date of birth or death is not securely known. Aj Wosal from Naranjo was still a child not older than 12 years when he acceded to the throne, but he ruled for at least 69 years and reached the status of a 5 K'atun lord, indicating an age of 78 or older. Itzamnaaj B'alam II was king of Yaxchilán for 60 years. The date of his birth is not known, but based on K'atun age statements from Structure 23 we can calculate that his birth must have occurred between AD 643 and 647, implying that Itzamnaaj B'alam was between 94.8 and 98.5 years old when he died in 742 (Riese 1980:168–17; Mathews 1997:139). Based on the K'atun count only, his mother, Lady Pakal, even reached her sixth K'atun, indicating that she was at least 98 years of age when she died in 705. At Copán, Smoke Imix also reached the status of

a 5 K'atun lord. Calculations drawn from his various K'atun-age statements place his birth around 612, making him about 15 years old when he
took the throne and 83 upon his death. This age was considered such an
important feature of his personality that he is the only one of the sixteen
kings shown on Altar Q who sits on his 5 K'atun age statement rather than
on his nominal glyph. Quirigua's K'ak' Tiliw must have reached a similar
age; once again the birth date is not known, but based on K'atun age statements, in order to have remained in office for the next 60 years, he had to
have been between 28 and 32 when he took power (Riese 1980:164–65).

In the future, researchers will certainly identify more kings with astonishingly long reigns; however, the long-living dynasts currently known
are clearly an exception. Of the seventeen kings with securely known birth
and death dates, twelve indeed died within plus or minus 10 years of the
average length of life of 54 years. It seems that Maya kings who went beyond their third K'atun of life were prepared for the possibility of their
demise and in some cases undertook steps to secure proper dynastic succession. This is most obvious at Caracol, where there is strong evidence of
preemptive accessions and co-rule during the latter years of certain rulers.
Yajaw Te' K'inich of Caracol was succeeded by his 23-year-old son Knot
Ajaw in June 599, but the father continued to live at least until 603 (Martin
and Grube 2000:88). A few years later K'ak' Ujol K'inich II of Caracol acceded to the throne twenty-nine days before the death of his predecessor,
K'an II, who was 70 years old and probably expecting his death. Yukno'm
the Great of Calakmul was 62 when he erected Stela 9 in 662, a monument dedicated to his future successor, Yukno'm Yich'aak K'ak'. Although
Yukno'm Yich'aak K'ak' took power only after the death of his father in
686, Stela 9 already bestows him with a full Calakmul emblem glyph, an
attribute otherwise reserved for the actual king. Perhaps the aged Yukno'm
the Great, ailing or infirm, passed the effective running of the state to the
younger man.

Pakal of Palenque certainly anticipated the end of his reign and started with the construction of his massive funerary monument, the Temple
of the Inscriptions, around 675, when he was 72 (Schele and Mathews
1998:97). The same can be said about Smoke Imix at Copán—the tomb
within the pyramid called Chorcha must have been ready to receive the
body of the king when he had died on 15.6.695, at an age of approximately
83 years. Maya lords considered themselves sacred and probably divine,

and their longevity was a visible sign of their exalted status and difference from the rest of the populace. At the same time, they were aware that their life was limited and that they could not expect to live beyond their third K'atun. In those few cases where kings had a particularly long life, they were well aware of the exceptional nature of this fact. Perhaps longevity added to the notion of divine protection and penultimately to a king's glory, fame, and power.

The Length of Interregnum Periods

The corpses of deceased kings were interred within a few days after death. The tropical climate does not permit extended periods of mourning. K'ak' Tiliw of Quirigua was buried ten days after his death. This is the longest period between death and burial known and can be taken as a sign that his body was elaborately prepared.

The next step was the coronation of a successor, a process that sometimes required only a few days and in other cases took years. At Copán, new kings were usually placed in power within less then forty days. However, we also know about long interregnums—a sure sign of dynastic trouble and unrest. The most famous interregnum period in Maya history is the 10-year interregnum between the death of Yaxchilán's Itzamnaaj B'alam II and Bird Jaguar IV, for which Proskouriakoff (1963, 1964) suggested a power struggle so intense that it kept any candidate from taking the throne. New evidence suggests the existence of an interregnum king who had only a short reign and whose monuments, if he left any, were destroyed and effaced by Bird Jaguar in an effort to rewrite Yaxchilán's history. Another period often described as an interregnum is between the 711 capture of K'an Joy Chitam II at Palenque and the investment of the next king, K'inich Ahkal Mo' Naab' in 721. A closer look at the inscriptions shows, however, that K'an Joy Chitam was not killed in 711 and that he continued to exert influence at Palenque until 720.

Interregnum periods of several years are clearly an exception. In the corpus of dynasties, nineteen successive reigns are currently known, where both the successor's date of death and his accession are recorded. The average interregnum period was 262 days. Of these nineteen successions, fourteen took place less than 200 days after the death of the king. In three cases, it took more than a year for a new king to take power: after the death of K'inich Ahkal Mo' Naab' I of Palenque on 29.11.524, more than 4 years elapsed before the accession of the next lord, K'an Joy Chitam I, on 23.2.529. One generation later, after the death of K'inich Ahkal Mo' Naab' II, who ruled for only 5 years and seems to have died unexpectedly early in 21.7.570, there was an interregnum of 624 days until Kan B'alam I entered the office on 6.4.572. At Toniná, there was a 3-year interregnum between the death of K'inich Hix Chapat on 5.2.665 and the inauguration of Ruler 2 on 20.8.668. Although these interregnum periods cannot yet be explained in every case, future investigation will certainly detect problems in dynastic succession as the principal reason.

The sample of interregnum periods does not include those from early Tikal, although there are four cases of succeeding death and accession dates. One reason for excluding Tikal is that some of the reconstructed dates still leave room for doubt. More important is the specific nature of the Tikal dynasty in this period. Tikal was taken over by a group of foreigners from central Mexico in AD 378, a fact that certainly has disturbed the pattern of succession (Martin and Grube 2000:28–31; Stuart 2000). Yax Nuun Ayiin was placed in the office 605 days after the death of Chak Tok Ich'aak, but he was the son of a Mexican lord and himself a foreigner at Tikal. After his death, there was an interregnum of 2,352 days, which may represent an internal conflict at Tikal, probably a vain attempt to restore the old, local dynasty. There is no written statement about this interregnum period, but whatever occurred, it resulted in the continuation of the foreign dynasty in the person of Siyaj Chan K'awiil, Yax Nuun Ayiin's son.

Maya kings certainly were aware of the immense insecurity created by interregnum periods. As mentioned earlier, those kings who foresaw their coming deaths seem to have taken preemptive steps to secure proper succession in order to avoid the vulnerability of an interregnum.

Evidence Against Primogeniture

Publications about Maya kingship often state that the first son of a king inherited the royal throne. Statements like this permeate the literature, although they actually lack supportive evidence. In fact, extremely little is known about the structure of royal families and about Classic Maya elite concepts of kinship in general. The written sources are astonishingly silent about the role of women at the court. Women are predominantly mentioned in the context of parentage, as the future king's mother. We also lack descriptions of marriage ceremonies. The joining of a local lord with a foreign bride is laconically described as the woman's "arrival" at the man's place. Our limited information about the king's wives comes mostly from Yaxchilán, where Itzamnaaj B'alam and Bird Jaguar give a great deal of prominence to their wives, emphasizing their role as alliance builders because many of them came from neighboring kingdoms. This limited information is not enough to claim that Maya kings in general practiced polygamy. Furthermore, the women at Yaxchilán were distinguished by titles and status, and it is possible that each king had only one principal or "real" wife (Houston and Stuart 2001:66). The Aztec comparison shows that some rulers boasted of having 150 wives pregnant at the same time (López-Austin 1988:302). Whether the principal wife also was the mother of the heir is impossible to say with our limited current understanding. However, an astonishing fact in regard to succession is that the kings were remarkably old when they were siring the offspring that finally became king. From all known cases of kings who had sons who also acceded to power, where the dates of birth of both father and son are known, the age of the father at the birth of the son can be calculated:

DOS PILAS
B'alaj Chan K'awiil: Birth 15.10.625
son: Itzamnaaj K'awiil: Birth 25.1.673, when the father was 47

CALAKMUL
Yukno'm the Great: Birth 11.9.600
son (?): Yukno'm Yich'aak K'ak': Birth 6.10.649, when the father was 49

YAXCHILÁN
Itzamnaaj B'alam II: Birth between 643 and 647
son: Bird Jaguar IV: Birth 23.8.709, when the father was between 62 and 66
son: Itzamnaaj B'alam III: Birth 14.2.752 (?), when the father was 42

PIEDRAS NEGRAS
Ruler 2: Birth 22.5.626
son: K'inich Yo'nal Ahk II: Birth 29.12.664, when the father was 38
Ruler 4: Birth 18.11.701
son (?): Ruler 7: Birth 7.4.750, when the father (?) was 48

PALENQUE
K'inich Janaab' Pakal I: Birth 23.3.603
son 1: K'inich Kan B'alam II: Birth 20.3.635, when the father was 32
son 2: K'inich K'an Joy Chitam II: Birth 2.11.644, when the father was 41
son 3: Batz' Chan Mat: Birth 14.3.648, when the father was 45
grandson: K'inich Ahkal Mo' Naab' III: Birth 13.9.678 when the father
    (Batz' Chan Mat) was 30

Although the sample is small and perhaps not representative because it
is biased in favor of famous kings with long life spans, it shows that there
was not a single king who procreated his heir before the age of 30. The
average age of the father at the birth of his successor was 43 years old. It
is extremely unlikely that kings had not produced other male offspring
previously, thus implying that primogeniture was not practiced; at least,
primogeniture was not a rule that had to be strictly obeyed. This is astonishing considering that primogeniture was a fundamental aspect of many
elite kinship systems (Sahlins 1958:141). It should be kept in mind that the
fathers in this sample had extremely long reigns. It is possible that first-
born sons had become too old, so that they were not considered appropriate charismatic heirs anymore. Old kings often outlive their heirs. Another
threat to smooth succession is that long-living kings produce too much
offspring, creating serious sources of internal conflict and feud. For this
reason, good administrations maintain alternative systems of ensuring
that the economic and social fabric is preserved, despite problems in the
transference of royal authority. We can only speculate about the processes
that finally led to the selection of a new king among the Maya. Because the
inscriptions were commissioned by kings after their accession, they are un-
derstandably silent about any conflict taking place before the inauguration.

The Palenque case is especially opaque with regard to the selection
of the heirs to the throne. Kan B'alam was born almost precisely at the
time when Pakal had celebrated his first K'atun in office. The parallel-

ism of these events—the K'atun celebration and the procreation of the heir—is one of the central themes of the Tablet of the Ninety-six Glyphs at Palenque. Pakal was 32 when Kan B'alam was born. After Pakal's death, Kan B'alam acceded at the age of 48, about twice as old as the mean accession age. It is unlikely that Kan B'alam was Pakal's first son, but the inscriptions are silent about any older brother. Why then did no younger brother take the power, such as K'an Joy Chitam, who was only 39 at the death of his father? Dynastic succession in Palenque becomes even murkier after the death of Kan B'alam, when the throne was taken by his younger brother K'inich K'an Joy Chitam and not by a son. K'an Joy Chitam was 57 upon accession and holds the record for the longest wait. Why did royal succession pass through this old man and not through a young and dynamic son of Kan B'alam (if he produced offspring at all)? Was this a strategy to keep the power within the inner circle of Pakal's family, perhaps among individuals who were directly connected to Pakal's male line and to Lady Tz'akb'u Ajaw's female line? The long interregnum period of 348 days between Pakal's death and the accession of Kan B'alam suggests that the transfer of power from father to son was less smooth than Kan B'alam makes us believe in the iconographic program of the Cross Group.

Summary and Conclusions

Pakal's long life and tenure were unusual but not unique. In any human population, certain individuals will reach maximum life spans of 90 years (Hammond and Molleson 1994:76). Although Pakal reached an age of 80, no portraits show him as an old man. The lack of naturalism in this regard is a common feature of Classic Maya royal portraiture in general. Kings are always shown as young, potent juveniles, emulating the beauty and unblemished face of the young Maize God (Miller 1999:161–63; see also Tiesler, chapter 2, in this volume for references on Pakal's mandible). Even at Palenque, where artists created human images that show particular individual features in the rendering of the faces, leaving no doubt that the artists could have displayed old kings if they had wished to do so, there is not a single image of a monarch with features of advanced age. Images of age and serenity are common in Maya art, but they are restricted to the depiction of gods and supernaturals, such as the old God N and Itzamnaaj, the first priest and master of scribes. Maya artists could have used the same iconographic devices to render images of their lords, but portrayals of Maya nobility never indicate aging, only vibrant youth.

At the same time, whenever it was deemed possible, kings emphasized their old age by using K'atun age statements. Their divine counterparts, God L and Itzamnaaj, who sit on the thrones in the underworld or in celestial palaces, are always rendered old, leaving no doubt that occupants of thrones were conceptually linked with old age (Taube 1992:88). The desire to be old and young at the same time is not a contradiction, but illustrates the dual nature of Maya kings. The combination of opposites seems to be a feature they share with many other cultures of divine kingship. Maya kings were gods and men at the same time; they had absolute power, yet knew that they had to die; they were eternally young and physically old, wise and brave, excellent ballplayers and at the same time well-fed lords carried around in palanquins. Absorbing and manifesting contradictions elevated Maya lords from the rest of the population and stressed their special connection to the divine world. In this regard, Maya rulers were considered stranger kings in the Polynesian sense, as described by Sahlins (1958:73–103). That they had a lifestyle that was different and more refined than everybody else's, that they used a different language, that they traced back their origin to distant places and divine ancestors, and that they enjoyed—on the average—a significantly longer life than the common people outside the palaces contributed to the idea that they enjoyed a special relationship to the divine world.

A comparison of Maya royal biographies with that of other dynasties in preindustrial societies shows the essential similarities. Pakal's long life stands out in the same way as the long life of some famous Egyptian pharaohs, such as Pepi II (with a reign of 94 years) and Ramesses II (with a reign of 67 years) (Clayton 1994). A comparative approach to Maya dynastic history not only emphasizes similar concerns and solutions in regard to dynastic succession, but also helps to develop a more sophisticated approach to the broader issue of the inscriptions' veracity and their propagandistic nature. As historians, Maya epigraphers now understand inscriptions as texts and not as faithful accounts of the past. But dismissing the written texts as pure propaganda often impels a cynical understanding of the written record as the product of a small number of nobles who used deceit and exaggeration as a means to manipulate the dull "masses." Indeed, the results of the recent restudy of Pakal's bones support the veracity of the information provided in these texts (see also chapters 4 and 5 in this volume). Maya inscriptions do not employ deceit; otherwise, we would expect to see more contradictions in the record. We know that where the written record can be tested archaeologically, it has proved robust. It is significant, for example, that no two sides claimed victory in the same battle. Defeats are sometimes recorded by the losers (Dos Pilas by Tikal and Calakmul, Caracol by Naranjo, Palenque by Calakmul, and so on), but they are usually embedded in larger narratives of ultimate victory. Historians and anthropologists can generally trust the information provided. However, a great deal of information is omitted—competing claims to power, a lost battle, and murky ancestry. Inconvenient events are passed over in silence. What kings wanted to let us know emphasizes their current needs and claims. Yet dark spots in the history very often can be discovered through the comparison of different texts and through the study of departures from the common patterns in royal biographies.

11

Discussion

John W. Verano

The decades that have passed since the discovery of the tomb of Janaab' Pakal have witnessed major advances in our knowledge of the ancient Maya. Significant developments in epigraphic decipherment and a rapidly growing corpus of new archaeological and bioanthropological data have restructured the playing field upon which debates about the ancient Maya are enacted. Whether or not Pakal would have wished for such attention, he has become a central figure in debates over the interpretation of Maya epigraphy and history. The identity of the skeletal remains in the sarcophagus in Palenque is not at issue, but Pakal's age at death continues to be a subject of debate among Maya specialists.

The chapters in this volume grew out of a multidisciplinary research project directed by Vera Tiesler and a symposium organized by Vera Tiesler and Andrea Cucina for the Sixty-eighth Annual Meeting of the Society of American Archaeology in Milwaukee, Wisconsin, in April 2003. They provide new and important data on Janaab' Pakal's life and death, drawing upon a reexamination of his skeletal remains in situ, new laboratory analyses of associated skeletal material, and comparative data from other archaeological and bioanthropological studies and from recent advances in Maya epigraphy. Although a consensus on Pakal's age at death has not been reached, the research and analyses presented here demonstrate the value of interdisciplinary approaches to reconstructing the lives of ancient Maya rulers.

The Central Issue

Multiple questions have emerged from both the previous and recent studies of materials in Pakal's tomb, such as the presence of possible congenital defects in his skeleton and the interpretation of additional skeletal remains found within it, but the key point of contention remains his age at death. Contributors to this volume take different approaches to this question, drawing on decades of fieldwork, laboratory analysis, and epigraphic research, as well as employing new analytical methods to revisit the question. Before reviewing these contributions individually, I briefly address some general issues and underlying problems inherent in any attempt to resolve the debate.

Pakal's Remains

The condition of Pakal's skeletal remains constitutes one of the principal problems in estimating his age at death, and one for which little can be done other than recognizing the limitations inherent in the analysis of fragmentary and poorly preserved skeletal material. Poor skeletal preservation is characteristic of the Maya area, as most contributors to this volume note, and Pakal's remains are no exception to the rule. Vera Tiesler's recent examination of the skeleton indicates that it is only about 75 percent complete and poorly preserved. Taphonomic changes were noted at both the macroscopic and microscopic level, making both age determination and other analyses problematic, and DNA extraction not possible. Despite these limitations, however, some observations were possible on degenerative changes in the vertebral column and joint surfaces of the appendicular skeleton. Also, Pakal's pubic symphyses and portions of his auricular surfaces were sufficiently preserved to allow for morphological observations. Preservation of a rib also was sufficient to attempt age assessment using histological methods.

Even disregarding the fragmentary condition of his remains, Pakal presents special challenges precisely because of the general age range that he falls into, whether one accepts the low (40–50 years) or the high estimate (80 years) of his age at death. Skeletal specialists are well aware of the great difficulty involved in estimating skeletal age in adults, particularly in those beyond 50 years. Few techniques attempt to enter this territory because of the great variability and idiosyncratic nature of age changes beyond the 50-year threshold. Some paleodemographers have developed mathematical approaches to simulate mortality profiles extending into older age classes. Although these models may be useful for predicting general tendencies, they are on less firm ground when applied to a single individual who may show atypical or inconsistent age indicators. Attempts to age Pakal by comparing his skeletal age indicators to those of other elite burials at Palenque face the same problem of imprecision. Despite these major challenges, contributors to this volume attempt to resolve this and other issues surrounding the life and death of Pakal by employing some novel approaches.

Individual Contributions

In chapter 2, Vera Tiesler reports on new findings made during a reexamination of Pakal's skeleton in 1999, including important new information on cranial modification, childhood health (no evidence of anemia, healed periostitis, or enamel hypoplasias), and mortuary treatment of Pakal's body. Her examination of the king's remains provides evidence that might be used to support either a younger or older age. A younger age might be argued based on a lack of pronounced osteoarthritis on the major and minor joints of the appendicular skeleton or based on an absence of visible entheseopathies. The lack of pronounced occlusal wear on the teeth can also be used to argue for a younger age, although Tiesler notes that the remains of Maya elite typically show only moderate tooth wear, presumably due to a soft, protein-rich diet. Caution must be used, therefore, in estimating Pakal's age at death based on dental attrition. Evidence for an older age comes primarily from the finding of generalized osteopenia, mainly in the axial skeleton. Barring some metabolic disease, osteopenia generally should not be expected in a male younger than 70 years of age. Tiesler notes also that Pakal has a "remarkably low mandible," which she suggests is an indication of degenerative changes associated with age.

Chapters 3 and 4 present the results of new osteological aging techniques that were applied to Pakal's remains in an attempt to reevaluate the conclusions of Dávalos and Romano's original study. Both analyses produce results suggesting a more advanced age at death for Pakal. Jane Buikstra, George Milner, and Jesper Boldsen employ a newly developed aging method known as Transition Analysis, which combines observations on standard skeletal indicators such as the pubic symphysis and auricular surface with mathematical modeling of mortality profiles in an attempt to improve on current skeletal aging methods—particularly for older adults. Stout and Streeter use histological examination of one of Pakal's ribs to estimate age at death.

Transition Analysis is a new technique that has yet to be tested independently by other researchers and thus is potentially more controversial than Stout and Streeter's histological aging method, which is well established in the literature and has been advocated as a method capable of extending age estimates beyond the traditional 50-year threshold. It should be noted, however, that not all agree that histological methods provide more accurate ages than macroscopic observations (Aiello and Molleson 1993; Hoppa and Vaupel 2002).

Given the poor preservation of Pakal's skeleton, only the morphology of the pubic symphyses could be fully scored for the Transition Analysis, although some observations were possible on auricular surface morphology and cranial suture closure. Results of Buikstra, Milner, and Boldsen's analyses are consistent, however, in suggesting an advanced age for Pakal, approximating the 80-year life span recorded in the inscriptions.

Results of Stout and Streeter's histological analysis, although not entirely consistent, are in general agreement with Buikstra, Milner, and Boldsen's results. Their age-estimation method produced an estimate for Pakal of only 52 years, but they note other features such as very small osteon size and substantial loss of cortical bone as being consistent with senile osteoporosis, which in males is normally a postseventies phenomenon. Their overall conclusion is that an age of 80–90 years is not unreasonable, taking all data into account.

In chapter 5, Lourdes Márquez, Patricia Hernández, and Carlos Serrano take a comparative approach to Pakal's age, employing a detailed paleodemographic and paleopathological study of the known skeletal sample from Palenque. To put Pakal in context, they reconstruct age profiles and demographic parameters for the sample, including life expectancy at birth and in adulthood, and frequencies of individuals in different age classes. Their paleopathological analysis indicates that all individuals, whether elite or commoner, were subject to a range of diseases and debilitating conditions that could affect both longevity and quality of life. They conclude that their demographic profile of the mortuary sample at Palenque is that of a young population, with very few adults living beyond 40 years. In fact, their analysis identified only one individual judged to be older than 50 years of age (an adult male from Tomb 1 of Group IV, with an estimated age of 55–59) at Palenque. Comparing the skeletal and dental observations made on this individual with those of Pakal and with modern comparative data on skeletal age published by Overfield (1995), they conclude that the 40–50 year age estimate originally made by Dávalos and Romano (1973) was more likely than an age of 80.

Márquez, Hernández, and Serrano's chapter is important in situating Pakal in the larger demographic context of Palenque to the degree that it can be reconstructed from the available skeletal data. Their results suggest that very few individuals at Palenque reached old age and that the one individual judged to be the oldest shows skeletal and dental changes substantially more advanced than what is seen in Pakal's remains. Unfortunately, any conclusions about Pakal's age face the same small-sample problem that complicates other studies in this volume: How closely does Pakal's skeletal age correspond with his chronological age?

In chapter 6, Arturo Romano provides additional observations on Pakal's skeleton, critically evaluating claims that Pakal had congenital defects such as clubfoot and polydactyly. These claims were based on portraits of Pakal at Palenque that appeared to some observers to show these defects. Romano convincingly argues that a careful examination of Pakal's foot bones shows no evidence of either condition. He suggests alternative interpretations for the depiction of foot position and polydactyly in Classic Maya sculpture, citing Nikolai Grube's (1996) observations on foot position in ancient Maya dance.

In chapter 7, Douglas Price and colleagues examine the question of the possible geographic origin of Pakal and the "Red Queen"—as well as of several sacrificial victims in the Red Queen's tomb—utilizing strontium isotope analysis of bone and teeth. Strontium analysis has been successfully applied to skeletal material from a variety of sites in central Mexico and the Maya area to examine questions of geographic origin and migration (Wright 1999b; Price, Manzanilla, and Middleton 2000; Buikstra et al. 2004). The analysis presented in chapter 7 produced $^{87}Sr/^{86}Sr$ ratios of both tooth enamel and bone consistent with strontium values extrapolated from local (Palenque-area) rock types, and the lack of difference in enamel and bone values support the hypothesis that Pakal, the Red Queen, and two sacrificial victims buried with her were natives of the Palenque area although they are not sure about their local on-site origin, especially in the case of the Red Queen. Given the small size of this sample, however, analyses of additional Palenque burials and of faunal remains from the site would be useful for confirming these results.

In chapter 8, Andrea Cucina and Vera Tiesler present the results of recent laboratory studies of other human skeletal remains from the tomb of Pakal and from the nearby tomb of the high-status female known as the "Red Queen." Using multiple lines of evidence, including data on burial position, patterns of articulation, and evidence of sharp-force trauma, they effectively argue that these other remains are of sacrificial victims placed in these tombs as companions or retainers to the principal interment. They use the location of cut marks on vertebrae and ribs to document peri-mortem and possible postmortem trauma on several of these skeletons. Position and articulation are offered as supportive evidence to argue that these interments were not secondary or sequential, but that they appear to represent single sacrificial events. The careful analysis of these remains provides important new data on retainer sacrifices in elite Maya tombs.

In chapter 9, Patricia Hernández and Lourdes Márquez take a comparative approach to the controversy over Pakal's age at death, comparing biological age as estimated from skeletal analysis with ages recorded in monuments for Maya rulers at Yaxchilán. They find multiple cases where epigraphic data provide ages at death that are substantially higher than those estimated from examination of the skeletal remains. For example, Bird Jaguar IV's age at death is estimated from skeletal data at 30–35 years, whereas monumental inscriptions suggest an age in excess of 59 years. Likewise, a 30-year gap is claimed between skeletal and epigraphic age for Shield Jaguar.

In interpreting their findings, Hernández and Márquez highlight the challenges involved in aging poorly preserved skeletons, in particular individuals older than 50 years of age, and they question aging techniques that attempt to push much beyond this range. In the case of Pakal, the authors appear to accept Dávalos and Romano's original age estimate and support the position of scholars such as Joyce Marcus (1992) who argue that Maya dynastic histories inscribed on monuments should be read with caution (but see Nikolai Grube's chapter and my concluding comments).

In chapter 10, Nikolai Grube makes a strong argument in support of the veracity of Pakal's life history as recorded in stone. He demonstrates that Pakal's long life, although unusual, was not unique among Maya rulers. Grube assembles a large body of data from inscriptions marking rulers' birth, accession to the throne, and death and examines issues such as length of reign, age at accession, primogeniture, and biases in the record with respect to short reigns for which no monuments were erected. Within his sample, a small group of rulers stands out for their unusually long reigns—Pakal being the foremost. Grube argues forcefully for the legitimacy of Pakal's long reign, noting that "any modification of the dates would involve an implausible and impossible rearrangement of the entire epigraphic basis of Palenque's history." In discussing the credibility of a Maya ruler living to 80, he notes examples of similarly long rulerships and life spans documented in other preindustrial societies such as ancient Egypt.

Conclusion

The purpose of the papers collected in this volume and of the field project that stimulated it was to conduct new research on the life of Janaab' Pakal. Reaching a consensus on his age at death was not its primary objective, and a careful reading of these chapters reveals continuing differences of opinion. Such is to be expected given the diverse data sets and analytical techniques employed, and given the complexities involved in both epigraphic interpretation and the determination of skeletal age in ancient and poorly preserved remains. The editors of this volume are to be commended for bringing together a group of scholars of such distinction, and Vera Tiesler in particular is to be praised for her vision and dedication in organizing the reexamination and conservation of Pakal's remains. Not only has this study produced important new information on Pakal's tomb and its contents, but it has also stimulated scholars to reevaluate previous research and to test new analytical methods. It shifts the debate over Pakal's age away from the simple "epigraphy versus biological anthropology" argument to a more nuanced discussion drawing on multiple lines of evidence.

In this volume, Nikolai Grube's chapter provides the primary defense for the veracity of Pakal's inscribed biography, but his chapter goes far beyond this in contextualizing Pakal within the larger world of Maya rulers and dynastic history. From the biological anthropology perspective, the new studies of Pakal's skeleton reach similar conclusions using different observations and techniques, although not all skeletal observations are consistent, and some analytical methods are new and relatively untested at the time of this writing. Some contributors to this volume continue to support Dávalos and Romano's original age assessment of Pakal, but the weight of new evidence suggests overall that there is indeed a correspondence between Pakal's biographic and biological age.

There may not be consensus on all issues, but this volume constitutes a new and important contribution to our understanding of the life and times of Maya ruler Janaab' Pakal.

Appendix A

Analytical Procedure for Strontium Isotope Analysis
(Chapter 7)

For dental enamel, we lightly abrade the surface of a single cusp of a molar using a Dremel "Moto-tool" fitted with sander bands, cut this cusp from the molar with a cross-cut blade, and remove dentine, if any remains, with a drill. If a clean cusp is not available, we, after abrading the surface, remove a small chip from the side of the molar or drill 5 milligrams of powder from the enamel for analysis by thermal ionization mass spectrometry (TIMS).

Enamel samples weighing 2–5 milligrams are dissolved in 5M HNO_3. The strontium fraction is purified using EiChrom SrSpec resin and elution with HNO_3 followed by H_2O. Isotopic compositions are obtained on the strontium fraction using a VG (Micromass) Sector 54 TIMS in the Department of Geological Sciences at the University of North Carolina (UNC) at Chapel Hill. This is a single-focusing, magnetic-sector instrument equipped with multiple Faraday collectors. Strontium is placed on single rhenium filaments and analyzed using a quintuple-collector dynamic mode of data collection. Internal precision for $^{87}Sr/^{86}Sr$ analyses is typically 0.0006 to 0.0009 percent standard error, based on one hundred dynamic cycles of data collection (±0.000006). Analyses of strontium standard NIST 987 average 0.710260±0.000010 (2s; n = 30). The $^{87}Sr/^{86}Sr$ ratios are corrected for mass fractionation using an exponential mass-fractionation law.

All $^{87}Sr/^{86}Sr$ ratios from the UNC laboratory are reported relative to a value of 0.710250 for the NIST 987 standard (e.g., if the $^{87}Sr/^{86}Sr$ ratios for the standards analyzed with the samples average 0.710260, a value of 0.000010 is subtracted from the ratio for each sample). Total procedural blanks for strontium typically are below 300 picograms, which is insignificant relative to the amounts of strontium in the samples.

For bone samples, which are more porous than enamel and more prone to diagenetic contamination, we abrade the surfaces, then repeatedly sonicate small (5-millimeter) pieces in ultrapure water until no visible material is being removed, and then repeat the sonication with diluted (5 percent) acetic acid to remove soluble salts. After another sonication in ultrapure water, the pieces are ashed for eight hours in a muffle furnace at 750°C. Five milligrams of this ash is then processed for TIMS analysis.

Appendix B
Biographic Dates from the Lives of Maya Kings
(Chapter 10)

PALENQUE

K'uk' B'alam I
Birth: 30.3.397 (8.18.0.13.6)
Accession: 10.3.431 (8.19.15.3.4) at age 33

Casper
Birth: 8.8.422 (8.19.6.8.8)
Accession: 9.8.435 (8.19.19.11.17) at age 13

B'utz'aj Sak Chi'k
Birth: 14.11.459 (9.1.4.5.0)
Accession: 28.7.487(9.2.12.6.18) at age 17

Ahkal Mo' Naab' I
Birth: 5.7.465 (9.1.10.0.0)
Accession: 3.6.501 (9.3.6.7.17) at age 35
Death: 29.11.524 (9.4.10.4.17) at age 59
Length of reign: 23 years

K'an Joy Chitam I
Birth: 3.5.490 (9.2.15.3.8)
Accession: 23.2.529 (9.4.14.10.4) at age 38
Death: 6.2.565 (9.6.11.0.16) at age 74
Length of reign: 35 years

Ahkal Mo' Naab' II
Birth: 3.9.523 (9.4.9.0.4)
Accession: 2.5.565 (9.6.11.5.1) at age 41
Death: 21.7.570 (9.6.16.10.7) at age 46
Length of reign: 5 years

Kan B'alam I
Birth: 18.9.524 (9.4.10.1.5)
Accession: 6.4.572 (9.6.18.5.12) at 47 years
Death: 1.2.583 (9.7.9.5.5) at age 58
Length of reign: 10 years

Lady Yohl Ik' Nal
Accession: 21.12.583 (9.7.10.3.8)
Death: 4.11.604 (9.8.11.6.12)
Length of reign: 10 years

Aj Nen Ohl Mat
Accession: 1.1.605 (9.8.11.9.10)

	Death: 8.8.612 (9.8.19.4.6)
	Length of reign: 7 years
Lady S'ak' K'uk'	Accession: 19.10.612 (9.8.19.7.18)
	Death: 9.9.640 (9.10.7.13.5)
	Length of reign: 27 years
K'inich Janaab' Pakal I	Birth: 23.3.603 (9.8.9.13.0)
	Death: 28.8.683 (9.12.11.5.18) at age 80
	Length of reign: 68 years
K'inich Kan B'alam II	Birth: 20.5.635 (9.10.2.6.6)
	Accession: 7.1.684 (9.12.11.12.10) at age 49
	Death: 16.2.702 (9.13.10.1.5) at age 66
	Length of reign: 18 years
K'an Joy Chitam II	Birth: 2.11.644 (9.10.11.17.0)
	Accession: 30.5.702 (9.13.10.6.8) at age 57
K'inich Ahkal Mo' Naab' III	Birth: 13.9.678 (9.12.6.5.8)
	Accession: 30.12.721 (9.14.10.4.2) at age 43

TORTUGUERO

B'alam Ajaw	Birth: 26.10.612 (9.8.19.8.5)
	Accession: 6.2.644 (9.10.11.3.10) at age 31
	Death: 21.5.679 (9.12.6.17.18) at age 66
	Length of reign: 35 years

TONINÁ

K'inich Hix Chapat	Birth: 13.4.606 (9.8.12.14.17)
	Accession: 30.1.615 (9.9.1.13.11) at age 8
	Death: 5.2.665 (9.11.12.9.0) at age 58
	Length of reign: 50 years
Ruler 2	Accession: 20.8.668 (9.11.16.0.1)
	Killed: 687 (Martin and Grube 2000: 180)
	Length of reign: 18 years
K'inich B'aknal Chaak	Birth: 23.12.652 (9.11.0.3.13)
	Accession: 16.6.688 (9.12.16.3.12) at age 36
Ruler 4	Birth: 12.9.706 (9.13.14.12.14)
	Accession: 24.11.708 (9.13.16.16.18) at age 2
K'inich Ich'aak Chapat	Birth: 20.3.696 (9.13.17.1.6)
	Accession: 15.11.723 (9.14.12.2.7) at age 27

MORALES

Cráneo de Halcón   Birth: 18.1.656 (9.11.3.5.14)

Accession: 7.5.661 (9.11.8.12.10) at age 5
(this was the first accession; his accession was confirmed twice by lords of
other kingdoms, see Martin 2003b)

Stela 2 Ruler   Birth: 18.5.711 (9.13.19.8.1)

Accession: 21.11.729 (9.14.18.4.3) at age 18

PIEDRAS NEGRAS

K'inich Yo'nal Ahk I   Accession: 14.11.603 (9.8.10.6.16)

Death: 3.2.639 (9.10.6.2.1)

Length of reign: 35 years

Ruler 2   Birth: 22.5.626 (9.9.13.4.1)

Accession: 12.4.639 (9.10.6.5.9) at age 12

Death: 15.11.686 (9.12.14.10.13) at age 60

Length of reign: 47 years

K'inich Yo'nal Ahk II   Birth: 29.12.664 (9.11.12.7.2)

Accession: 2.1.687 (9.12.14.13.1) at age 22

Death: 729 at age 65

Length of reign: 42 years

Ruler 4   Birth: 18.11.701 (9.13.9.14.15)

Accession: 9.11.729 (9.14.18.3.13) at age 28

Death: 26.11.757 (9.16.6.11.17) at age 56

Length of reign: 28 years

Yo'nal Ahk III   Accession: 10.3.758 (9.16.6.17.1)

Death: ca. 766 (Martin and Grube
2000:151)

Length of reign: 8 years

Ha' K'in Xook   Accession: 14.2.767 (9.16.16.0.4)

Death: 24.3.780 (9.17.9.5.11)

Length of reign: 13 years

Ruler 7   Birth: 7.4.750 (9.15.18.16.7)

Accession: 31.5.781 (9.17.10.9.4) at age 31

Killed: 808 at age 58

Length of reign: 27 years

EL CAYO

Chak Lakamtuun

Birth: 16.6.639 (9.10.16.8.14)
Accession: 7.4.697 (9.13.5.2.9) at age 58
Death: 13.12.731 (9.15.1.6.3) at age 92
Length of reign: 34 years

Chan Panak Wayib'

Birth: 29.6.755 (9.16.4.3.16)
Accession: 3.5.772 (9.17.1.5.9) at age 16

YAXCHILÁN

Itzamnaaj B'alam II

Accession: 20.10.681 (9.12.9.8.1)
Death: 15.6.742 (9.15.10.17.14)
Length of reign: 60 years

Bird Jaguar IV

Birth: 23.8.709 (9.13.17.12.10)
Accession: 29.4.752 (9.16.1.0.0) at age 42
Death: ca. 768 (Martin and Grube 2000: 132) at age 59
Length of reign: 17 years

ITZAN

Uchan B'alam

Birth: 26.5.736 (9.15.4.15.3)
Accession: 13.11.748 (9.15.17.8.17) at age 12

LAGUNA PERDIDA

Aj K'an Chow

Birth: 4.7.702 (9.13.10.8.3)
Accession: 30.11.722 (9.14.11.2.17) at age 20

CALAKMUL

Tajo'm Uk'ab' K'ak'

Accession: 28.3.622 (9.9.9.0.5)
Death: 1.10.630 (9.9.17.11.14)
Length of reign: 8 years

Yukno'm the Great

Birth: 11.9.600 (9.8.7.2.17)
Accession: 28.4.636 (9.10.3.5.10) at age 35
Death: 11.1.686 (9.12.13.13.5) at age 85
Length of reign: 49 years

Yukno'm Yich'aak K'ak'

Birth: 6.10.649 (9.10.16.16.19)
Accession: 3.4.686 (9.12.13.17.7) at age 36

Killed: 6.8.695 (9.13.3.7.18) at age 45
Length of reign: ca. 9 years

LOS ALACRANES
Sak B'aah Witzil

Birth: 8.11.504 (9.3.9.16.11)
Accession: 30.4.561 (9.6.7.3.18) at age 56

BALAKBAL
Stela 5 Ruler

Accession: 27.8.386 (8.17.9.17.18)
Death: 15.4.406 (8.18.9.16.9)
Length of reign: 19 years

LA CORONA
Chak Naab

Birth: 7.5.615 (9.9.2.0.8)
Accession: 11.2.658 (9.11.5.7.9) at age 42
Death: 5.9.668 (9.11.16.2.8) at age 53
Length of reign: 10 years

Yohel

Birth: 18.2.645 (9.10.12.4.8)
Accession: 19.9.667 (9.11.15.2.16) at age 22

TIKAL
Spearthrower Owl

Accession: 4.5.374 (8.16.17.9.0)
Death: 10.6.439 (9.0.3.9.18)
Length of reign: 65 years

Yax Nuun Ayiin

Accession: 12.9.379 (8.17.2.16.17)
Death: 17.6.404 (8.18.8.1.2)
Length of reign: 24 years

Siyaj Chan K'awiil

Accession: 26.11.411 (8.18.15.11.0)
Death: 3.2.456 (9.1.0.8.0)
Length of reign: 44 years

K'an Chitam

Birth: 26.11.415 (8.18.19.12.1)
Accession: 8.8.458 (9.1.2.17.17) at age 42

Lady of Tikal

Birth: 1.9.504 (9.3.9.13.3)
Accession: 19.4.511 (9.3.16.8.4) at age 6

NARANJO

Aj Wosal
Accession: 5.5.546 (9.5.12.0.4)
Death: ca. 615 (Martin and Grube 2000:71)
Length of reign: around 69 years

K'ak' Tiliw Chan Chaak
Birth: 3.1.688 (9.12.15.13.7)
Accession: 28.5.693 (9.13.1.3.19) at age 5

K'ak' Ukalaw Chan Chaak
Accession: 8.11.755 (9.16.4.10.18)
Death: after 780 (Martin and Grube 2000:80–81)
Length of reign: around 25 years

Itzamnaaj K'awiil
Birth: 13.3.771 (9.17.0.2.12)
Accession: 4.2.784 (9.17.13.4.3) at age 12
Death: Between 810 and 814 (Martin and Grube 2000:83)

CARACOL

Knot Ajaw
Birth: 28.11.575 (9.7.2.0.3)
Accession: 24.6.599 (9.8.5.16.12) at age 23

K'an II
Birth: 18.4.588 (9.7.14.10.8)
Accession: 6.3.618 (9.9.4.16.2) at age 29
Death: 21.7.658 (9.11.5.15.9) at age 70
Length of reign: 40 years

DOS PILAS

Itzamnaaj K'awiil
Birth: 25.1.673 (9.12.0.10.11)
Accession: 24.3.698 (9.13.6.2.0) at age 25
Death: 22.10.726 (9.14.15.1.19) at age 53
Length of reign: 53 years

Ruler 3
Accession: 6.1.727 (9.14.15.5.15)
Death: 28.5.741 (9.15.9.16.11)
Length of reign: 14 years

Ruler 5 (Aguateca)
Birth: 22.1.748 (9.15.16.12.1)
Accession: 8.2.770 (9.16.19.0.14) at age 22

Lachan K'awiil Ajaw Bot
Birth: 25.6.760 (9.16.9.4.19)
Accession: 1.5.802 (9.18.11.13.4) at age 42

MACHAQUILA
Ochk'in Kalo'mte'   Birth: 1.9.770 (9.16.19.10.19)
                     Accession: 20.9.798 (9.18.8.1.5) at age 28

QUIRIGUA
K'ak' Tiliw Chan Yoaat   Accession: 29.12.724 (9.14.13.4.17)
                          Death: 27.7.785 (9.17.14.13.12)
                          Length of reign: 61 years

COPÁN
K'inich Yax K'uk' Mo'   Accession: ca. 426 (Stuart and Schele 1986)
                         Death: ca. 435 (Martin and Grube 2000: 193)
                         Length of reign: around 9 years
Moon Jaguar   Accession: 24.5.553 (9.5.19.3.0)
               Death: 24.10.578 (9.7.4.17.4)
               Length of reign: 25 years
Butz' Chan   Accession: 17.11.578 (9.7.5.0.8)
              Death: 20.1.628 (9.9.14.16.9)
              Length of reign: 49 years
Smoke Imix   Accession: 5.2.628 (9.9.14.17.5)
              Death: 15.6.695 (9.13.3.5.7)
              Length of reign: 67 years
Waxaklajun Ub'aah-K'awiil   Accession: 6.7.695 (9.13.3.6.8)
                             Killed: 29.4.738 (9.15.6.14.6)
                             Length of reign: 42 years
K'ak' Joplaj Chan   Accession: 7.6.738 (9.15.6.16.5)
                     Death: 31.1.749 (9.15.17.12.16)
                     Length of reign: 11 years
K'ak' Yipyaj Chan   Accession: 14.2.749 (9.15.17.13.10)
                     Death: ca. 763 (Martin and Grube 2000: 208)
                     Length of reign: ca. 14 years
Yax Pasaj Chan Yoaat   Accession: 28.6.763 (9.16.12.5.17)
                        Death: ca. 820 (Martin and Grube 2000:212)
                        Length of reign: around 57 years

Notes

Chapter 1. Studying Janaab' Pakal and Reconstructing
Maya Dynastic History

1. Bioarchaeology is a field that consolidated during the 1970s and can be defined as a thematic specialization between archaeology and physical anthropology, wherein human remains are studied from a biocultural perspective, in their cultural context, and jointly with other information in the material record.

Chapter 2. Life and Death of the Ruler

1. This figure was calculated from the bottom's surface area of 9,900 square centimeters and the line's distance from the floor. The subtraction of the volume displaced by the body's solid parts and the offerings below this line should give a rough estimate of the displaced body liquids, provided that the evaporation process was extremely slow, which we expect was the case in the sealed condition of the sarcophagus's inner cavity.

Chapter 8. The Companions of Janaab' Pakal and the "Red Queen"
from Palenque, Chiapas

1. *Primary burials* are defined here according to Duday (1997:93) as the depositions of fresh corpses in their final resting places in which total body decomposition takes place. *Secondary burials* are those in which the skeleton has been removed from its original funerary space and placed elsewhere. Remains that have been rearranged in the original primary burial and have lost the anatomical connections should be considered as *primary disturbed.* Nonetheless, it is often difficult to sort them from the true secondary remains and for this reason are considered within the secondary burial category (Duday 1997).

Chapter 9. Maya Rulers of Yaxchilán Longevity

1. The day of death is different from the burial day (personal communication by Joyce Marcus, 2004).

2. The implications of "taking office" are not the same as those of "rise to the throne." Attempts to assess the age at death and the age at ascent to the throne can be confusing.

3. Damage inflicted by the hyperactivity of muscles and tendons in their insertion places.

4. See table 5-4 of Mathews 1997:171, with the dates of death for Lady Pakal, Shield Jaguar I, Lady Fist-Fish, and Lady Ik' Skull.

5. Periosteal growth is importantly associated with infectious problems. However, as a nonspecific health indicator, it might well be associated with any other problem, such as scurvy or something similar.

6. Mathews mentions that Lady Ik' Skull might have been between 15 and 35 years old when she gave birth to Bird Jaguar (1997:174–75). If we take her date of death into consideration, she would have been between 56 and 75 when she passed away. The term "K'atun" refers to the number twenty, the basic unit of the Maya vigesimal system. The literal translation of the term is "20 years" (Longhena 2000:103).

7. Mathews describes the references to Shield Jaguar's life events on step I and mentions a reference to a Lady Pakal "of six K'atuns," which would give this woman a very old age.

Chapter 10. Ancient Maya Royal Biographies in a Comparative Perspective

1. The earliest use of the birth glyph is in Tomb 1 at Río Azul. Here, the glyph occurs in a context that suggests that its meaning was different, probably referring to a "rebirth" or birth into the Underworld. In its primary meaning, the birth glyph is found first on Tikal Stela 40, recording the birth of Tikal's king K'an Chitam.

2. This figure seems to be low because of underrepresentation of infants. "Life expectancy" for individuals who reached age 15 seems to have been 25–30 years (Cohen et al. 1997:79).

3. In this chapter and in appendix B, Gregorian calendar dates are given as three numbers for month, day, and year: 2.11.644 stands for 2 November 644.

4. This mean is based on the eighty-three pharaohs from the Old Kingdom, the Middle Kingdom, the New Kingdom, and the Late Period, excluding the Intermediate and Graeco-Roman periods (Clayton 1994).

Bibliography

Åberg, G., G. Fosse, and H. Stray. 1998. "Man, Nutrition, and Mobility: A Comparison of Teeth and Bone from the Medieval Era and the Present from Pb and Sr Isotopes." *Science of the Total Environment* 224: 109–19.

Aiello, Leslie C., and Theya Molleson. 1993. "Are Microscopic Ageing Techniques More Accurate Than Macroscopic Ageing Techniques?" *Journal of Archaeological Science* 20: 689–704.

Almaguer, C. 2002. "Paleodieta como desarrollo diferencial dentro de la población del sitio arqueológico de San Buenaventura, Ixtapaluca, México." Master's thesis, Escuela Nacional de Antropología e Historia, Mexico City.

Alvarado, José Luis. 1999. *Análisis de materiales orgánicos presentes en restos óseos procedentes del Templo de las Inscripciones, Palenque, Chiapas.* Report on file, Laboratorio de Paleobotánica, Subdirección de Laboratorios y Apoyo Académico. Mexico City: Instituto Nacional de Antropología e Historia.

Anda, Guillermo de, Vera Tiesler, and Pilar Zabala. 2004. "Cenotes, espacios sagrados y la práctica del sacrificio humano en Yucatán." *Los Investigadores de la Cultura Maya* 2: 376–86.

Aufderheide, A. C., and C. Rodríguez. 1998. *The Cambridge Encyclopedia of Human Paleopathology.* Cambridge: Cambridge University Press.

Bassie-Sweet, Karen. 1991. *From the Mouth of the Dark Cave.* Norman: University of Oklahoma Press.

Bell, E. E. 2002. "Engendering a Dynasty: A Royal Woman in the Margarita Tomb, Copán." In *Ancient Maya Women,* edited by Tracy Arden, 89–104. New York: Altamira Press.

Berlin, Heinrich. 1958. "Glifos nominales en el sarcófago de Palenque: Un ensayo." *Humanidades* 2: 1–8.

———. 1977. *Signos y significados en las inscripciones mayas.* Guatemala City: Instituto Nacional del Patrimonio Cultural de Guatemala.

Bernal, Guillermo. 2005. "El linaje de *Ox Te' K'uh,* una localidad provincial de Palenque. Comentarios sobre la identidad histórica de las señoras Tz'ak-b'u Ajaw y Kinuuw Mat." *Mayab* 18: 77-87.

Binford, Lewis R. 1971. "Mortuary Practices: Their Study and Their Potential." In *Approaches to the Social Dimensions of Mortuary Practices,* edited by J. A. Brown, 6–29. Memoirs of the Society for American Archaeology no. 25. Washington, D.C.: Society for American Archaeology.

Bocquet-Appel, Jean-Pierre, and Claude Masset. 1982. "Farewell to Palaeodemography." *Journal of Human Evolution* 11: 321–33.

Boldsen, Jesper L., George R. Milner, Lyle W. Konigsberg, and James W. Wood. 2002. "Transition Analysis: A New Method for Estimating Age-Indicator Methods." In *Paleodemography: Age Distribution from Skeletal Samples,* edited by Robert D. Hoppa and James W. Vaupel, 72–106. Cambridge: Cambridge University Press.

Boone, Elizabeth H., ed. 1984. *Ritual Human Sacrifice in Mesoamerica.* Washington, D.C.: Dumbarton Oaks Research Library and Collection.

Bourdillon, M. F. C. 1980. "Introduction." In *Sacrifice,* edited by M. F. C. Bourdillon and M. Fortes, 1–27. Edinburgh: Academic Press.

Braswell, Geoffrey, ed. 2003. *The Maya and Teotihuacán: Interpreting Early Classic Interaction.* Austin: University of Texas Press.

Brito, Eva L. 2000. "Análisis de la población prehispánica de Monte Albán a través del estudio de la dieta." Ph.D. diss., Universidad Nacional Autónoma de México, Mexico City.

Brooks, S., and Judith Suchey. 1990. "Skeletal Age Determination Based on the Os Pubis: A comparison of the Acasádi-Nemeskéri and Suchey-Brooks Methods." *Human Evolution* 5: 227–38.

Brothwell, Don. 1967. "Major Congenital Anomalies of the Skeleton: Evidence from Earlier Populations." In *Diseases in Antiquity: A Survey of the Diseases, Injuries, and Surgery of Early Populations,* edited by Don Brothwell and A. T. Sandison, 423–46. Springfield, Ill.: Charles C. Thomas.

———. 1987. *Desenterrando huesos.* Mexico City: Fondo de Cultura Económica.

Budd, P., J. Montgomery, B. Barreiro, and R. G. Thomas. 2000. "Differential Diagenesis of Strontium in Archaeological Human Dental Tissues." *Applied Geochemistry* 15: 687–94.

Buikstra, Jane E. 1997. "Paleodemography: Critiques and Controversies." *American Anthropologist* 87: 316–33.

Buikstra, Jane E., Douglas T. Price, Lori E. Wright, and James A. Burton. 2004. "Tombs from the Copán Acropolis: A Life History Approach." In *Understanding Early Classic Copán,* edited by Ellen E. Bell, Marcelo A. Canuto, and Robert J. Sharer, 191–212. Philadelphia: Museum of Archaeology and Anthropology, University of Pennsylvania.

Buikstra, Jane E., and Douglas Ubelaker. 1994. *Standards for Data Collection from Human Skeletal Remains.* Research Series no. 44. Fayetteville: Arkansas Archaeological Survey.

Burke, W. H., R. E. Denison, E. A. Hetherington, R. B. Koepnick, H. F. Nelson, and J. B. Otto. 1982. "Variation of Seawater $^{87}Sr/^{86}Sr$ Throughout Phanerozoic Time." *Geology* 10: 516–19.

Burton, James H., T. Douglas Price, L. Cahue, and Lori E. Wright. 2003. "The Use of Barium and Strontium Abundances in Human Skeletal Tissues to Determine Their Geographic Origins." *International Journal of Osteoarchaeology* 13: 88–95.

Calvino Italo. 1998. *Las ciudades invisibles.* Barcelona: Minotauro.

Camargo, Lourdes, Lourdes Márquez, and Minerva Prado. 1999. "Paleodemografía del México prehispánico." In *Hacia la demografía del siglo XXI,* edited by R. Benítez and R. Jiménez, 227–48. Mexico City: Sociedad Mexicana de Demografía, Instituto de Investigaciones Sociales, Universidad Nacional Autónoma de México.

Camargo, Lourdes, and Virgilio Partida. 1998. "Algunos aspectos demográficos de cuatro poblaciones prehispánicas de México." In *Perfiles demográficos de poblaciones antiguas de México,* edited by Lourdes Márquez and Josepha Gómez de León, 77–94. Mexico City: Diversa and Instituto Nacional de Antropología e Historia.

Carrasco, Pedro. 1970. "Social Organization of Ancient Mexico." In *Handbook of Middle American Indians,* edited by G. F. Ekholm and I. Bernal, 10: 349–75. Austin: University of Texas Press.

Carrasco, Ramón. 2000. "El cuchcabal de la cabeza de la serpiente." *Arqueología Mexicana* 7, no. 42: 12–21.

Carrasco, Ramón, Sylviane Boucher, Paula Álvarez, Vera Tiesler, Valeria García, Renata García-Moreno, and Javier Vázquez. 1998. "A Dynastic Tomb from Campeche, Mexico: New Evidence on Jaguar Paw, a Ruler of Calakmul." *Latin American Antiquity* 10: 47–59.

Chase, Diane Z. 1992. "Postclassic Maya Elites: Ethnohistory and Archaeology." In *Mesoamerican Elites: An Archaeological Assessment,* edited by Diane Z. Chase and Arlen F. Chase, 118–34. Norman: University of Oklahoma Press.

———. 1997. "Southern Lowland Maya Archaeology and Human Skeletal Remains: Interpretations from Caracol (Belize), Santa Rita Corozal (Belize), and Tayasal (Guatemala)." In *Bones of the Maya: Studies of Ancient Skeletons,* edited by Stephen L. Whittington and David M. Reed, 15–27. Washington, D.C.: Smithsonian Institution Press.

Cho, Helen. 2002. "Age-Associated Bone Loss in an Imperial Roman Population: A Histological Analysis of Inter-skeletal and Intra-skeletal Variability." Ph.D. diss., University of Missouri, Columbia.

Cho, Helen, Sam D. Stout, R. W. Madsen, and Margaret Streeter. 2002. "Population-Specific Histological Age-Estimating Method: A Model for Known African-American and European-American Skeletal Remains." *Journal of Forensic Science* 47: 12–18.

Civera, Magalí, and Lourdes Márquez. 1996. "Perfiles demográficos de alguans poblaciones prehispánicas mesoamericanas." In *La antropología física en México: Estudios de poblaciones antiguas y contemporáneas,* edited by S. López Alonso, Carlos Serrano, and Lourdes Márquez, 153–70. Mexico City: Instituto de Investigaciones Antropológicas, Universidad Nacional Autónoma de México.

———. 1998. "Tlatilco, población aldeana del Preclásico en la Cuenca de México: Sus perfiles demográficos." In *Perfiles demográficos de poblaciones antiguas de México,* edited by Lourdes Márquez and Josepha Gómez de León, 30–76. Mexico City: Diversa and Instituto Nacional de Antropología e Historia.

Clayton, Peter A. 1994. *Chronicle of the Pharaohs: The Reign-by-Reign Record of the Rulers and Dynasties of Ancient Egypt.* London: Thames and Hudson.

Coale, Ansley J., and Paul Demeny. 1966. *Regional Model Life Tables and Stable Populations.* Princeton, N.J.: Princeton University Press.

Coale, Ansley J., Paul Demeny, and Bruce Vaughan. 1983. *Regional Model Life Tables and Stable Populations.* New York: Academic Press.

Cohen, Mark, and George J. Armelagos. 1984. *Paleopathology at the Origins of Agriculture.* New York: Academic Press.

Cohen, Mark, Kathleen O'Connor, Marie Elaine Danforth, Keith P. Jacobi, and Carl Armstrong. 1997. "Archaeology and Osteology of the Tipu Site." In *Bones of the Maya: Studies of Ancient Skeletons,* edited by Stephen L. Whittington and David M. Reed, 78–86. Washington, D.C.: Smithsonian Institution Press.

Comar C., R. S. Russell, and R. H. Wasserman. 1957. "Strontium-Calcium Movement from Soil to Man." *Science* 126: 485–96.

Cook, Della C. 1976. "Pathological States and Diseases in Illinois Woodland Populations: An Epidemiological Approach." Ph.D. diss., University of Chicago.

Coyston, Shanon, Christine D. White, and Henry Schwarcz. 1999. "Dietary Carbonate Analysis of Bone and Enamel for Two Sites of Belize." In *Reconstructing Ancient Maya Diet,* edited by Christine D. White, 221–44. Salt Lake City: University of Utah Press.

Cucina, Andrea, and Vera Tiesler. 2003. "Dental Caries and Antemortem Tooth Loss in the Northern Petén Area, México: A Biocultural Perspective on Social Status Differences among the Classic Maya." *American Journal of Physical Anthropology* 122: 1–10.

Dávalos, Eusebio, and Arturo Romano. 1955. "Estudio preliminar de los restos osteológicos encontrados en la Tumba del Templo de las Inscripciones, Palenque (A. Ruz 'Exploraciones en Palenque: 1952')." *Anales del Instituto Nacional de Antropología e Historia, México, 6a época* 6, no. 1: 107–10.

———. 1973. "Estudio preliminar de los restos osteológicos encontrados en la tumba del Templo de las Inscripciones, Palenque." In *El Templo de las Inscripciones,* edited by Alberto Ruz, 253–54. Mexico City: Instituto Nacional de Antropología e Historia.

Del Ángel, Andrés, and Hector B. Cisneros. 2004. "Technical Note: Modification of Regression Equations Used to Estimate Stature in Mesoamerican Skeletal Remains." *American Journal of Physical Anthropology* 125: 264–65.

Demarest, Arthur. 1984. "Overview: Mesoamerican Human Sacrifice in Evolutionary Perspective." In *Ritual Human Sacrifice in Mesoamerica,* edited by Elizabeth H. Boone, 227–47. Washington, D.C.: Dumbarton Oaks Research Library and Collection.

Demarest, Arthur A., Hector Escobedo, Juan Antonio Valdés, Stephen Houston, Lori E. Wright, and Ketty F. Emery. 1991. "Arqueología, epigrafía y el descubrimiento de una tumba real en el centro ceremonial de Dos Pilas, Petén, Guatemala." *U tz'ib* 1, no. 1: 14–28.

Dembo, Adolfo, and José Imbelloni. 1938. *Deformaciones intencionales del cuerpo humano de carácter étnico.* Buenos Aires: Biblioteca Humanior.

Drew, D. 1999. *The Lost Chronicles of the Maya Kings*. Berkeley: University of California Press.

Duday, Henry. 1987. "Contribution des observations ostéologiques à la chronologie interne des sépultures collectives." In *Anthropologie physique et archéologie: Méthodes d'etude des sepultures*, edited by Henry Duday and Claude Masset, 51–59. Paris: Éditions du CNRS.

———. 1997. "Antropología biológica de campo, tafonomía y arqueología de la muerte." In *El cuerpo humano y su tratamiento mortuorio*, edited by Elsa Malvido, Gregory Pereira, and Vera Tiesler, 91–126. Mexico City: Colección Científica, Instituto Nacional de Antropología e Historia.

Duday, Henry, P. Courtaud, E. Crubezy, Pascal Sellier, and A. M. Tillier. 1990. "L'anthropologie 'de terrain': Reconnaissance et interprétation des gestes funéraires." *Bulletins et Mémoires de la Société d'Anthropologie de Paris* 2, nos. 3–4: 29–50.

Duday, Henry, and Pascal Sellier. 1990. "L'archéologie des gestes funéraires et la taphonomie." *Les Nouvelles de L'archéologie* 40: 12–14.

Dumond, Don E. 1997. "Seeking Demographic Causes for Changes in Population Growth Rates." In *Integrating Archaeological Demography: Multidisciplinary Approaches to Prehistoric Population*, edited by Richard R. Paine, 175–90. Carbondale: Southern Illinois University Press.

Eberl, Markus. 2005. *Muerte, entierro y ascensión: Ritos funerarios entre los antiguos mayas*. Mérida: Universidad Autónoma de Yucatán.

Elias, R. W., Y. Hirao, and C. C. Patterson. 1982. "The Circumvention of the Natural Biopurification of Calcium along Nutrient Pathways by Atmospheric Inputs of Industrial Lead." *Geochimica et Cosmochimica Acta* 46: 2561–580.

Epker, B. N., M. Kelin, and H. M. Frost. 1965. "Magnitude and Location of Cortical Bone Loss in Human Rib with Aging." *Clinical Orthopedics* 41: 198–203.

Ezzo, Joseph, Clark Johnson, and T. Douglas Price. 1997. "Analytical Perspectives on Prehistoric Migration: A Case Study from East-Central Arizona." *Journal of Archaeological Science* 24: 447–66.

Fastlicht, Samuel. 1971. *La odontología en el México prehispánico*. Mexico City: Ediciones Mexicanas.

Faure, Gunter. 1986. *Principles of Isotope Geology*. New York: John Wiley.

Faure, Gunter, and T. Powell. 1972. *Strontium Isotope Geology*. New York: Springer-Verlag.

Ferembach, D., I. Schwidetzky, and M. Stloukal. 1979. "Recomendations pour determiner l'age et le sexe sur le squelette." *Bulletin et Mémoirs de le Societé de Antropologie de Paris* 6, no. 3: 7–45.

Frost, Harold M. 1987. "Secondary Osteon Population Density: An Algorithm for Estimating Missing Osteons." *Yearbook of Physical Anthropology* 30: 239–54.

Gage, Timothy B. 1988. "Mathematical Hazard Models of Mortality: An Alternative to Model Life Tables." *American Journal of Physical Anthropology* 76: 429–41.

García-Moll, Roberto. 1996. "Yaxchilán, Chiapas." *Arqueología Mexicana* 4, no. 22: 36–45.

García-Moreno, Renata, and Josefina Granados. 2000. "Tumbas reales de Calakmul." *Arqueología Mexicana 7*, no. 42: 28–33.

García-Vierna, Valeria A., and Renata Schneider. 1996. "El proceso de rescate, conservación, restauración y análisis como una fuente primaria de investigación antropológica: El caso de la tumba 1 de la estructura XV de Calakmul, Campeche." Bachelor's thesis, Escuela Nacional de Conservación, Restauración y Museografía "Manuel del Castillo Negrete," Mexico City.

Garza, Mercedes de la. 1992. *Palenque.* Tuxla, Mexico: Instituto Nacional de Antropología e Historia, Gobierno del Estado de Chiapas.

———. 1998. *Rostros de lo sagrado en el mundo maya.* Mexico City: Paidós.

Genovés, Santiago. 1967. "Proportionality of the Long Bones and Their Relation to Stature among Mesoamericans." *American Journal of Physical Anthropology* 26: 67–78.

Gilbert, Robert I., and T. W. McKern. 1973. "A Method of Aging the Female Os Pubis." *American Journal of Physical Anthropology* 38: 31–38.

Gillespie, Susan D. 1989. *The Aztec Kings: The Constitution of Rulership in Mexico History.* Tucson: University of Arizona Press.

———. 2000. "Personhood, Agency, and Mortuary Ritual: A Case Study from the Ancient Maya." *Journal of Anthropological Archaeology* 20: 73–112.

Glassman, David M., and James F. Garber. 1999. "Land Use, Diet, Under Effects on the Biology of the Prehistoric Maya of Northern Ambergris Caye, Belize." In *Reconstructing Ancient Maya Diet,* edited by Christine D. White, 119–32. Salt Lake City: University of Utah Press.

Gómez, Almudena. 1999. "Estratificación social y condiciones de salud en Palenque, Chiapas, en el periodo Clásico Tardío: Un estudio bioarqueológico." Master's thesis, Escuela Nacional de Antropología e Historia, Mexico City.

González-Cruz, Arnoldo. 1998. "El Templo de la Reina Roja, Palenque, Chiapas." *Arqueología Mexicana* 5, no. 30: 61.

———. 2001. "The Red Queen." Pre-Columbian Art Research Institute, San Francisco. Available at: *www.mesoweb.com/palenque/features/red_queen/01.html.*

González-Oliver, Angélica, Lourdes Márquez Morfín, José Jiménez, and Alfonso Torre-Blanco. 2001. "Founding Amerindian Mitochondrial DNA Lineages in Ancient Maya from Xcaret, Quintana Roo." *American Journal of Physical Anthropology* 116: 230–35.

González-Torres, Yolotl. 1985. *El sacrificio humano entre los Mexicas.* Mexico City: Instituto Nacional de Antropología e Historia, Fondo de Cultura Económica.

Goodman, Alan H., and Thomas L. Leatherman, eds. 1998. *Building a New Biocultural Synthesis: Political-Economic Perspectives on Human Biology.* Ann Arbor: University of Michigan Press.

Goodman, Alan H., and Debra L. Martin. 2002. "Reconstructing Health Profiles from Skeletal Remains." In *The Backbone of History: Health and Nutrition of the Western Hemisphere,* edited by Richard H. Steckel and Jerome C. Rose, 11–60. Cambridge: Cambridge University Press.

Goody, Jack. 1996. *Succession to High Office.* Cambridge Papers in Social Anthropology no. 4. Cambridge: Cambridge University Press.

Greene, Merle. 1980. "El Templo de las Inscripciones y sus tesoros." In *Palenque: Esplendor del arte maya,* edited L. Gutiérrez Muñoz, 264–81. Mexico City: Editora del Sureste.

———. 1983. *The Temple of Inscriptions.* Vol. 1 of *The Sculpture of Palenque.* Princeton, N.J.: Princeton University Press.

———. 1985. *The Late Buildings of the Palace.* Vol. 2 of *The Sculpture of Palenque.* Princeton, N.J.: Princeton University Press.

———. 1991. *The Cross Group.* Vol. 4 of *The Sculpture of Palenque.* Princeton, N.J.: Princeton University Press.

Greene, Merle, Marjorie S. Rosenblum Scandizzo, and John R. Scandizzo. 1976. "Physical Deformities in the Ruling Lineage of Palenque and the Dynastic Implications." In *The Art, Iconography, and Dynastic History of Palenque, Part III,* edited by Merle Greene, 59–86. Pebble Beach, Calif.: Pre-Columbian Art Research Institute, Robert Louis Stevenson School.

Grube, Nikolai. 1988. "'Städtegründer' und 'Erste Herrscher' in Hieroglyphentexten der Klassischen Mayakultur." *Archiv für Völkerkunde* 42: 69–90.

———. 1996. "Classic Maya Dance: Evidence from Hieroglyphs and Iconography." *Ancient Mesoamerica* 3: 201–18.

———. 2002. "Onomástica de los gobernantes mayas." In *La organización social entre los mayas prehispánicos, coloniales y modernos: Memoria de la Tercera Mesa Redonda de Palenque,* edited by Vera Tiesler, Rafael Cobos, and Merle Greene, 2: 323–53. Mérida, Mexico: Instituto Nacional de Antropología e Historia.

———. 2003. "Hieroglyphic Inscriptions from Northwest Yucatán: An Update of Recent Research." In *Escondido en la selva: Arqueología en el norte de Yucatán,* edited by Hanns J. Prem, 339–70. Mexico City and Bonn: Instituto Nacional de Antropología e Historia and University of Bonn.

Hammond, Norman. 1989. "Maya Alchemy: Emic Understanding of Chemically-Based Color Change in Mineral Pigments in Preclassic and Classic Maya Culture." Unpublished paper.

Hammond, Norman, and Theya Molleson. 1994. "Huguenot Weavers and Maya Kings: Anthropological Assessment versus Documentary Record of Age at Death." *Mexicon* 16: 75–77.

Haviland, William. 1967. "Stature at Tikal, Guatemala: Implications for Ancient Maya Demography and Social Organization." *American Antiquity* 32: 316–25.

———. 2003. "Settlement, Society, and Demography at Tikal." In *Tikal: Dynasties, Foreigners, and Affairs of State,* edited by Jeremy Sabloff, 111–42. Santa Fe: School for American Research Press.

Hernández, Patricia. 2002. "La regulación del crecimiento de la población en el México prehispánico." Ph.D. diss., Escuela Nacional de Antropología e Historia, Mexico City.

Hernández, Patricia, and Lourdes Márquez. 2004. "La población maya prehispánica: Una interpretación sobre su dinámica demográfica." Paper presented at the Quinta Mesa Redonda de Palenque, Palenque, Chiapas.

Hernández, Patricia, Richard S. Meindl, and Lourdes Márquez. 2000. "Los antiguos chinamperos de Xochimilco en el Posclásico: Su dinámica demográfica." Paper presented at the Cuarta Reunión de Investigación Demográfica en México, Mexico City.

Hillson, Simon W. 1986. *Teeth*. Cambridge Manuals in Archaeology. Cambridge: Cambridge University Press.

———. 1996. *Dental Anthropology*. Cambridge: Cambridge University Press.

———. 2000. "Dental Pathology". In *Biological Anthropology of the Human Skeleton*, edited by M. Anne Katzenberg and Shelley R. Saunders, 249–86. New York: Wiley-Liss.

———. 2002. *Dental Anthropology*. 3rd ed. Cambridge: Cambridge University Press.

Hodell, David A., Rhonda L. Quinn, Mark Brenner, and George Kamenov. 2004. "Spatial Variation of Strontium Isotopes (^{87}Sr/^{86}Sr) in the Maya Region: A Tool for Tracking Ancient Human Migration." *Journal of Archaeological Science* 31: 585–601.

Hooton, Earnest A. 1930. *The Indians of Pecos Pueblo: A Study of Their Skeletal Remains*. New Haven, Conn.: Yale University Press.

Hoppa, Robert D., and James W. Vaupel, eds. 2002. *Paleodemography: Age Distributions from Skeletal Samples*. Cambridge: Cambridge University Press.

Houston, Stephen D. 1993. *Hieroglyphs and History at Dos Pilas: Dynastic Politics of the Classic Maya*. Austin: University of Texas Press.

Houston, Stephen D., Héctor L. Escobedo, Andrew Scherer, Mark Child, and James L. Fitzsimmons. 2003. "Classic Maya Death at Piedras Negras, Guatemala." In *Antropología de la eternidad: La muerte en la cultura maya*, edited by Andrés Ciudad, Mario H. Ruz-Sosa, and María J. Iglesias, 113–43. Madrid and Mexico City: Sociedad Española de Estudios Mayas and Centro de Estudios Mayas, Universidad Nacional Autónoma de México.

Houston, Stephen D., and David Stuart. 1996. "Of Gods, Glyphs, and Kings: Divinity and Rulership among the Classic Maya." *Antiquity* 70: 289–312.

———. 2001. "Peopling the Classic Maya Court." In *Theory, Comparison, and Synthesis*, vol. 1 of *Royal Courts of the Ancient Maya*, edited by Takeshi Inomata and Stephen D. Houston, 54–83. Boulder, Colo.: Westview Press.

Houston, Stephen D., David Stuart, and Karl Taube. 1989. "Folk Classification of Classic Maya Pottery." *American Antiquity* 91: 720–26.

Hrdlička, Alex. 1920. *Anthropometry*. Philadelphia: Wistar Institute of Anatomy and Biology.

———. 1939. *Practical Anthropometry*. Philadelphia: Wistar Institute of Anatomy and Biology.

Iglesias, María J. 2003. "Contenedores de cuerpos, cenizas y almas: El uso de las urnas funerarias en la cultura maya." In *Antropología de la eternidad: La muerte en la cultura maya*, edited by Andrés Ciudad, Mario H. Ruz-Sosa, and María J. Iglesias, 209–54. Madrid and Mexico City: Sociedad Española de Estudios Mayas and Centro de Estudios Mayas, Universidad Nacional Autónoma de México.

Imbelloni, José. 1938. "Formas, esencia y metódica de las deformaciones cefálicas intencionales." *Revista del Instituto de Antropología de la Universidad de Tucumán* 1: 5–37.

Iscan, Mehmet Y., and Susan R. Loth. 1989. "Osteological Manifestation of Age in the Adult." In *Reconstruction of Life from the Skeleton*, edited by Mehmet Y. Iscan and Kenneth A. R. Kennedy, 23–40. New York: Alan R. Liss.

Jackes, Mary. 1992. "Paleodemography: Problems and Techniques." In *Skeletal Biology of Past Peoples: Research Methods*, edited by Shelley R. Saunders and M. Anne Katzenberg, 189–224. New York: Wiley-Liss.

———. 2000. "Building the Bases for Paleodemographic Analysis: Adult Age Estimation." In *Biological Anthropology of the Human Skeleton*, edited by M. Anne Katzenberg and Shelley R. Saunders, 417–66. New York: Wiley-Liss.

Jett, S., K. Wu, and H. M. Frost. 1967. "Tetracycline-Based Histological Measurement of Cortical-Endosteal Bone Formation in Normal and Osteoporotic Rib." *Henry Ford Hospital Medical Bulletin* 15: 325–41.

Jones G., T. V. Nguyen, P. N. Sambrook, P. J. Kelly, and J. A. Eisman. 1994. "Femoral Neck Bone Loss Progresses in the Elderly: Longitudinal Findings from the Dubbo Osteoporosis Epidemiology Study." *British Medical Journal* 309: 691–95.

Josserand, Kathleen J. 2002. "Woman in Classic Maya Hieroglyphic Texts." In *Ancient Maya Women*, edited by Tracy Arden, 114–51. New York: Altamira Press.

Kemkes-Grotenthaler, Ariane. 2002. "Aging Through the Age: Historical Perspectives on Age Indicator Methods." In *Paleodemography: Age Distributions from Skeletal Samples*, edited by Robert D. Hoppa and James W. Vaupel, 48–72. Cambridge: Cambridge University Press.

Kohn, Matthew J. 1996. "Predicting Animal $\delta^{18}O$: Accounting for Diet and Physiological Adaptation." *Geochimica et Cosmochimca Acta* 60: 4811–830.

Konigsberg, Lyle, and Susan R. Frankenberg. 1994. "Paleodemography: Not Quite Dead." *Evolutionary Anthropology* 3: 92–105.

Konigsberg, Lyle, Susan R. Frankenberg, and Robert Walker. 1997. "Regress What on What? Paleodemographic Age Estimation as a Calibration Problem." In *Integrating Archaeological Demography: Multidisciplinary Approaches to Prehistoric Population*, edited by Richard R. Paine, 64–88. Carbondale: Southern Illinois University Press.

Konigsberg, Lyle, and Nicholas P. Herrmann. 2002. "Markov Chain Montecarlo Estimation of Hazard Model Parameters in Paleodemography." In *Paleodemography: Age Distributions from Skeletal Samples*, edited by Robert D. Hoppa and James W. Vaupel, 222–42. Cambridge: Cambridge University Press.

Konigsberg, Lyle, and Darryl Holman. 1999. "Estimation of Age at Death from Dental Emergence and Its Implications for Studies of Prehistoric Somatic Growth." In *Human Growth in the Past: Studies from Bones and Teeth*, edited by Robert D. Hoppa and Charles M. Fitzgerald, 264–89. Cambridge: Cambridge University Press.

Landa, Fray Diego de. 1982. *Relación de las cosas de Yucatán*. Mexico City: Porrúa.

Laporte, Juan Pedro. 1988. "El complejo manik: Dos depósitos sellados grupo 6C-XVI, Tikal." In *Ensayos de alfarería prehispánica histórica de Mesoamérica: Homenaje a Eduardo Noguera Auza*, edited by M. C. Serra Puche and C. Navarrete, 173–86. Mexico City: Instituto de Investigaciones Antropológicas, Universidad Nacional Autónoma de México.

———. 1999. "Contexto y función de los artefactos de hueso en Tikal, Guatemala." *Revista Española de Antropología Americana* 29: 31–64.

Larsen, Clark Spencer. 1997. *Bioarchaeology: Interpreting Human Behavior from the Skeleton*. Cambridge: Cambridge University Press.

Larsen, Clark Spencer, Rebecca Shavit, and Mark C. Griffin. 1991. "Dental Caries Evidence for Dietary Change: An Archaeological Context." In *Advances in Dental Anthropology*, edited by Mark A. Kelley and Clark Spencer Larsen, 179–202. New York: Wiley-Liss.

Leclerc, F., and Henry Duday. 1990. "La notion de sépulture." *Bulletin et Mémoirs de la Société d'Anthropologie de Paris* 2, nos. 3–4: 13–18.

Liendo, Rodrigo. 2002. "Organización social y producción agrícola en Palenque." In *La organización social entre los mayas prehispánicos, coloniales y modernos: Memoria de la Cuarta Mesa Redonda de Palenque*, edited by Vera Tiesler, Rafael Cobos, and Merle Greene, 305–27. Mexico City: Instituto Nacional de Antropología e Historia.

Livi-Bacci, Massimo. 1990. *Historia mínima de la población mundial*. Barcelona: Editorial Ariel.

Logan, William H. G., and R. Kronfeld. 1933. "Development of the Human Jaws and Surrounding Structures from Birth to the Age of Fifteen Years." *Journal of the American Dental Association* 20: 379–427.

Longhena, Maria. 2000. *Maya Script*. New York: Abbeville Press.

López-Austin, Alfredo. 1988. *The Human Body and Ideology: Concepts of the Ancient Nahuas*. 2 vols. Salt Lake City: University of Utah Press.

López-Bravo, Roberto. 1995. "El grupo B de Palenque, Chiapas: Una unidad habitacional maya del Clásico Tardío." Bachelor's thesis, Escuela Nacional de Antropología e Historia, Mexico City.

López-Jiménez, Fanny. 1994. "Entierros humanos en el Templo de la Cruz y la Cruz Foliada de Palenque, Chiapas." In *Cuarto Foro de Arqueología de Chiapas: Serie Memorias, Comitán*, 83–97. Tuxtla Gutiérrez, Mexico: Gobierno del Estado de Chiapas.

———. 1996. "El Templo de la Calavera: Estudio arqueológico de un edificio maya tardío." Bachelor's thesis, Escuela Nacional de Antropología e Historia, Mexico City.

———. 2003. "Referentes de la identidad entre los linajes mayas del periodo Clásico: El caso de Palenque. (En busca de la identidad de la Reina Roja)." In *Memoria del Cuarto Congreso Internacional de Mayistas*, 602–19. Mexico City: Centro de Estudios Mayas, Universidad Autónoma de Yucatán.

López-Jiménez, Fanny, and Arnoldo González-Cruz. 1995. "El Templo de la Reina Roja en Palenque, Chiapas." *Coordinación de Humanidades, Universidad Nacional Autónoma de México, Mexico (CIHMECH)* 5, no. 1–2: 121–34.

Lounsbury, Floyd G. 1974. "The Inscription of the Sarcophagus Lid at Palenque." In *Primera Mesa Redonda de Palenque, Part 2*, edited by Merle Greene, 5–19. Pebble Beach, Calif.: Robert Louis Stevenson School.

————. 1991. "Distinguished Lecture: Recent Work in the Decipherment of Palenque's Hieroglyphic Inscriptions." *American Anthropologist* 93: 809–25.

Lovejoy, C. Owen. 1985. "Dental Wear in the Libben Population: Its Functional Pattern and Role in the Determination of Adult Skeletal Age at Death." *American Journal of Physical Anthropology* 68: 47–56.

Lovejoy, C. Owen, Richard S. Meindl, Robert P. Mensforth, and Timothy J. Barton. 1985. "Multifactorial Determination of Skeletal Age at Death: A Method and Blind Test of Its Accuracy." *American Journal of Physical Anthropology* 68: 1–14.

Lovejoy, C. Owen, Richard S. Meindl, Thomas R. Pryzbeck, K. G. Heiple, and D. Kotting. 1977. "Paleodemography of the Libben Site, Ottawa County, Ohio." *Science* 198: 291–93.

Lovejoy, C. Owen, Richard S. Meindl, Thomas R. Pryzbeck, and Robert P. Mensforth. 1985. "Chronological Metamorphosis of the Auricular Surface of the Ilium: A New Method for the Determination of Adult Skeletal Age." *American Journal of Physical Anthropology* 68: 15–28.

MacLeod, Barbara. 1990. "The God N/Step Set in the Primary Standard Sequence." In *A Corpus of Roll-Out Photographs*, vol. 2 of *The Maya Vase Book*, edited by Justin Kerr, 331–47. New York: Kerr Associates.

Magennis, Ann L. 1999. "Dietary Change of the Lowland Maya Site of Kichpanha, Belize." In *Reconstructing Ancient Maya Diet*, edited by Christine D. White, 133–50. Salt Lake City: University of Utah Press.

Marcus, Joyce. 1976. *Emblem and State in the Classic Maya Lowlands: An Epigraphic Approach to Territorial Organization*. Washington, D.C.: Dumbarton Oaks Center for Pre-Columbian Studies.

————. 1992a. *Mesoamerican Writing Systems: Propaganda, Myth, and History in Four Ancient Civilizations*. Princeton, N.J.: Princeton University Press.

————. 1992b. "Royal Families, Royal Texts: Examples from the Zapotec and Maya." In *Mesoamerican Elites: An Archaeological Assessment*, edited by Diane Z. Chase and Arlen F. Chase, 221–41. Norman: University of Oklahoma Press.

Márquez, Lourdes, Antonio Benavides, and Peter Schimdt. 1982. *La exploración de la gruta de Xcan, Yucatán, México*. Mérida, Mexico: Centro Regional de Yucatán, Instituto Nacional de Antropología e Historia.

Márquez, Lourdes, and Andrés del Ángel. 1997. "Height among Prehispanic Maya of the Yucatán Peninsula: A Reconsideration." In *Bones of the Maya: Studies of Ancient Skeletons*, edited by Stephen L. Whittington and David M. Reed, 51–61. Washington, D.C.: Smithsonian Institution Press.

Márquez, Lourdes, and Patricia Hernández. 2001. *Principios básicos, teóricos y metodológicos de la paleodemografía.* Mexico City: Escuela Nacional de Antropología e Historia.

Márquez, Lourdes, Patricia Hernández, and Almudena Gómez. 2002. "La población urbana de Palenque en el Clásico Tardío." In *La organización social entre los mayas prehispánicos, coloniales y modernos: Memoria de la Tercera Mesa Redonda de Palenque,* edited by Vera Tiesler, Rafael Cobos, and Merle Greene, 2: 13–31. Mexico City: Instituto Nacional de Antropología e Historia.

Márquez, Lourdes, Patricia Hernández, and Ernesto González. 2001. "La salud en las grandes urbes prehispánicas." *Estudios de Antropología Biológica* 10: 291–313.

Márquez, Lourdes, M. Teresa Jaén, and José C. Jiménez. 2002. "Impacto biológico de la colonización en Yucatán: La población de Xcaret, Quintana Roo, México." *Antropología Física Latinoamericana* 3: 25–42.

Márquez, Lourdes, María E. Peraza, María T. Miranda, and José Gamboa. 1982. *Playa del Carmen: Una población de la costa oriental en el Postclásico (un estudio osteológico).* Mexico City: Instituto Nacional de Antropología e Historia.

Marquina, Ignacio. 1964. *Arquitectura prehispánica.* 2d ed. Mexico City: Instituto Nacional de Antropología e Historia.

Martin, Simon. 2003a. "A Biography of Pakal." Unpublished museum guide on file, San Francisco Fine Arts Museum.

———. 2003b. "Moral-Reforma y la contienda por el oriente de Tabasco." *Arqueología Mexicana* 11, no. 61: 44–47.

Martin, Simon, and Nikolai Grube. 2000. *Chronicle of the Maya Kings and Queens.* London: Thames and Hudson.

———. 2002. *Crónicas de los reyes y reinas mayas: La primera historia de las dinastías mayas.* Mexico City: Editorial Planeta.

Martínez, Sofía, and Laura Filloy. 2004. "La restauración de las máscaras funerarias de jade: Un reencuentro con los rostros del pasado." *Arqueología Mexicana* 16: 12–13.

Massey, Virginia K. 1994. "Osteological Analysis of the Skull Pit Children." In *Continuing Archaeology at Colha, Belize,* edited by T. Hester, H. Shafer, and J. Eaton, 209–20. Texas Archaeological Research Laboratory Studies in Archaeology no. 16. Austin: University of Texas Press.

Massey, Virginia K., and D. Gentry Steele. 1982. "Preliminary Notes on the Dentition and Taphonomy of the Colha Human Skeletal Material." In *Archaeology at Colha, Belize: The 1981 Interim Report,* edited by T. Hester, 198–202. San Antonio: University of Texas Press.

———. 1997. "A Maya Skull Pit from the Terminal Classic Period, Colha, Belize." In *Bones of the Maya: Studies of Ancient Skeletons,* edited by Stephen L. Whittington and David M. Reed, 62–77. Washington, D.C.: Smithsonian Institution Press.

Matheson, Carney. 2005. *Palenque Research Report.* Unpublished manuscript on file, Thunder Bay, Canada.

Matheson, Carney, Renée Praymak, Arlene Lahti, P. Luukkonen, Vera Tiesler, and Kim Vernon. 2003. "The Ancient Populations of the Maya: Moving Towards a Regional Genetic Study." *Los Investigadores de la Cultura Maya* 11, no. 2: 602–10.

Mathews, Peter. 1997. *La escultura de Yaxchilán*. Serie Arqueología. Mexico City: Instituto Nacional de Antropología e Historia.

Mathews, Peter, and Linda Schele. 1974. "Lords of Palenque: The Glyphic Evidence." In *Primera Mesa Redonda de Palenque, Part I*, edited by Merle Greene, 63–76. Pebble Beach, Calif.: Robert Louis Stevenson School.

Mayne, Pamela C. 1997. "Fire Modification of Bone: A Review of the Literature." In *Forensic Taphonomy: The Postmortem Fate of Human Remains*, edited by William D. Haglund and Marcella H. Sorg, 275–93. Boca Raton, Fl.: CRC Press.

McAnany, Patricia. 1995. *Living with the Ancestors: Kinship and Kingship in Ancient Maya Society*. Austin: University of Texas Press.

———. 1998. "Ancestors and Classic Maya Built Environment." In *Function and Meaning in Classic Maya Architecture*, edited by Stephen D. Houston, 271–98. Washington, D.C.: Dumbarton Oaks.

McAnany, Patricia A., and Shannon Plank. 2001. "Perspectives on Actors, Gender Roles, and Architecture at Classic Maya Courts and Households." In *Theory, Comparison, and Synthesis*, vol. 1 of *Royal Courts of the Ancient Maya*, edited by Takeshi Inomata and Stephen D. Houston, 84–129. Boulder, Colo.: Westview Press.

McArthur John M., R. J. Howarth, and T. R. Bailey. 2001. "Strontium Isotope Stratigraphy: LOWESS Version 3. Best-fit Line to the Marine Sr-Isotope Curve for 0 to 509 Ma and Accompanying Look-up Table for Deriving Numerical Age." *Journal of Geology* 109: 155–69.

Meindl, Richard S. 2003. "Current Methodological Issues in the Study of Prehistoric Demography." *Estudios de Antropología Biológica* 11: 679–92.

Meindl, Richard S., and C. Owen Lovejoy. 1985. "Ectocranial Suture Closure: A Revised Method for the Determination of Skeletal Age at Death Based on the Lateral-Anterior Sutures." *American Journal of Physical Anthropology* 68: 57–66.

———. 1989. "Age Changes in the Pelvis: Implications for Paleodemography." In *Age Markers in the Human Skeleton*, edited by Mehmet Y. Iscan, 137–68. Springfield, Ill.: Charles C. Thomas.

Meindl, Richard S., and Robert P. Mensforth. 1985. "A Revised Method of Age Determination Using the Os Pubis, with a Review and Tests of Accuracy of Other Current Methods of Pubic Symphyseal Aging." *American Journal of Physical Anthropology* 68: 29–45.

Meindl, Richard S., Robert P. Mensforth, and Heather York. 2001. "Mortality, Fertility, and Growth in the Kentucky Late Archaic: The Paleodemography of the Ward Site." In *Archaic Transitions in Ohio and Kentucky Prehistory*, edited by Olaf H. Prufer, Sara E. Pedde, and Richard S. Meindl, 87–109. Kent, Ohio: Kent State University Press.

Meindl, Richard S., and Katherine F. Russell. 1998. "Recent Advances in Method and Theory in Paleodemography." *Annual Review of Anthropology* 27: 375–99.

Merbs, Charles F. 1983. *Patterns of Activity-Induced Pathology in a Canadian Inuit Population*. Archaeological Survey of Canada no. 119. Ottawa: Archaeological Survey of Canada.

Merriwether, Andrew D., David M. Reed, and Robert E. Ferrell. 1997. "Ancient and Contemporary Mitochondrial DNA Variation in the Maya." In *Bones of the Maya: Studies of Ancient Skeletons,* edited by Stephen L. Whittington and David M. Reed, 208–17. Washington, D.C.: Smithsonian Institution Press.

Miller, Mary E. 1999. *Maya Art and Architecture: World of Art.* London: Thames and Hudson.

Miller, Mary E., and Karl Taube. 1993. *The Gods and the Symbols of Ancient Mexico and the Maya.* London: Thames and Hudson.

Milner, George R., James W. Wood, and Jesper L. Boldsen. 2000. "Paleodemography." In *Biological Anthropology of the Human Skeleton,* edited by M. Anne Katzenberg and Shelley R. Saunders, 467–97. New York: Wiley-Liss.

Mock, Shirley B. 1994. "Destruction and Denouement during the Late-Terminal Classic: The Colha Skull Pit." In *Continuing Archaeology at Colha, Belize,* edited by T. Hester, H. Shafer, and J. Eaton, 221–31. Texas Archaeological Research Laboratory Studies in Archaeology no. 16. Austin: University of Texas Press.

Molleson, Theya I. 1995. "Rates of Ageing in the Eighteenth Century." In *Grave Reflections: Portraying the Past Through Cemetery Studies,* edited by Shelley R. Saunders and Ann Herring, 199–222. Toronto: Canadian Scholars' Press.

Molnar, Stephen. 1971. "Human Tooth Wear, Tooth Function, and Cultural Variability." *American Journal of Physical Anthropology* 34: 175–90.

Montgomery, J., P. Budd, A. Cox, P. Krause, and R. G. Thomas. 1999. "LA-ICP-MS Evidence for the Distribution of Pb and Sr in Romano-British Medieval and Modern Human Teeth: Implications for Life History and Exposure Reconstruction." In *Metals in Antiquity: Proceedings of the International Symposium,* edited by S. M. M. Young, A. M. Pollard, P. Budd, and R. A. Ixer, 258–61. Oxford: Archaeopress.

Montgomery, J., P. Budd, and J. Evans. 2000. "Reconstructing the Lifetime Movements of Ancient People: A Neolithic Case Study from Southern England." *European Journal of Archaeology* 3: 407–22.

Montgomery, J., J. Evans, and T. Neighbour. 2003. "Sr Isotope Evidence for Population Movement within the Hebridean Norse Community of NW Scotland." *Journal of the Geological Society* 160: 649–53.

Montgomery, J., J. Evans, and C. A. Roberts. 2003. "Mineralization, Preservation, and Sampling of Teeth: Strategies to Optimize Comparative Study and Minimize Age-Related Change for Lead and Strontium Analysis." *American Journal of Physical Anthropology* (supplement) 36: 153–54.

Morse, D. 1978. *Ancient Disease in the Midwest.* State Museum Report of Investigations no. 15. Springfield: Illinois State Museum.

Mosekilde, Lis. 1999. "Trabecular Microarchitecture and Aging." In *Osteoporosis in Men,* edited by Eric S. Orwoll, 313–34. Boston: Academic Press.

Moser, C. L. 1973. *Human Decapitation in Ancient Mesoamerica.* Washington, D.C.: Dumbarton Oaks Research Library and Collection.

Murray, Ronald O., and Harold G. Jacobson. 1982. *Radiología de los trastornos esqueléticos.* Vol. 1. Barcelona: Salvat.

Nájera, Martha I. 1987. *El don de la sangre en el equilibrio cósmico: El sacrificio y el autosacrificio sangriento entre los antiguos maya.* Mexico City: Universidad Nacional Autónoma de México.

Orea-Magaña, Haydée. 1999. *Informe de los trabajos de conservación de los restos óseos de Pakal, ubicado en el Templo de las Inscripciones.* Mexico City: Coordinación de Restauración, Instituto Nacional de Antropología e Historia.

Ortega, F., L. M. Mitre, J. Roldan, J. Aranda, D. Moran, S. Alaniz, and A. Nieto. 1992. *Carta geológica de la Republica Mexicana: Consejo de Recursos Minerales de Mexico and Instituto de Geologia de la UNAM, scale 1:2,000,000.* Mexico City: Universidad Nacional Autónoma de México.

Ortner, Donald J. 2003. *Identification of Pathological Conditions in Human Skeletal Remains.* 2d ed. Amsterdam: Academic Press.

Ortner, Donald J., and Walter G. Putschar. 1981. *Identification of Pathological Conditions in Human Skeletal Remains.* Washington, D.C.: Smithsonian Institution Press.

O'Shea, J. M. 1984. *Mortuary Variability and Archaeological Investigation.* Orlando, Fl.: Academic Press.

Overfield, Theresa. 1995. *Biologic Variation in Health and Illness: Race, Age, and Sex Differences.* Boca Raton, Fl.: CRC Press.

Paine, Richard R., ed. 1997. *Integrating Archaeological Demography: Multidisciplinary Approaches to Prehistoric Population.* Carbondale: Southern Illinois University.

Peebles, Christopher S., and Susan M. Kus. 1977. "Some Archaeological Correlates of Ranked Societies." *American Antiquity* 42: 421–48.

Phenice, Terry. 1969. "A Newly Developed Visual Method of Sexing in the Os Pubis." *American Journal of Physical Anthropology* 30: 297–301.

Pirok, D. J., J. R. Ramser, H. Takahashi, A. R. Villanueva, and H. M. Frost. 1966. "Normal Histological, Tetracycline, and Dynamic Parameters in Human, Mineralized Bone Sections." *Henry Ford Hospital Medical Bulletin* 14: 195–218.

Prager, Christian. 2002. "Enanismo y gibosidad: Las personas afectadas y su identidad en la sociedad maya del tiempo prehispánico." In *La organización social entre los mayas prehispánicos, coloniales y modernos: Memoria de la Tercera Mesa Redonda de Palenque,* edited by Vera Tiesler, Raphael Cobos, and Merle Greene, 2: 35–67. Mérida, Mexico: Instituto Nacional de Antropología e Historia.

Price, T. Douglas, R. A. Bentley, D. Gronenborn, J. Lüning, and J. Wahl. 2001. "Human Migration in the Linearbandkeramik of Central Europe." *Antiquity* 75: 593–603.

Price, T. Douglas, J. Blitz, James Burton, and Joseph Ezzo. 1992. "Diagenesis in Prehistoric Bone: Problems and Solutions." *Journal of Archaeological Science* 19: 513–29.

Price, T. Douglas, James H. Burton, and R. A. Bentley. 2002. "The Characterization of Biologically Available Strontium Isotope Ratios for the Study of Prehistoric Migration." *Archaeometry* 44: 117–35.

Price, T. Douglas, Gisela Grupe, and P. Schrorter. 1994. "Reconstruction of Migration Patterns in the Bell Beaker Period by Stable Strontium Isotope Analysis." *Applied Geochemistry* 9: 413–17.

———. 1998. "Migration and Mobility in the Bell Beaker Period in Central Europe." *Antiquity* 72: 405–11.

Price, T. Douglas, Clark M. Johnson, Joseph A. Ezzo, James H. Burton, and Jonathan A. Ericson. 1994. "Residential Mobility in the Prehistoric Southwest United States: A Preliminary Study Using Strontium Isotope." *Journal of Archaeological Science* 21: 315–30.

Price, T. Douglas, Linda Manzanilla, and William D. Middleton. 2000. "Immigration and the Ancient City of Teotihuacán in Mexico: A Study Using Strontium Isotope Ratios in Human Bone and Teeth." *Journal of Archaeological Science* 27: 903–13.

Proskouriakoff, Tatiana. 1960. "Historical Implications of a Pattern of Dates at Piedras Negras, Guatemala." *American Antiquity* 25: 454–75.

———. 1963. "Historical Data in the Inscriptions of Yaxchilán, Part I." *Estudios de Cultura Maya* 3: 149–67.

———. 1964. "Historical Data in the Inscriptions of Yaxchilán, Part II." *Estudios de Cultura Maya* 4: 177–201.

Quenon, Michel, and Genevieve Le Fort. 1997. "Rebirth and Resurrection in Maize God Iconography." In *A Corpus of Rollout Photographs of Maya Vases,* vol. 5 of *The Maya Vase Book,* edited by Justin Kerr and Barbara Kerr, 884–902. New York: Kerr Associates.

Richter, Frank M., D. B. Rowley, and D. L. DePaolo. 1992. "Sr Isotope Evolution of Seawater: The Role of Tectonics." *Earth and Planetary Science Letters* 109: 11–23.

Riese, Berthold. 1980. "Katun-Altersangaben in Klassischen Maya-Inschriften." *Baessler-Archiv (NF), Band* 28: 155–79.

———. 1984. "Hel Hieroglyphs." In *Phoneticism in Maya Hieroglyphic Writing,* edited by John S. Justeson and Lyle Campbell, 263–86. Institute for Mesoamerican Studies Publication no. 9. Albany: State University of New York Press.

Ringle, William M. 1996. "Birds of a Feather: The Fallen Stucco Inscription of Temple XVIII, Palenque, Chiapas." In *Eighth Palenque Round Table, 1993,* edited by Martha J. Macri and Jan McHargue, 10: 45–61. San Francisco: Pre-Columbian Art Research Institute.

Robicsek, Francis, and Donald M. Hales. 1981. *The Maya Book of the Dead: The Ceramic Codex.* Charlotte: University of Virginia Art Museum.

———. 1984. "Maya Heart Sacrifice: Cultural Perspective and Surgical Technique." In *Ritual Human Sacrifice in Mesoamerica,* edited by Elizabeth H. Boone, 49–89. Washington, D.C.: Dumbarton Oaks Research Library and Collection.

Robling, Alex G., and Sam D. Stout. 2000. "Histomorphometry of Human Cortical Bone: Applications to Age Estimation." In *Biological Anthropology of the Human Skeleton,* edited by Mary A. Katzenberg and Shelley R. Saunders, 187–213. New York: Wiley-Liss.

Rogers, Graeme, and C. J. Hawkesworth. 1989. "A Geochemical Traverse across the North Chilean Andes: Evidence for Crust Generation from the Mantle Wedge." *Earth and Planetary Science Letters* 91: 271–85.

Romano, Arturo. 1965. *Estudio morfológico de la deformación craneana en Tamuín, S.L.P., y en la Isla del Idolo, Veracruz.* Serie de Investigaciones 10. Mexico City: Instituto Nacional de Antropología e Historia.

———. 1975. "Balance y proyecciones de los estudios de poblaciones desaparecidas en Mesoamérica y el norte de México." *Sociedad Mexicana de Antropología, Mesa Redonda* 13: 4–14.

———. 1977. "Los restos craneales del personaje de la cámara sepulcral del Templo de las Inscripciones en Palenque, Chiapas: Su estado de conservación." Unpublished report on file in the Dirección de Antropología Física, Instituto Nacional de Antropología e Historia.

———. 1980. "La tumba del Templo de las Inscripciones." In *Palenque: Esplendor del arte maya,* edited by L. Gutiérrez Muñoz, 284–301. Mexico City: Editora del Sureste.

———. 1989. "El entierro del Templo de las Inscripciones en Palenque." In *Memorias del Segundo Coloquio Internacional de Mayistas,* 1413–473. Mexico City: Universidad Nacional Autónoma de México.

Romano, Arturo, and Vera Tiesler. 2002. *Reporte del análisis tafo-osteológico de los restos humanos, recuperados en el recinto funerario dentro del Templo XIII, Palenque, Chiapas.* Mérida, Mexico: Instituto Nacional de Antropología e Historia.

Romero, Javier. 1986. *Catálogo de la colección de dientes mutilados prehispánicos IV parte.* Colección Fuentes. Mexico City: Instituto Nacional de Antropología e Historia.

Rosenthal, Harold L. 1981. "Content of Stable Strontium in Man and Animal Biota." In *Handbook of Stable Strontium,* edited by S. C. Skoryna, 503–14. New York: Plenum Press.

Ruz, Alberto. 1953. "The Mystery of the Mayan Temple." *Saturday Evening Post* 226, no. 9: 95–98.

———. 1955. "Exploraciones en Palenque: 1952." *Anales del Instituto Nacional de Antropología e Historia* 6: 79–106.

———. 1958. "Exploraciones arqueológicas en Palenque: 1953–1956." *Anales del Instituto Nacional de Antropología e Historia* 10: 69–299.

———. 1973. *El Templo de las Inscripciones, Palenque.* Colección Científica no. 7. Mexico City: Instituto Nacional de Antropología e Historia.

———. 1978. "Gerontocracy at Palenque?" In *Social Process in Maya Prehistory,* edited by Norman Hammond, 287–95. London: Academic Press.

———. 1991. *Costumbres funerarias entre los antiguos mayas.* Mexico City: Universidad Nacional Autónoma de México.

Sahlins, Marshall. 1958. *Social Stratification in Polynesia.* Seattle: University of Washington Press.

Saul, Frank P. 1972. *The Human Skeletal Remains of Altar de Sacrificios: An Osteobiographic Analysis.* Papers of the Peabody Museum of Archaeology and Ethnology, vol. 63, no. 2. Cambridge, Mass.: Harvard University.

Saul, Judy M., and Frank P. Saul. 1997. "The Preclassic Skeletons from Cuello." In *Bones of the Maya: Studies of Ancient Skeletons,* edited by Stephen L. Whittington and David M. Reed, 28–50. Washington, D.C.: Smithsonian Institution Press.

Saunders, Shelley R., and Lisa Barrans. 1999. "What Can Be Done about the Infant Category in Skeletal Samples?" In *Human Growth in the Past: Studies from Bones and Teeth*, edited by Robert D. Hoppa and C. M. Fitzgerald, 183–209. Cambridge: Cambridge University Press.

Schele, Linda. 1979. "Genealogical Documentation on the Three-Figure Panels at Palenque." Paper presented at the Third Palenque Round Table, Monterey, Calif.

———. 1984a. "Human Sacrifice among the Classic Maya." In *Ritual Human Sacrifice in Mesoamerica*, edited by Elizabeth H. Boone, 7–48. Washington, D.C.: Dumbarton Oaks Research Library and Collection.

———. 1984b. "Some Suggested Readings for the Event and Office of Heir-Designate at Palenque." In *Phoneticism in Maya Hieroglyphic Writing*, edited by John S. Justeson and Lyle Campbell, 287–305. Institute for Mesoamerican Studies Publication no. 9. Albany: State University of New York Press.

Schele, Linda, and David Freidel. 1990. *The Forest of Kings*. New York: William Morrow.

Schele, Linda, and Peter Mathews. 1998. *The Code of Kings*. New York: Scribner.

Schele, Linda, and Mary E. Miller. 1986. *The Blood of Kings*. New York: G. Baziller.

Scholes, F., and E. Adams. 1938. *Don Quijada: Alcalde mayor de Yucatán (1561–1565)*. Vol. 1. Mexico City: Porrúa.

Schroeder, H. A., A. P. Nason, and I. H. Tipton. 1972. "Essential Metals in Man: Strontium and Barium." *Journal of Chronic Diseases* 25: 491–517.

Schultz, Michael. 1988. "Paläopathologische Diagnostik." In *Anthropologie, Wesen und Methoden der Anthropologie*, edited by R. Knussmann, 1: 480–96. Stuttgart: Gustav Fischer.

Sealy, Judy C., R. Armstrong, and C. Schrire. 1995. "Beyond Lifetime Averages: Tracing Life Histories Through Isotopic Analysis of Different Calcified Tissues from Archaeological Human Skeletons." *Antiquity* 69: 290–300.

Sealy, Judy C., N. J. van der Merwe, Andrew Sillen, F. J. Kruger, and H. W. Krueger. 1991. "^{87}Sr/^{86}Sr as a Dietary Indicator in Modern and Archaeological Bone." *Journal of Archaeological Science* 18: 399–416.

Sedlin, E. D. 1964. "The Ratio of Cortical Area to Total Cross-Section Area in Rib Diaphysis: A Quantitative Index of Osteoporosis." *Clinical Orthopedics* 36: 161–68.

Sempowski, Martha L., and Michael W. Spence. 1994. "Mortuary Practices in Skeletal Remains at Teotihuacán." In *Urbanization at Teotihuacán, Mexico*, edited by R. Millon, 3: 45–122. Salt Lake City: University of Utah Press.

Sillen, Andrew, and Judy C. Sealy. 1995. "Diagenesis of Strontium in Fossil Bone: A Reconsideration of Nelson et al. (1986)." *Journal of Archaeological Science* 22: 313–20.

Solano, Arturo. 1978. "Informe de los trabajos de consolidación realizados en los restos del sacerdote que se encuentra en la tumba del Templo de las Inscripciones de la Zona Arqueológica de Palenque, Chis., México, durante los días del 11 al 24 de octubre de 1977." Unpublished report on file in the Coordinación de Restauración, Instituto Nacional de Antropología e Historia.

Spence, Michael W., Christine D. White, Fred J. Longstaffe, and Kimberly R. Law. 2004. "Victims of the Victims: Human Trophies Worn by Sacrificed Soldiers from the Feathered Serpent Pyramid, Teotihuacán." *Ancient Mesoamerica* 15: 1–15.

Steckel, Richard H., and Jerome C. Rose, eds. 2002. *The Backbone of History: Health and Nutrition in the Western Hemisphere.* Cambridge: Cambridge University Press.

Steele, Gentry, and Claude A. Bramblett. 1988. *The Anatomy and Biology of the Human Skeleton.* Austin: University of Texas Press.

Steinbock, Ted R. 1976. *Paleopathological Diagnosis and Interpretation: Bone Disease in Ancient Human Population.* Springfield, Ill.: Charles C. Thomas.

Steiniche, Torben, and E. Eriksen. 1999. "Age Related Changes in Bone Remodeling." In *Osteoporosis in Men,* edited by E. Orwoll, 299–312. Boston: Academic Press.

Stephens, John Lloyd. [1841] 1969. *Incidents of Travel in Central America, Chiapas, and Yucatán.* New York: Dover.

Stewart, T. Dale. 1979. *Essentials of Forensic Anthropology.* Springfield, Ill.: Charles C. Thomas.

Storey, Rebecca. 1992. *Life and Death at Teotihuacán.* Dumbarton: University of Oklahoma.

———. 1997. "Individual Frailty, Children of Privilege, and Stress in Late Classic Copán." In *Bones of the Maya: Studies of Ancient Skeletons,* edited by Stephen L. Whittington and David M. Reed, 116–26. Washington, D.C.: Smithsonian Institution Press.

Storey, Rebecca, and Kenneth Hirth. 1997. "Archaeological and Paleodemographic Analysis of the El Cajon Skeletal Population." In *Integrating Archaeological Demography: Multidisciplinary Approaches to Prehistoric Population,* edited by Richard R. Paine, 131–49. Carbondale: Southern Illinois University Press.

Storey, Rebecca, Lourdes Márquez, and Vernon Schmidt. 2002. "Social Disruption and the Maya Civilization of Mesoamerica: A Study of Health and Economy of the Last Thousand Years." In *The Backbone of History: Health and Nutrition in the Western Hemisphere,* edited by Richard H. Steckel and Jerome C. Rose, 281–306. New York: Cambridge University Press.

Stout, Sam D., and Rhonda Lueck. 1995. "Bone Remodeling Rates and Skeletal Maturation in Three Archaeological Skeletal Populations." *American Journal of Physical Anthropology* 98: 161–71.

Stout, Sam D., and Robert R. Paine. 1992. "Histological Age Estimation Using Rib and Clavicle." *American Journal of Physical Anthropology* 87: 111–15.

Stuart, David. 1998. "'The Fire Enters His House': Architecture and Ritual in Classic Maya Texts." In *Function and Meaning in Classic Maya Architecture,* edited by Stephen D. Houston, 373–425. Washington, D.C.: Dumbarton Oaks Research Library and Collection.

———. 2000. "The Arrival of Strangers: Teotihuacán and Tollan in Classic Maya History." In *Mesoamerica's Classic Heritage: From Teotihuacán to the Aztecs,* edited by David Carrasco, Lindsay Jones, and Scott Sessions, 465–513. Boulder: University of Colorado Press.

Stuart, David, and Stephen D. Houston. 1994. *Classic Maya Place Names*. Studies in Pre-Columbian Art and Archaeology no. 33. Washington, D.C.: Dumbarton Oaks Research Library and Collection.

Stuart, David, and Linda Schele. 1986. *Yax K'uk' Mo', the Founder of the Lineage of Copán*. Copán Note 6 Report. Honduras: Instituto Hondureño de Antropología e Historia.

Stuart-Williams, H. L., H. P. Schwarcz, C. D. White, and M. Spence. 1996. "The Isotopic Composition and Diagenesis of Human Bone from Teotihuacán and Oaxaca, Mexico." *Palaeogeography, Palaeoclimatology, Palaeoecology* 126: 1–14.

Suchey, Judy M., and Darryl Katz. 1997. "Applications of Pubic Age Determination in a Forensic Setting." In *Forensic Osteology: Advances in the Identification of Human Remains*, edited by Kathleen J. Reichs, 204–36. Springfield, Ill.: Charles C. Thomas.

Suchey, Judy M., Patricia A. Owings, Dean V. Wiseley, and Thomas T. Noguchi. 1984. "Skeletal Aging of Unidentified Persons." In *Human Identification: Case Studies in Forensic Anthropology*, edited by Ted A. Rathbun and Jane E. Buikstra, 278–97. Springfield, Ill.: Charles C. Thomas.

Takahashi, H., and Harold M. Frost. 1966. "Age and Sex Related Changes in the Amount of Cortex of Normal Human Ribs." *Acta Orthopedica Scandinavica* 37: 122–30.

Tate, Carolyn E. 1992. *Yaxchilán: The Design of a Maya Ceremonial City*. Austin: University of Texas Press.

Taube, Karl A. 1992. *The Major Gods of Ancient Yucatán*. Studies in Pre-Columbian Art and Archaeology no. 32. Washington, D.C.: Dumbarton Oaks Research Library and Collection.

Tejeda, Samuel. 2000. *Informe técnico de los resultados de elementos traza obtenidos en el individuo de la cámara secreta, Palenque, Chiapas*. Mexico City: Instituto Nacional de Investigación Nuclear.

Tiesler, Vera. 1998. *La costumbre de la deformación cefálica entre los antiguos mayas: Aspectos morfológicos y culturales*. Mexico City: Colección Científica, Instituto Nacional de Antropología e Historia.

———. 1999. "Rasgos bioculturales entre los antiguos mayas: Aspectos arqueológicos y sociales." Ph.D. diss., Facultad de Filosofía y Letras, Universidad Nacional Autónoma de México, Mexico City.

———. 2000. "Eres lo que comes: Patrones de desgaste oclusal en poblaciones mayas prehispánicas." *TRACE* 38: 67–79.

———. 2001a. *Decoraciones dentales de los antiguos mayas*. Mexico City: Ediciones Euroamericanas, Instituto Nacional de Antropología e Historia.

———. 2001b. "La estatura entre los mayas prehispánicos: Consideraciones bioculturales." *Estudios de Antropología Biológica* 10: 257–73.

———. 2002. "Un caso de decapitación prehispánica de Calakmul, Campeche." *Antropología Física Latinoamericana* 3: 129–42.

———. 2003a. *Re-evaluación de los entierros de Calakmul*. Campeche, Mexico: Universidad Autónoma de Campeche.

———. 2003b. *Reporte de los restos humanos recuperados en el sitio arqueológico de Calakmul, Campeche.* Mexico City: Instituo Nacional de Antropología e Historia.

———. 2004. "Maya Mortuary Treatments of the Elite: An Osteotaphonomic Perspective." In *Continuity and Change: Maya Religious Practices in Temporal Perspective,* Acta Mesoamericana, vol. 14, edited by Daniel Graña Behrens, Nikolai Grube, Christian M. Prager, Frauke Sachse, Stefanie Teufel, and Elisabeth Wagner, 143–56. Markt Schwaben, Germany: Verlag Anton Saurwein.

Tiesler, Vera, and Andrea Cucina. 2003. "Sacrificio, tratamiento y ofrenda del cuerpo humano entre los mayas del Clásico: Una mirada bioarqueológica." In *Antropología de la eternidad: La muerte en la cultura maya,* edited by Andrés Ciudad, Mario H. Ruz-Sosa, and María J. Iglesias, 337–54. Madrid and Mexico City: Sociedad Española de Estudios Mayas and Centro de Estudios Mayas, Universidad Nacional Autónoma de México.

———. 2004. "Stress Indicators, Sex, and Social Status Differences in Ancient Maya Society." Paper presented at the Fifteenth European Conference of the Paleopathology Association, Durham, United Kingdom, 10–14 August.

———. 2006. "Procedures in Human Heart Extraction and Ritual Meaning: A Taphonomic Assessment of Anthropogenic Marks in Classic Maya Skeletons." *Latin American Antiquity* (in press).

Tiesler, Vera, Andrea Cucina, and Arturo Romano. 2002. "Vida y muerte del personaje hallado en el Templo XIII-sub, Palenque: I Culto funerario y sacrificio humano." *Mexicon* 24: 75–78.

———. 2003. "Vida y muerte del personaje del Templo XIII-sub, Palenque, Chiapas: Una mirada bioarqueológica." In *Culto funerario en la sociedad maya: Memoria de la Cuarta Mesa Redonda de Palenque,* edited by Rafael Cobos, 455–82. Mexico City: Instituto Nacional de Antropología e Historia.

———. 2004. "Who Was the Red Queen? The Identity of the Female Maya Dignitary from the Sarcophagus Tomb of Temple XIII, Palenque, Mexico." *HOMO Journal of Comparative Human Biology* 55, nos. 1–2: 65–76.

Todd, Thomas W. 1920. "Age Changes in the Pubic Bones. I. The Male White Pubis." *American Journal of Physical Anthropology* 3: 285–334.

———. 1921a. "Age Changes in the Pubic Bones. II. The Pubis of the Male Negro-White Hybrid. III. The Pubis of the White Female. IV. The Pubis of the Female Negro-White Hybrid." *American Journal of Physical Anthropology* 4: 4–70.

———. 1921b. "Age Changes in the Pubic Bones. V. Mammalian Pubic Bone Metamorphosis. VI. The Interpretation of Variations in the Symphyseal Area." *American Journal of Physical Anthropology* 4: 333–424.

Todd, Thomas W., and D. W. Lyon. 1924. "Endocranial Suture Closure: Its Progress and Age Relationship. Part I. Adult Males of White Stock." *American Journal of Physical Anthropology* 7: 325–84.

———. 1925a. "Cranial Suture Closure: Its Progress and Age Relationship. Part II. Ectocranial Closure in Adult Males of White Stock." *American Journal of Physical Anthropology* 8: 23–45.

————. 1925b. "Cranial Suture Closure: Its Progress and Age Relationship. Part III. Endocranial Closure in Adult Males of Negro Stock." *American Journal of Physical Anthropology* 8: 47–71.

————. 1925c. "Cranial Suture Closure: Its Progress and Age Relationship. Part IV. Ectocranial Closure in Adult Males of Negro Stock." *American Journal of Physical Anthropology* 8: 149–68.

Tozzer, Alfred M. 1941. *Landa's relación de las cosas de Yucatán.* Papers of the Peabody Museum of American Archaeology and Ethnology, vol. 18. Cambridge, Mass.: Harvard University.

Ubelaker, Douglas H. 1989. *Human Skeletal Remains: Excavation, Analysis, Interpretation.* 2d ed. Washington, D.C.: Taraxacum.

Urcid, Javier. 1993. *Bones and Epigraphy: The Accurate Versus the Fictitious?* Texas Notes on Pre-Columbian Art, Writing, and Culture no. 42. Austin: Center for the History and Art of Ancient American Cultures, Department of Art and Art History, University of Texas.

Valencia, Ariel. 1978. *Official Letter (Of. No. 401-2-0460), Addressed to Arturo Romano Pacheco, March 28, 1978.* Mexico City: General Secretary, Instituto Nacional de Antropología e Historia.

Vázquez, Javier. 2000. *Análisis químicos de los pigmentos y materiales empleados en la preparación mortuoria del personaje depositado en el recinto funerario del Templo de las Inscripciones en Palenque, Chiapas.* Report on file. Mexico City: Escuela Nacional de Conservación, Restauración y Museografía, Instituto Nacional de Antropología e Historia.

Veizer, James, and W. Compston. 1974. "$^{87}Sr/^{86}Sr$ Composition of Seawater during the Phanerozoic." *Geochimica et Cosmochimica Acta* 38: 1461–484.

Weiss, Kenneth W. 1973. *Demographic Models for Anthropology.* Society for American Archaeology Memoir no. 27. Washington, D.C.: Society for American Archaeology.

Weiss-Krejci, Estella. 2001. "Restless Corpses: 'Secondary Burial' in the Babenberg and Habsburg Dynasties." *Antiquity* 75: 769–80.

————. 2003. "Victims of Human Sacrifice in Multiple Tombs of the Ancient Maya: A Critical Review." In *Antropología de la eternidad: La muerte en la cultura maya,* edited by Andrés Ciudad, Mario H. Ruz-Sosa, and María J. Iglesias, 355–81. Madrid and Mexico City: Sociedad Española de Estudios Mayas and Centro de Estudios Mayas, Universidad Nacional Autónoma de México.

Welsh, Bruce W. 1988. *An Analysis of Classic Lowland Maya Burials.* British Archaeological Reports International Series no. 409. Oxford: British Archaeological Reports.

White, Christine D. 1997. "Ancient Diet at Lamanai and Pacbitun: Implications for the Ecological Model of Collapse." In *Bones of the Maya: Studies of Ancient Skeletons,* edited by Stephen L. Whittington and David M. Reed, 171–80. Washington, D.C.: Smithsonian Institution Press.

————, ed. 1999. *Reconstructing Ancient Maya Diet.* Salt Lake City: University of Utah Press.

White, Christine D., Fred J. Longstaffe, and Kimberly R. Law. 2001. "Revisiting the Teotihuacán Connection at Altun Ha: Oxygen-Isotope Analysis of Tomb f-8/1." *Ancient Mesoamerica* 12: 65–72.

White, Christine D., Fred J. Longstaffe, Michael W. Spence, and Kimberly Law. 2000. "Testing the Nature of Teotihuacán Imperialism at Kaminaljuyu Using Phosphate Oxygen-Isotope Ratios." *Journal of Anthropological Research* 56, no. 4: 535–58.

White, Christine D., Michael W. Spence, Fred J. Longstaffe, Hillary Stuart-Williams, and Kimberly R. Law. 2002. "Geographic Identities of the Sacrificial Victims from the Feather Serpent Pyramid, Teotihuacán: Implications for the Nature of State Power." *Latin American Antiquity* 13: 217–36.

White, Christine D., Michael W. Spence, Hillary L. Stuart-Williams, and Henry P. Schwarcz. 1998. "Oxygen Isotopes and the Identification of Geographical Origins: The Valley of Oaxaca versus the Valley of Mexico." *Journal of Archaeological Science* 25, no. 7: 643–55.

White, Christine D., Rebecca Storey, Michael W. Spence, and Fred J. Longstaffe. 2004. "Immigration, Assimilation, and Status in the Ancient City of Teotihuacán: Isotopic Evidence from Tlajinga 33." *Latin American Antiquity* 15: 176–98.

Whittington, Stephen L., and David M. Reed. 1997. "Commoner Diet at Copán: Insights from Stable Isotopes and Porotic Hyperostosis." In *Bones of the Maya: Studies of Ancient Skeletons,* edited by Stephen L. Whittington and David M. Reed, 157–70. Washington, D.C.: Smithsonian Institution Press.

Wood, James W., Darryl H. Hoilman, Kathleen A. O'Connor, and Rebecca J. Ferrel. 2002. "Mortality Models for Paleodemography." In *Paleodemography: Age Distributions from Skeletal Samples,* edited by Robert H. Hoppa and James W. Vaupel, 129–68. Cambridge: Cambridge University Press.

Wood, James W., George R. Milner, Henry C. Harpending, and Kenneth M. Weiss. 1992. "The Osteological Paradox: Problems of Inferring Prehistoric Health from Skeletal Samples." *Current Anthropology* 33: 343–70.

Wright, Lori E. 1996. "Human Biology in the Classic Maya Collapse: Evidence from Paleopathology and Paleodiet." *Journal of World Prehistory* 10, no. 2: 147–98.

———. 1997. "Ecology or Society? Paleodiet and the Collapse of the Pasión Maya Lowlands." In *Bones of the Maya: Studies of Ancient Skeletons,* edited by Stephen L. Whittington and David M. Reed, 181–95. Washington D.C.: Smithsonian Institution Press.

———. 1999a. "The Elements of Maya Diets: Alkaline Earth Baselines and Paleodietry Reconstruction in the Pasión Region. Part III: Bone Chemistry." In *Reconstructing Ancient Maya Diet,* edited by Christine D. White, 197–219. Salt Lake City: University of Utah Press.

———. 1999b. "Los Niños de Kaminaljuyu: Isótopos, dieta y etnicidad en el Altiplano Guatemalteco." In *Acts of the XII Simposio de Investigaciones Arqueológicas en Guatemala,* edited by Juan Pedro Laporte and Hector Escobedo, 485–97. Guatemala City: Ministerio de Cultura y Deportes, IDAEH, Asociación Tikal.

Wu, K., K. E. Schubeck, H. M. Frost, and A. R. Villanueva. 1970. "Haversian Bone Formation Rates Determined by a New Method in a Mastodon, and in Human Dia-
betes Mellitus and Osteoporosis." *Calcified Tissue Research* 6: 204–19.

Wurster, W. 2000. *El sitio de Topoxté: Investigaciones en una isla del Lago Yaxhá, Petén.*
Mainz, Germany: KAVA, Philipp von Zabern.

Contributors

Jesper L. Boldsen is professor of paleodemography at the Danish Center for Demographic Research and the Institute for Community Health, Odense University; head of the Anthropological Data Base, Odense University; and adjunct professor of anthropology at the University of Utah. He received his Ph.D. in biology from Aarhus University in Denmark. His research interests include human population biology, epidemiology, demography, evolution, growth and sexual maturation, the spread of HIV, and the structure of the medieval population of Denmark. He has published widely in biological and anthropological journals.

Jane E. Buikstra is currently professor of bioarchaeology and director of the Center for Bioarchaeological Research at the School of Human Evolution and Social Changes, Arizona State University. She was formerly the Leslie Spier Distinguished Professor of Anthropology at the University of New Mexico, the Harold H. Swift Distinguished Service Professor of Anthropology at the University of Chicago, and a professor at Northwestern University. She has edited or authored fourteen books and more than one hundred articles on a variety of subjects, including bone chemistry in eastern North America; ancient treponematosis and tuberculosis in the Americas and Egypt; leprosy in the Americas; the diet and health of Argaric peoples (Bronze Age, Spain); australopithecine spinal pathology; trauma in Copán's founding dynasty (Maya); and coca chewing, cranial deformation, tuberculosis, and funerary rituals of ancient Andeans.

James H. Burton is currently associate director of the Laboratory of Archaeological Chemistry of the Department of Anthropology at the University of Wisconsin at Madison. He received his Ph.D. in anthropology at Arizona State University in 1986. His primary research interests include the development of new archaeometric methods, in particular the use of elemental and isotopic analyses for paleodietary assessments and isotopic analyses of traditional materials and of humans who relocated. Current projects include exploration of the utility of alkaline earth elements and of various isotopic systems in the study of human remains.

Andrea Cucina is currently a full-time research professor "A" at the Facultad de Ciencias Antropológicas of the Universidad Autónoma de Yucatán in Mérida, Mexico. He received his Ph.D. in paleopathology at the School of Medicine, Catholic University of Rome. His research interests include skeletal biology, with an emphasis on dental anthropology. He is currently investigating the ancient Maya populations for different biological and biocultural indicators of sacrifice, as well as studying paleonutrition, biological affinities, and population movement.

Nikolai Grube received a Ph.D. in pre-Columbian studies from the University of Hamburg and taught anthropology and pre-Columbian studies at the University of Bonn. Since 1986, he has worked as project epigrapher for various archaeological projects in the Maya region. In 1999, he became the first holder of the Linda and David Schele Chair in the Art and Writing of Mesoamerica at the University of Texas at Austin. His publications feature the dynastic history and political structure of the Classic Maya; early writing systems, especially Maya hieroglyphic writing; and ethnolinguistics.

Patricia Hernández is a professor of demographic anthropology and skeletal biology in the undergraduate and graduate biological anthropology programs at the Escuela Nacional de Antropología e Historia in 2002, where she received a Ph.D. in anthropology. She has been a researcher for the Instituto Nacional de Antropología e Historia since 1990. Her specializations include demographic anthropology, paleodemography, paleoepidemiology, skeletal biology, and the health and demographic patterns of ancient populations, and she has authored several works in these research areas.

Lourdes Márquez is a professor in the Graduate Division of the National School of Anthropology in Mexico. Former director of the Department of National Physical Anthropology at the Instituto Nacional de Antropología e Historia in Mexico, she has conducted research on ancient Mesoamerican populations, especially Maya and Zapotecs; on colonial skeletons from Mexico City; and on pathology, health, and nutrition. She is one of the pioneers of paleodemographic studies of pre-Hispanic Mesoamerican populations and has published several books on health, nutrition, and demographic profiles.

Simon Martin is the research specialist in Maya epigraphy at the University of Pennsylvania Museum of Archaeology and Anthropology. He was one of the creators of the exhibition "Courtly Art of the Ancient Maya" hosted by the National Gallery of Art, Washington, D.C., and the San Francisco Fine Arts Museum in 2004–2005. His current fieldwork is conducted at Calakmul for the Proyecto Arqueológico de la Biosfera de Calakmul, Mexico.

George R. Milner is a professor of anthropology at Pennsylvania State University. Before coming to Penn State, he was a postdoctoral fellow in physical anthropology at the Smithsonian Institution and director of the University of Kentucky Museum of Anthropology, where he was responsible for organizing Great Depression–era collections from archaeological sites to facilitate current researchers' work. His areas of specialization include human osteology and archaeology, with an emphasis on the late-prehistoric peoples of eastern North America. He has participated in excavations in several midwestern states, Egypt, Micronesia, and Denmark, and has published several books on prehistoric societies.

T. Douglas Price is Weinstein Professor of European Archaeology and director of the Laboratory for Archaeological Chemistry at the University of Wisconsin at Madison, where he has been on the faculty for more than 30 years. His current field research involves the beginnings of agriculture on the island of Zealand, Denmark, and projects using strontium isotopes in human tooth enamel to look at questions of prehistoric migration.

Arturo Romano is currently emeritus investigator at the Instituto Nacional de Antropología e Historia in Mexico. He received his B.A. and M.A. in physical anthropology from the Escuela Nacional de Antropología e Historia and the Universidad Nacional Autónoma de México. He has participated in numerous research projects, including Tamuín, Tlatilco, Texcoco Lake, the Candelaria cave (Coahuila), Tepexpán, Peñón de los Baños, Yagul and Zaachila (Oaxaca), former convent San Jerónimo, and the Janaab' Pakal tomb in Palenque. He has published more than thirty articles on skeletal anthropology, focusing on artificial head shaping, craneometry, and forensic studies. Additional interests include the excavation process of human remains and ancient microfauna, as well as anthropological documentary photography.

Carlos Serrano is professor of anthropology at the Universidad Nacional Autónoma de México (UNAM) and at the Escuela Nacional de Antropología e Historia, Mexico. He is also currently chair of the Instituto de Investigaciones Antropológicas at UNAM and president of the Latin-American Association of Biological Anthropology. His research interests include skeletal biology, disease, nutrition, evolution of Holocene populations, and dermatoglyphics in indigenous populations.

Sam D. Stout is professor emeritus in the Department of Anthropology at the University of Missouri and professor in the Department of Anthropology at Ohio State University. He received his Ph.D. in biological anthropology from Washington University in St. Louis, Missouri. His general research interests are in skeletal biology, with specific focus on microstructural analysis of bone (histomorphometry) and its applications in bioarchaeology, forensic anthropology, and paleontology.

Margaret Streeter received her M.A. and Ph.D. in anthropology from the University of Missouri at Columbia. She is currently associate professor in the Department of Anthropology at Boise State University. Her general research interests include skeletal biology and its applications in paleontological and forensic studies. She focuses on histomorphometry and the histology of bone.

Vera Tiesler is a full professor at the Facultad de Ciencias Antropológicas at the Universidad Autónoma de Yucatán in Mérida, Mexico, where she is in charge of the bioarchaeology section. She received her M.A. in archaeology from the Escuela Nacional de Antropología e Historia and her Ph.D. in anthropology from the Universidad Nacional Autónoma de México. She formerly served as the academic chair of the Palenque Round Tables (1998–2001). She has published more than thirty articles and authored or edited several books. Her research interests center on bioarchaeology and mortuary research, Maya studies, and biocultural theory. Her recent work has focused on understanding the skeletal signatures and meanings of human sacrifice and posthumous body treatments among the ancient Maya.

John W. Verano is an associate professor in the Department of Anthropology at Tulane University, where he teaches courses in human osteology, paleopathology, forensic anthropology, and South American archaeology. He received his M.A. and Ph.D. degrees in anthropology from the University of California at Los Angeles. His principal research interests include the physical anthropology and paleopathology of prehistoric South American populations, with a particular focus on the northern coast of Peru; disease in ancient skeletal and mummified remains; trepanation, amputation, and other ancient surgery; and warfare, human sacrifice, and mortuary practices in Andean South America.

Index